WHAT WOULD JEFFERSON DO?

ALSO BY THOM HARTMANN

The Prophet's Way

Attention Deficit Disorder: A Different Perception

Focus Your Energy

Beyond ADD

Best of the DTP Forum
    (edited with Brad Walrod and Don Arnoldy)

ADD Success Stories

Think Fast!
    (edited with Janie Bowman and Susan Burgess)

Healing ADD

Thom Hartmann's Complete Guide to ADHD

Unequal Protection

ADHD Secrets of Success

The Greatest Spiritual Secret

The Last Hours of Ancient Sunlight

The Edison Gene

We the People

WHAT WOULD JEFFERSON DO?

A RETURN TO DEMOCRACY

THOM HARTMANN

 HARMONY BOOKS NEW YORK

Published by Harmony Books, New York, New York.
Member of the Crown Publishing Group, a division of Random House, Inc.
www.crownpublishing.com

Harmony Books is a registered trademark and the Harmony Books colophon is
a trademark of Random House, Inc.

Portions of this book have previously appeared on the author's website,
www.thomhartmann.com, and on www.commondreams.org.

Printed in the United States of America

Design by Barbara Sturman

Library of Congress Cataloging-in-Publication Data
Hartmann, Thom
    What would Jefferson do? : a return to democracy /
Thom Hartmann. — 1st ed.
    Includes bibliographical references.
    1. Democracy. 2. Democracy—United States. I. Title.
JC423.H3737   2004
321.8—dc22   2004002781

ISBN 1-4000-5208-4

10 9 8 7 6 5 4 3 2 1

First Edition

To my wife, Louise Hartmann,
whose love and patient encouragement have helped bring this
book and so many other projects to fruition.

———————

Contents

Acknowledgments   xi

Introduction   xiii

1 AMERICA'S DEMOCRACY IS ERODING   1

Bad for democracy, good for giant corporations   4

The loss of democratic participation   7

The rise of the new corporate feudal lords   7

The three threats   9

2 WHAT IS DEMOCRACY, AND WHAT DIFFERENCE DOES IT MAKE?   10

Democracies don't attack each other.   10

How democracy is defined   14

Antidemocracies   19

The characteristics of a healthy democracy   20

The Goddess of Democracy   22

Beware: Tight control can look very good, at first . . .   22

Is this what the Founders fought for?   23

3 PEOPLE AND EVENTS THAT INFLUENCED AMERICA'S FOUNDERS   24

Jefferson encounters ancient wisdom.   24

Native Americans   28

Tacitus on the natives of England   31
Paul de Rapin Thoyras on the history of England   34
The truth about the Tea Party   41

4 WHEN DEMOCRACY FAILED   56

Sunset provisions and gradual increases in terror   58
Creating a new homeland security bureau   60
The lies that convinced the people war was necessary   61
Two nations take two different paths—in the 1930s.   63

5 MYTHS ABOUT DEMOCRACY IN AMERICA   65

Myth: "Even our Founders knew democracies eventually
    self-destruct."   65
Myth: "America was created by rich white men to
    protect their wealth."   67
Myth: "The Founders wrote slavery into the Constitution."   76
Myth: "A woman's place is in the home, and the Founders
    knew it."   87
Myth: "The Republican Party has always been the party of
    big business and cheap labor."   89
Myth: "The Founders thought the Constitution was perfect
    and should never change."   91
Myth: "Government is an evil entity that's against the people."   94
Myth: "The Founders and Framers were impractical, idealistic
    Enlightenment-era dreamers."   95
Myth: "The Constitution offers no right to privacy."   96
Myth: "Jefferson said it's wrong for the rich to pay more in taxes."   99
Myth: "Working women are responsible for the loss of
    good-paying jobs."   104
Myth: "Liberals wrote child labor laws to create a shortage
    and drive up wages."   107
Myth: "Left to themselves, people would drain the Treasury."   109
Myth: "Liberal democratic policies are socialism."   110
Myth: "Free markets are nature's way of making the winner
    fit and strong (it's Darwin)."   111
Myth: "Taxes are an unfair burden and a waste of money."   116

Myth: "Social programs are the liberals' way of buying votes." 119
Myth: "Unlimited growth and concentration of power is
    nature's way and it's good for us." 121
Myth: "Media conglomerates are just nature taking its course." 122
Myth: "The media have a liberal bias." 123
Myth: "There's too much regulation: Get government off the
    backs of big companies." 124
Myth: "NAFTA/GATT/WTO 'free trade' is good for all nations." 127
Myth: "Unions harm economies by driving up wage expenses." 129
It's time to set aside the myths. 130

6 WHAT BECAME OF REAL
   AMERICAN CONSERVATIVES? 132

The modern conservative movement: Russell Kirk 133
The shift to pseudoconservative values 135
Awakening to the antidemocratic conservative damage 136

7 DEMOCRACY, NOT DOMINANCE,
   IS THE WAY OF NATURE 140

The biology of democracy 142
Democracy in nature 144
Is democracy the same thing as enlightened self-interest? 146
But what about "survival of the fittest"? 147
Tribal democracy 148
Democracy always wins. 153

8 WARLORDS, THEOCRATS, AND
   ARISTOCRATS RISE AGAIN 155

Warlord presidents use "national security" to grab power. 156
Theocrats attack democracy. 164
The new aristocracy: corporatism and monopolies 174

9 MODERN DEMOCRACY:
   ITS HISTORY AND WHY IT WORKS 183

The oldest democratic cultures 183
Roots in Rome and Greece 188

10 THE STATE OF DEMOCRACY
IN THE WORLD TODAY   204

Democracy spreads across the world in a single century,
1920–2000.   204
Where we are now   209
Democracy is inevitable.   210

11 A VISION FOR THE FUTURE OF AMERICA
AND THE WORLD   219

Register and vote.   220
Return war powers to Congress and end nonwars.   221
Repeal the PATRIOT Act and other antiliberty laws.   224
Provide free high-quality public education for all—
through college.   224
Require that any benefits Congress gives itself, it gives to
all citizens.   227
Provide health care for all.   227
Require a living wage.   228
Support organized labor or organize your workplace.   230
Use tariffs and trade policy to balance labor's playing field.   231
Strengthen the social safety net.   232
Bring back the middle class by restoring the tax laws that
created it.   237
Keep Social Security out of corporate hands.   238
Institute universal conscription.   239
Clean up the environment and public lands.   241
Strengthen the Sherman Anti-Trust Act and break up
monopolies.   242
Bust up the media conglomerates and restore a robust
free press.   243
Make the "revolving door" between industry and regulatory
agencies illegal.   245
Use tax incentives and grants to jump-start alternative energy.   245
Reserve human rights for humans, not "aggregated capital."   246
Keep church and state separate.   247
Make the United States more democratic in its elections.   248

Abolish the Electoral College.   251
Get corporations out of the voting process.   251
Make the UN more democratic.   252
Take action.   253

12 WHAT WOULD JEFFERSON DO?   254

We can speak out.   256
Transforming democracy for the better   257

Afterword by robert wolff   261
Notes   267
Index   277

ACKNOWLEDGMENTS

Are the special privilege boys going to run the country, or are the people going to run it?

—PRESIDENT HARRY S. TRUMAN (1945–1953)

I t may seem strange to express gratitude to somebody dead nearly two centuries, but the simple reality is that without Thomas Jefferson neither this book nor our nation would exist as they do today. I acknowledge not only the greatness of his mind, but the extraordinary amount of research he did, which captured for all time an extensive library of thought that might otherwise have been lost to us.

Several years ago Louise and I bought an 1850 Gothic house in central Vermont, where we now live. Going through the dusty attic over the carriage house, we found a 20-volume set of *The Works of Thomas Jefferson,* published in 1904 in Washington, D.C., by the Thomas Jefferson Memorial Association.

I'd read several biographies of Jefferson during the course of my life, and back in 1974 I particularly enjoyed Fawn Brodie's classic *Thomas Jefferson: An Intimate History* (which I still consider the best Jefferson biography ever written). More recently, I've been saddened by the distortions of his perspective and life that I've repeatedly found in the more recent Jefferson biographies and books about his era, most coming from historians or authors who are also political or philosophical conservatives.

But finding a complete collection of Jefferson's own words—as opposed to works about him—was a life-changing event for me. I thought I knew something about Jefferson, but nothing prepared me for the impact of reading his personal and private correspondence straight through in large chunks.

These fragile and badly time-damaged books led me to discover on the Internet several nearly identical collections of this now-public-domain collection in easily searchable digital form on CD-ROMs. His *Autobiography,* his *Notes on Virginia,* and his thousands of letters offer a compelling insight into the mind and soul of one of America's most extraordinary men, and I've spent much of the last decade immersed in them. All of the unfootnoted quotes in this book by Jefferson and his correspondents (Adams, Lafayette, etc.) come from these original-source collections.

In addition to Jefferson's inspiration, I was helped in completing this book by the extraordinary editorial skills of Toinette Lippe, herself an accomplished author whose books I recommend to you.

Joe MacPherson, who worked for some months as producer of my radio program, provided useful research that has found its way into this book, and Rob Kall, whose online quote collection at www.futurehealth.org is extraordinary, provided some great epigraphs and ongoing encouragement. Jim Walsh did great work as an editor and proofreader, and many thanks also go to my old friend Jerry Schneiderman.

And Dave deBronkart, an old and dear friend who has edited several of my other books, spent an extraordinary week with me just when I thought this book was all finished and ready to submit, for which I am extremely grateful. This book is substantially better for his efforts.

To all, and particularly to Louise Hartmann, who kept me on task through the years it took to research and write this book, I offer my most heartfelt thanks.

INTRODUCTION

I am not among those who fear the people. They, and not the rich, are our dependence for continued freedom.

—PRESIDENT THOMAS JEFFERSON, in a July 12, 1816, letter

There is a nearly continuous arc of despotically controlled nations, starting just north of South Africa, arching up over the African continent, across the Middle East, and extending over much of Asia, across China, all the way to Southeast Asia. The good news is that this is a minority of the world's nations (fewer than 50), most have strong internal prodemocracy movements already agitating for change, and the rest of the world has moved or is quickly moving into the camp of democracy.

Of the 191 member nations of the United Nations in 2003, 140 hold multiparty elections and 81 are considered "fully democratic" by the UN's standards.[1] Through democratically elected representatives, citizens themselves rule nearly all of North and South America, Europe, Australia and most Pacific Islands, South Africa, and many parts of Asia.

Since the formation of the first modern democracies in the late 1700s, no two democratic nations have ever gone to war (assuming that England didn't really become democratic until after the reforms of 1832). And no fully democratic nation has ever spawned or sponsored terrorism, or intentionally harbored terrorists.

Yet at the same time, there is real danger—both in the United

States and across the world—from the changes that are happening to American democracy. Among democratic nations, democracy is increasingly under assault by corporate forces that promote multilateral agreements like NAFTA and GATT/WTO to override the laws and actions of democratically elected legislatures.

Specific measurements of human well-being have declined as our government has become less and less oriented toward serving and protecting its human citizens while making itself available to corporate overlords. Even business overall (particularly small and medium-sized business) is adversely affected when monopolists influence the halls of power.

The decline of democracy usually happens when power gets massed into a very few hands, which defeats the equal opportunity that makes democracy work. Indeed, the hallmark of democracy is widespread access to the processes and protections of government: equal opportunity, access to creation of laws, access to all levels of the courts, and protection from harm by those more powerful. When power is concentrated in too few hands and democratic protections are curtailed, the average person's quality of life declines, and so do many business conditions.

The power of democracy

In many parts of the world, democracy has taken on a mythic significance. Despite the fact that prodemocracy activists are regularly beaten, arrested, tortured, and killed in dictatorships like those in China, Saudi Arabia, and Pakistan, they keep coming back. From Burma to Tibet to Nigeria to the United States of America, the archetype of democracy has taken such strong root that somebody is always willing to step up and speak out when it's being repressed or under attack.

Thus, the trend worldwide is still toward more and more democracy.

Many political thinkers say democracy is an aberration in human history, an unnatural do-gooder sort of government held together by people of goodwill overriding the forces of human nature.

Many claim that the natural state of humans is evil and must be controlled, and, as in the science fiction worlds of *Star Wars* and *The Lord of the Rings,* the best and most stable government is one ruled by a warlord king or queen who's powerful enough to destroy enemies yet still righteous and compassionate to his/her subjects.

But the noble warlord is an aberration: democracy is common in the animal kingdom—perhaps universally so—and it's the oldest, most resilient, and historically most universal form of governance there is.

The threat to the commons

In a constitutionally limited democratic republic like the United States, there are some things we all own together. Often referred to as "the commons," these include the necessities and commonalities of life: our air, water, waste/sewage systems, transportation routes, educational systems, radio and television spectrums, and, in every developed nation in the world except America, a national health-care system. They also include those things held in common trust for us by our government: the nation's parks and forestlands; the mineral wealth and grazing rights under and on public lands; and our beaches, sky, waterways, and oceans.

But the most important of the commons in a democracy is the government itself. We're supposed to own our government, and it is meant to be solely responsible to us, the individual voters, and not to corporate special interests.

And make no mistake—it's democracy itself that some conservatives want to replace with a new corporate aristocracy.

Democracy fights back.

———————

The price of democracy is eternal vigilance. That doesn't apply just to invaders from outside; it applies to internal forces that try to dismantle the fundamental protections that make democracy work. Repeatedly throughout history the train of democracy has been partly derailed, and the duty has fallen on those generations to get it back on track. We, today, are one of those generations.

This book is about the extraordinary power and resilience of democracy. It will show you that democracy is actually built into our genetic code, and it will tell you how democracy is played out across the biological spectrum. You'll get a solid grasp of the democratic concepts that were rediscovered by America's Founders and feel the hot touch of the powers in the world today that are working against democracy.

You'll learn how we can revitalize and restore democracy to the developed nations that are under corporate assault and how we can work to spread to the rest of the world this greatest political force ever known for peace and human happiness.

Democracy can heal our world and set its people free. And you and I, by being born into this era and having the information we now hold, are destined to help bring that about.

WHAT WOULD JEFFERSON DO?

AMERICA'S DEMOCRACY
IS ERODING

The fortunes amassed through corporate organization are now so large, and vest such power in those that wield them, as to make it a matter of necessity to give to the sovereign—that is, to the Government, which represents the people as a whole—some effective power of supervision over their corporate use. In order to insure a healthy social and industrial life, every big corporation should be held responsible by, and be accountable to, some sovereign strong enough to control its conduct.

—PRESIDENT THEODORE ROOSEVELT (1901–1909)

For the past year, I've been on radio stations coast to coast for three hours a day, five days a week, going up against Rush Limbaugh in the 12–3 P.M. time slot (eastern time). Callers from California to North Carolina, Iowa to Texas, and even a few expatriate Web listeners who've phoned in from Australia, Germany, Taiwan, and Scotland repeatedly stress a consistent set of concerns.

"I feel as though our country has lost its democracy," said one caller in New York.

"Our politicians are for sale to the highest corporate bidder," said another in New Mexico.

"I was arrested for standing a block away from a Bush fund-raiser with a 'No War for Oil' sign," said another in South Carolina.

A caller in Dallas told the story of how his master's degree in engineering and service as an officer in the army didn't qualify him to compete with the engineer in India who took his job. "I've been unemployed for 42 months," he said, "although I'm still looking every day for a good job."

A pervasive concern is sweeping across our nation, a fear that both the economic American dream is slipping away while the ideals of American democracy are under an organized and powerful attack.

Both worker productivity and wages increased 108 and 101 percent, respectively, between 1947 and 1973, the golden years of the American middle class. Since then, though, many of the key indicators of a functioning democracy have been eroding in America.

One of the most significant indicators is that from the time Ronald Reagan became president until today the income of the middle class in real dollars has declined 10 percent (adjusted for inflation) while the minimum wage has fallen 17 percent (also adjusted for inflation). Worker productivity went up 52 percent—Americans are working harder and working longer hours—but pay has fallen, causing middle-class debt to explode, doubling in just the past two decades.[2]

Today's middle class spends 21 percent less on clothes than 20 years ago (cheap imports), while an unprecedented 80 percent of homeowners in low- and moderate-income categories spend more than half their income on housing.[3] Bankruptcies are at an all-time high, and half of all people filing are doing so because of devastating medical bills (another 40 percent file because they're wiped out by job loss or divorce).[4]

Democracy in America *is* eroding. And with it are going many of the essential rights that democracy is supposed to ensure.

Instead of democracy—government for, by, and of the people—we increasingly have "corporatism"—a term that Benito Mussolini invented. He defined it as a merger of state and corporate power, and in the past few decades it's been adopted as a guiding tenet of conservative thought. The effect has been a steady shift of wealth away from the middle class and into corporate coffers and large investor portfolios, combined with a dramatic loss of the freedoms on which this country was founded:

▶ The First Amendment to the Constitution clearly states: "Congress shall make no law . . . abridging the freedom of speech, or of the press, or of the right of the people to peaceably assemble to petition the government for redress of grievances." Nonetheless, George W. Bush has, with virtually no mention in the mainstream corporate media, ordered his Secret Service to direct local police departments to create "free speech zones," out of the view of the press and sometimes as much as a mile away from the events at which he speaks. All persons carrying anti-Bush signs or showing an inclination to speak out against Bush are herded into these zones—often at gunpoint—and those who refuse to go have been arrested in nearly a dozen states.

▶ The Fourth Amendment says: "The right of the people to be secure in their persons, houses, papers, and effects, against unreasonable searches and seizures, shall not be violated. . . ." Yet in 2003 parts of PATRIOT II were passed that give the government the right to search through your doctor's records, credit card records, pawnshop records, bank records, and any other information about you from any source it deems relevant—without a warrant, without a court's order or oversight, and without informing you. This extraordinary assault on the Bill of Rights was unnoticed by the press, buried in a 2004 Intelligence Authorization bill, and signed into law without fanfare by George W. Bush.

▸   Legislation introduced and pending in 2003 and 2004, supported by the Bush administration, would extend the death penalty to crimes related to terrorism while redefining terrorism to include crimes "against commerce." Some suggest that, at least in theory, you can now be put to death for any interference with corporate activity. Additionally, under these various legislative provisions, the ACLU notes that the government would have the ability to defy the Eighth Amendment and deny bail, and to defy the Fifth Amendment and "compel testimony."[5]

▸   The PATRIOT Act itself includes a broad reduction in citizen privacy rights and the presumption of innocence.

Bad for democracy, good for giant corporations

In other cases, the move away from democratic principles doesn't involve just suppression of fundamental freedoms; the government is being substantially reprioritized to serve business, with less and less regard for the impact this has on citizens.

▸   Our unemployment statistics don't count how many people are unemployed; they leave out a large number of jobless:

▷ If you're unemployed for more than 18 months, the government eliminates your eligibility for unemployment benefits and no longer counts you in the unemployment statistics—even if your family is starving.

▷ Worse, if your career simply disappears to India, your education is down the drain, you lose your life savings, and you finally give up and take a job at a quarter of your former pay, you don't count as unemployed at all.

▸   Lobbyists roam freely in the halls of Congress and even write the specific language for much (if not most) of our nation's legislation. In early American history it was a crime for businesses to interfere with the citizens' legislation—and it's still illegal in many democratic nations. Meanwhile, average citizens, unable to get their elected representatives on the phone, rightly feel that their politicians are not there for them but are instead for sale to the highest bidder.

▶ Executives from regulated industries frequently head up the agencies that regulate them. Examples:

▷ Because of industries being their own regulators, the number two person in the USDA responsible for managing the Mad Cow situation was the head lobbyist for the Cattlemen's Association. And the Bush administration vetoed an appropriation to increase the inspection of beef. Up until the actual outbreak in January 2004, only one-tenth of "downer cows" (cows with symptoms of Mad Cow) were inspected.

▷ When new overtime rules were introduced in 2004, the White House touted how much increased overtime laborers would get. Meanwhile, the Department of Labor published guidelines to employers on how to avoid paying any more. Example: "Lower the base wage."

▷ In January 2004, an ad for a "Margaritas and Mulligans" get-together at a posh Arizona resort invited industry executives to play golf with Republican lawmakers, for a fee of $3,000 each, to help plan the changes "for the upcoming rewrite of the Clean Air Act." For $5,000, industry executives could support the keynote speech by Interior deputy secretary J. Steven Griles, the man responsible for overseeing the nation's public lands so coveted by oil, gas, mining, and timber industries, and himself a former lobbyist for the coal and oil industries.

▶ Profits of "managed-care" health-care providers such as HMOs are at record levels, while according to the American Medical Association (AMA), over 43 million Americans have no medical insurance of any sort.

▷ This is a true crisis of human well-being, because under today's rules, it's often impossible to get health care if you don't have insurance.

▷ For-profit hospitals have succeeded in putting uninsured people who can't pay their bills into jail.

▷ Prescription drug costs have risen dramatically.

▶ The very heartbeat of our democracy—our vote—has been turned over to fewer than a half-dozen large corporations with conspicuous conservative political connections. These corporations assert that voters have no right to examine the programs that run voter machines, even though many of the machines have repeatedly failed security and reliability tests.

▶ From mercury in the air to arsenic in the water to logging of old-growth forests to increasing greenhouse gas emissions, our environment is in a crisis exacerbated by conservative policies. Global warming poses one of the greatest threats to humankind, the average person has over a hundred detectable carcinogenic chemicals in his bloodstream, and one in three of us will get cancer in our lifetimes.

▶ Thomas Jefferson said, "Our liberty depends on the freedom of the press, and that cannot be limited without being lost." In that spirit, until the eras of Reagan and Clinton, radio and television stations were largely required to be locally owned and operated in ways that served their local communities. These protections are being stripped from us, as Fairness and Accuracy In Reporting (FAIR) chronicles: "Big media spent nearly $11 million from 1996–1998 to defeat bills mandating free airtime for candidates." At the same time, FAIR notes, "broadcasters earned at least $771 million from political TV ads in 2000, almost double the 1996 revenues."[6]

Things like this could not happen if the government's priority was to protect its people. President Grover Cleveland (1885–1889) said, "As we view the achievements of aggregated capital, we discover the existence of trusts, combinations, and monopolies, while the citizen is struggling far in the rear or is trampled to death beneath an iron heel. Corporations, which should be the carefully restrained creatures of the law and the servants of the people, are fast becoming the people's masters."[7] He was right about corporate dominance during the Gilded Age, and it's happening again today.

The loss of democratic participation

There's plenty of evidence that people are giving up: only half of eligible voters actually register and vote.[8] Nonvoters typically say lawmaking is already in the hands of special interests that are far bigger than them, so their own preference is largely irrelevant.

This is tragic in the nation that gave birth to modern democracy. According to the Federal Election Commission's website, some of those who learned from us do far better: in Australia, 96 percent of those registered to vote actually show up and cast a ballot.

The rise of the new corporate feudal lords

We're watching the transformation of many democracies around the world into what are essentially feudal states. They are not feudal in the sense that people are wheeling hand-pulled carts through muddy streets as in medieval days, but that the government increasingly runs solely for the benefit of those with the greatest wealth. And it makes little difference to the ordinary citizen whether the wealthiest are old-style feudal lords or today's very large corporate interests.

Government's activities are increasingly oriented toward business and away from advancing democracy. Worse, we increasingly see that the government's reports to us on unemployment, inflation, and other key issues can be juggled (and actively are) to conceal from us the truth about the well-being of our society.

In just the past 50 years, the United States has inspired a

boom in democracies worldwide. This trend was most powerfully influenced by our highly visible participation in the United Nations and our stand there against dictatorships. Yet in a 2002 report, the UN Development Programme found it necessary to report that its old mentor the United States was in trouble, by the very standards we taught them: "Imbalances in resources and political power often subvert the principle of one person, one voice, and the purpose of democratic institutions [in the United States]."9

It's a remarkable commentary when the UN, to whom *we taught democracy,* and where we once served as role model, says political power often subverts the principle of one person, one voice in America.

The report went on to say, "One critical problem is money in politics, which subverts democratic institutions when it exerts undue influence on who gets elected and what legislators vote for." They cited the example of Enron corrupting politics.

And, the report observed: "Presidential candidates in the 2000 U.S. election spent $343 million on their campaigns, up from $92 million in 1980. Including spending by political parties [for so-called 'issue ads,' which circumvent the legal spending limits], more than $1 billion was probably spent on the 2000 campaigns. In 2001 Michael Bloomberg spent a record $74 million to become New York City's mayor, the equivalent of $99 a vote. His main opponent spent $17 million." The losing candidate had 47 percent of the vote, at a "cost" of just $25 a vote; he was outspent 4:1 and barely lost.

The UN report concludes: "As campaign costs rise, so does the risk that politicians will be disproportionately influenced by business interests. In the 2000 U.S. election cycle, corporations gave $1.2 billion in political contributions—about 14 times the already considerable amount contributed by labour unions and 16 times the contributions of other interest groups. Although many European countries have more stringent limits on corporate funding, similar patterns emerge in many other countries. In

India large corporations provided 80% of the funding for the major parties in 1996."

The three threats

"Corporatism" is one of three threats to democracy:

▶ Muslim and Christian religious extremists, both wanting to limit individual freedoms in favor of theocracy (government by their religious standards).

▶ The deceptive, pseudoconservative corporatist influencers and their supporters, who seek changes in our laws that would take us away from democracy and toward government of, by, and for *corporations*—with complete disregard for the freedom and well-being of our citizens.

▶ A presidency that is oriented toward personal power, not the good of the country. Masterfully manipulating television images, and openly allowing unelected corporate friends into the halls of power while suppressing dissent, several recent conservative presidents have spent unprecedented amounts of borrowed money, while simultaneously cutting funding from education and social programs and running up the biggest deficits in history.

But citizens are not without power. This has happened before, democracy has recovered (and even improved—we've freed slaves and women), and we can—we must—take it back again.

This raises the question, what *is* democracy? Does it really make a difference? If freedoms and choice are curtailed, does it really make that much difference?

2

WHAT IS DEMOCRACY, AND WHAT DIFFERENCE DOES IT MAKE?

Democracy is the recurrent suspicion that more than half of the people are right more than half the time.
—E. B. WHITE, American author (1899–1985)

Much has been written and said over the years about the many blessings of democracy: individual liberty, civil society, religious freedom, and so on. But it's only in the last few decades that people living in democracies have begun to discover what anthropologist Peter Farb pointed out a half-century ago about the two most important elements of democracy as practiced among tribal peoples: it prevents both wars and famines.

Democracies don't attack each other.

Back in 1795, when the idea of a stable and enduring democracy was only a flickering experiment in faraway North America and just catching fire in France, Immanuel Kant suggested that it might be possible to eliminate the worst scourge that had, since the days of Gilgamesh, afflicted humankind: he believed that, through the simple institution of a political system, war could be ended for all time.

Kant's treatise on the topic, *Zum Ewigen Frieden: Ein Philosophischer Entwurf (Toward Eternal Peace: A Philosophical Draft)*, suggested that when a nation was ruled democratically—that is, by the will of the majority of the people—those people would never choose war unless it was in self-defense. Therefore, Kant reasoned, if all nations were democratic, there would never be aggressors (because no majority of citizens would ever vote to send their own children off to die), and war would be eliminated.

Kant's prediction didn't come out of the blue. Similar sentiments had been implied by Adam Smith in his 1776 book *The Wealth of Nations* and were openly advocated by America's Founders, particularly Thomas Jefferson. Perhaps that's why in the U.S. Constitution, the Founders wrote that the ability to declare war rests exclusively with Congress. (In those days, nobody imagined that in some future time our executive branch would lie to Congress to get war powers.)

Modern scholars rediscover Jefferson's dream of peace

The concept of democracy preventing wars wasn't much discussed—other than among philosophers—between the Civil War and World War I. But in the twentieth century, scholars rediscovered Kant's work on democracy. One of the first was former Princeton University president Woodrow Wilson, later U.S. president, who echoed Kant in his belief that the promotion of democracy around the world (through the Treaty of Versailles and the League of Nations) could end war for all time. He believed this so strongly that he referred to World War I as "the war to end all wars."

Later, social and political scientists began a more methodical analysis of the world since the widespread creation of liberal democracies. What they found shocked them, because it didn't just indicate a possibility or a trend, but pointed to what Kant had predicted—an immutable law of human behavior.

▶   In a 1962 article, Dean Babst, a research scientist with New York State, found that in a study of 116 wars that involved 438 countries, "No wars have been fought between independent nations with elective governments between 1789 and 1941."

If you were to consider that even though Germany was theoretically a democracy when Hitler was elected, it was no longer a "liberal democracy" when it went to war (because he had banned opposition parties), the date stretches well into the present era. (Babst pointed out that the War of 1812, between England and the United States, wasn't a war between two democracies because "if a hereditary ruler, such as a king, can choose the prime minister or president [as was the case in the U.K. in 1812], then the country is not considered to have an elective government."[10])

▶   After Babst piqued the interest of the international research community, a number of papers and books were published confirming his perspective. Among the best known are two books by J. David Singer and Melvin Small that examined all 50 wars from 1816 to 1965 that produced more than one thousand deaths in battle.[11] Not one of them was fought between two democracies.

▶   One of the world's leading experts on democracy and the author of several books on it, including *Saving Lives, Enriching Life*,[12] Professor Randolph J. Rummel of the University of Hawaii used a similar definition of a war (producing over a thousand casualties) in an exhaustive analysis of 353 dyads (pairs) of nations that had engaged in battle between 1816 and 1991.[13] Rummel, like Babst, defined a democracy as a nation with universal suffrage, a free press, and active multiple political parties. Dr. Rummel found that dictatorships fought each other in 198 of 353 conflicts, and democracies fought against nondemocracies in 155 wars, but he was unable to find evidence of any war between two democracies.

As author Jack S. Levy pointed out in his 1988 article "Domestic Politics and War," "the absence of war between democracies comes as close as anything to an empirical law in international relations."[14]

**Where there is freedom of information,
famines don't develop.**

Famine, according to the Nobel Prize–winning economist Amartya Sen, simply doesn't happen in functioning democracies.

Per Ahlmark, the former deputy prime minister of Sweden, addressed the European Parliament in 1999, saying: "Again, the crucial factor is freedom. Where there is an active opposition and a free press, governments cannot neglect tens of thousands of people starving to death. When the opposition is silenced and mass media give voice only to the propaganda of the dictator, the fate of millions of people dying from famine could be kept secret and ignored—because of ideology, incompetence, systematic lying and total lack of compassion."

Ahlmark recounts how democracies don't initiate wars, commit democide, or experience famine and then concludes:

"Since the last century, liberals [citizens of liberal democracies] have imagined or felt these connections to be true. And later we have seen how mass murderers have torn peoples and nations to pieces when Lenin, Stalin, Hitler and Mao seized power. Now the peace researchers have confirmed our fears and convictions with figures, analysis and the collection of countless documents.

"So my report today to the liberal parties of Europe is that you have been right about freedom the whole time. The resistance by liberals and by democrats of other political hues against Nazism and Communism, against apartheid and military or colonial rule, has been built partly on facts and observations, partly on values and intuition. When we have cursed the tyrants and their ideas it has been an ideological conviction as well as a result of our knowledge about the world and its realities. It has been a notion close to creed and to our basic approach to life."[15]

How democracy is defined

To fully assess whether there's a problem at hand, we must first think seriously about what we mean by *freedom* and *democracy*. These aren't airy concepts—they're real, down-to-earth, gut-level principles, things that have a very big effect on the quality of people's lives. They're things for which people will lie down in front of a tank or starve themselves to death in political prisons.

There are many ways to assess how "democratic" a government is. Everyone agrees it's about freedom and free elections, in one sense or another. But how much freedom? Freedom from what? And who gets the freedom?

Surely not everyone, because mass murderers aren't allowed to roam free.

But what about people of all sorts—including women, people of all races, and adults of all ages, religions, and sexual preferences? Not all democracies have given them fair voice.

Many great books, articles, and academic papers have been written on these issues, because so much is at stake. In this book we will concern ourselves only with the most fundamental issues, because the danger we see today has nothing to do with splitting hairs.

Rights and privileges

The core concept that holds democracies together is the allocation of rights and privileges.

Rights are not negotiable. They're absolute. Whether you believe they were ordained by the Creator (as did several of America's Founders) or are simply the application of natural law (as other Founders believed), they're absolute and cast in stone. All power flows from rights.

Privileges, on the other hand, are a form of "qualified rights." The *Merriam-Webster's Dictionary* defines *privileges* as "a right or immunity granted as a peculiar benefit, advantage, or favor."[16]

The key word is "granted," because—unlike rights, which are forever—privileges can be taken away just as quickly as they're granted.

The Founders knew that through most of the recent history of what we call civilization, rulers held rights and ordinary people held only privileges, granted by those rulers. In the past, three systems of government had risen up and seized control of nations and their peoples, and in each of those three types of government those in charge held the rights and the people were left with only privileges.

Historically, those who ruled had always been kings, theocrats, and feudal lords. Kings held power by threat of violence and continual warfare; theocrats and popes, by the people's fear of a god or gods; and feudal lords, by wealth and the power that comes from threatening people with poverty or hiring private armies.

The "new" idea of our Founders in 1776 was to throw off all three of these tyrannies and replace them with democracy— people ruling themselves.

At its core, it's a very simple concept, an inversion of the pyramid. Instead of the government holding the rights and passing out privileges to people as it sees fit, the people would hold all the rights. Whenever some of the people got together to form an institution—whether it was a corporation, a civic organization, a union or guild, a church, or even a government—that institution would have only privileges.

And those privileges would be granted—and could be revoked—by the sovereign action of the sole holders of the rights, We the People.

Democracy under assault

The concept that people—and only people—have rights is not new; in fact it's among the most ancient ways that tribes have organized themselves, as our Founders and Framers discovered when they began their research in the 1770s and 1780s. And it's been the power and force behind the rise of democracy world-wide, bringing peace and prosperity in its wake.

Democracy now, however, is under assault in the land of its birth. Corporations have funded massive projects to put into place judges who will assert that *corporations should have rights*—even civil rights—along with people, and they're getting results. Corporate CEOs have moved into the highest levels of American government and are threatening to do the same in other nations, "privatizing" many of the functions of government to keep them secret and take them out of the hands of We the People.

At the urging of corporate lawyers, South Africa recently wrote into its constitution that humans have rights, but, they added, so do corporations. The government would have only privileges, as would unions, churches, and unincorporated small businesses. But humans and corporations alike would share in the powers that come from being the holders of rights.

Other nations are considering similar provisions, and the movement toward "corporate rights" has rapidly gathered steam since it was first tacitly endorsed by the Reagan/Bush administration. It is now a cornerstone of the "conservative" movement and represents the greatest threat to democracy since this nation's founding.

So today the world confronts two struggles. One is the struggle for basic democracy by people who are ruled by dictators and tyrants. That struggle is being won, and the past 50 years have seen an explosion in democracy across the world. The second struggle is that of mature democracies to stay democratic.

Democracy

When all is said and done, in all its different forms around the world and through the years, democracy is *government by the people, of the people, and for the people.*

It is about whether the government responds to the needs and wants of ordinary, everyday citizens, or responds to the needs and wants of a selected few.

There are many different models of democracy. Although these may differ, they have the same fundamentals in common. And as the ideal has taken hold around the world, no matter how it's measured, democracy has shown a substantial increase in the twentieth century.

Modern democracy

Modern liberal democracies are heirs to the Athens experiment. As we'll discuss in more detail, Athens was one of the first "civilized" nations to adopt democracy, and it survived for several centuries. The democracy of Athens was more a "pure democracy" than a "modern democracy," however.

George Washington wasn't talking about a political point of view when, in 1790, he said, "As Mankind becomes more liberal, they will be more apt to allow that all those who conduct themselves as worthy members of the community are equally entitled to the protections of civil government. I hope ever to see America among the foremost nations of justice and liberality."[17] Most of the advanced democracies of the world—including the United States—refer to themselves as liberal democracies. Although it's less often used in the United States since the rise of Ronald Reagan and Newt Gingrich (with his list of words for conservatives to use and abuse), the phrase is common worldwide and is well understood.

The liberal concepts of modern democracy are grounded in several principles. First, if people are inherently good and democracy is a normal thing, then we don't need an elite class to control us. Second, liberal democrats (small "l" and small "d") believe that any sort of unbalanced power is inherently a force that will corrupt democracy, be it governmental force, individual force, organized religious force, or corporate force.

These core concepts are diametrically opposed to the conservative "people are essentially evil" worldview that has so long rationalized and thus sustained autocratic regimes. They underlie both ancient tribal democracies, modern democracies around the world, and liberal democratic institutions like the United Nations and NATO.

Liberals find in the rationalism of natural law the idea that all people should have equal opportunity, living free from oppression by political, military, or economic power. Thus, personal liberty on a local level is most effectively sustained when peace is achieved on a national and international level through shared goals and cooperation rather than through force or coercion.

Republic

It's popular today to assert that "America is not a democracy, it's a republic." In particular, conservative talk-show hosts and authors often use this argument, quoting the Founders who explicitly were not trying to create the "mob rule" of "pure democracy" but the "rule of law" in a constitutionally limited democratic republic. In this, they are technically correct, although the suggestion made to Republicans in the 1980s that it would be wise to stop refer-ring to "democracy" in America because it sounds too much like "Democrat" is probably closer to why today's conservatives are so fond of the term "republic," which sounds like "Republican."

In a republic, elected representatives make the laws, and in a "pure" democracy there are no representatives: the people them-selves vote on each issue. (California and other states' ballot initiatives are closer to pure democracy.) Nonetheless, the dis-tinction between the terms has been lost on most of the world, which defines a modern republic as a "modern democracy," and even James Madison—who first separated the definitions of the words "democracy" and "republic" in *Federalist* #10 in 1787—changed his mind in his later years to suggest that America is a democracy.

Antidemocracies

Fascism

The *American Heritage Dictionary* defines fascism as "a system of government that exercises a dictatorship of the extreme right, typically through the merging of state and business leadership, together with belligerent nationalism."[18]

Fascism was named by Italian dictator Benito Mussolini. This is relevant to our discussion because Mussolini noted in the entry he wrote for the *Encyclopedia Italiana,* "Fascism should more appropriately be called corporatism because it is a merger of state and corporate power."

Feudalism

In the classical sense, the feudal system in medieval times (the ninth to fifteenth centuries) was characterized by a concentration of most power in the hands of the few who owned property. All others were serfs: laborers who had no say in how anything was run.

Since the nineteenth century some observers have noted the increasing concentration of government power in corporate hands, coupled with the decline of human influence in government, and have called it feudalism. In 1873, Wisconsin's Supreme Court chief justice Edward G. Ryan spoke to a graduating class of law students on the topic, saying: "The enterprises of the country are aggregating vast corporate combinations of unexampled capital, boldly marching, not for economical conquests only, but for political power. . . . The question will arise and arise in your day, though perhaps not fully in mine, which shall rule—wealth or man; which shall lead—money or intellect; who shall fill public stations—educated and patriotic freemen, or the feudal serfs of corporate capital."[19]

The greatest threat to democracy worldwide is the shift of power to vast concentrations of capital called corporations, while power erodes away from the "educated and patriotic freemen" who form the cornerstone of democracy. Particularly worrisome and ironic is the fact that 15 years after Ryan gave his speech, a U.S. Supreme Court case resulted in human rights being given to corporations. It was in fact an error (the Court never made that ruling), but the result was that corporations began claiming civil rights, as if they were humans, and continue to do so today.

A later chapter will discuss in detail the damage that has resulted from this, as the "vast corporate combinations of capital" cited by Ryan have vastly outweighed the voices of actual humans in recent government decisions.

The characteristics of a healthy democracy

The hallmark of democracy is widespread access to the processes and protections of government.

To be sure, in different countries and eras there have been different levels of perfection or shortcoming. But at a practical level, these are the fundamental protections present in a functioning democracy and absent without it:

▶   EQUAL OPPORTUNITY: There should be no arbitrary restriction of a person's ability to better themselves through individual efforts.

▶   ACCESS TO CREATION OF LAWS: There should be no arbitrary restriction of a person's freedom to influence the lawmaking process. Nor should there be a case where an ordinary citizen can't afford to get involved, and influence is limited to those who give the most money to politicians or political parties. (Most democracies accomplish this by limiting campaign contributions or expenditures, or public financing of elections.)

▶ PROTECTION FROM HARM BY THOSE MORE POWERFUL: Thomas Jefferson said, "The legitimate powers of government extend to such actions as are injurious to others," meaning that government ought to protect citizens from such harm. But note that the same philosophy mandates a hands-off policy regarding issues where no harm is done. For example, on the particular issue of the religious beliefs of one's neighbor, Jefferson observed "It neither picks my pocket nor breaks my leg," and so, he said, the government should separate itself from religious power.

▶ ACCESS TO ALL LEVELS OF THE COURTS: Unlike the eighteenth century English system that our Founders rejected, citizens of all sorts should have comparable access to the courts.

As a more concrete and measurable version of the same criteria, the UN Development Programme says in its overview, "Deepening Democracy in a Fragmented World,"[20] that liberal democracy has six essential components:

1. A system of representation, with well-functioning political parties and interest associations
2. An electoral system that guarantees free and fair elections as well as universal suffrage
3. A system of checks and balances based on the separation of powers, with independent judicial and legislative branches
4. A vibrant civil society, able to monitor government and private business—and provide alternative forms of political participation
5. A free, independent media
6. Effective civilian control over the military and other security forces

The Goddess of Democracy

The Greek-Roman-Enlightenment-Iroquois-American idea of a government "deriving its just powers from the consent of the governed" is one of the most powerful and timeless ideas in the world.

Since democracy came into the modern world in America, American expressions of the ideal have been the beacon that has lit the path. From the French Revolution in 1789 to the people's uprising in Beijing in 1989, people around the world have used language and icons from the pen of Thomas Jefferson and his peers.

On May 29, 1989, over 20,000 people gathered around a 37-foot-tall papier-mâché statue in Beijing's Tiananmen Square. They called their statue the "Goddess of Democracy": it was a scale replica of the Statue of Liberty. That statue was such a powerful archetypal representation that many were willing to die for it . . . and some did.

It is tremendously ironic that today some conservative students of American history assert that modern democracy's Founders intended that power should rest in a moneyed elite.

Those prodemocracy protesters in China, like America's Founders, fought and died for the oppressed, and for their own hopes for personal freedom—not to create a nation ruled by the wealthy, such as the English monarch our Founders fought to escape.

Beware: Tight control can look very good, at first . . .

When Germany faced the last depression, its government turned to a hand-in-glove partnership with corporations (including some American corporations, as has been shown in recent years) to solidify its power over its own people and to wage war on others.

When Benito Mussolini named this new form of corporate/state partnership "fascism," referring to the Roman *fasces,* or bundle of sticks held together with a rope, that was the Caesars' symbol of power, he said that the bundle represented the police and military power of the state combined with the economic power of industry. The fascist system was adopted by Italy, Spain, Japan, and Germany.

Mussolini also said, "Fascism should more appropriately be called corporatism because it is a merger of state and corporate power." Advocates speak of the advantage of running things in a businesslike fashion, managing for results. And in the early days of fascist Italy, Mussolini (like many business leaders) had a reputation for getting things done: a common remark was, "He made the trains run on time."

Indeed, the results of fascism can look very good, at first; in Germany it brought such dramatic changes to that nation ravaged by World War I and crushed by the Treaty of Versailles that Adolf Hitler was named *Time* magazine's Man of the Year on February 2, 1939.

Is this what the Founders fought for?

Government must operate for the benefit of We the People, not corporations, churches, would-be warlords, or any other special interest group.

In these first chapters I have often referred to the Founders' intent and implicitly asked, "Is this what the Founders fought for?" Before I move forward to look at the attacks being waged on democracy, it's appropriate to step back and look at what inspired the Founders to fight back against the mightiest army in the world, and then, having won their freedom, create the type of government we have inherited.

3

PEOPLE AND EVENTS THAT INFLUENCED AMERICA'S FOUNDERS

The preservation of the sacred fire of liberty and the destiny of the republican model of government are justly considered as deeply, perhaps as finally staked, on the experiment entrusted to the hands of the American people.

—PRESIDENT GEORGE WASHINGTON (1789–1797)

I shall therefore conclude with a proposal that your watchmen be instructed, as they go on their rounds, to call out every night, half-past twelve, "Beware of the East India Company."

—Pamphlet signed by "RUSTICUS," 1773

Jefferson encounters ancient wisdom.

There was a full moon that Virginia night in 1762, and the sky was cloudless, cooling the ancient forest after a warm day. Thomas Jefferson watched respectfully as the elders and the "head women," as he'd come to call them, gathered to sit on blankets in a place of great honor near where the famous Cherokee warrior Ontasseté was about to speak. Although only 19, at six foot two

Jefferson was conspicuously tall among the Indians and was treated the same respectful way as his companion, the 28-year-old Thomas Sumter.

He watched as the sparks from the fire flew toward the dark moonlit sky, listening to the strange language of the Cherokee and the Creek around him. He understood none of their words, but later in life he would study their languages with the same mind that had enabled him to already learn to read and write Greek, Latin, and French.

His companion, Sumter, was a strong and aggressive man; the contrast between the two—the lanky, red-haired, freckle-faced scholar and the bold fighter—was distinct. Jefferson was in his last year of studies at the College of William and Mary, about to study law in a few months, while Sumter, who had left home as a teenager to fight in the French and Indian Wars, would leave the next day to escort Ontasseté across the Atlantic to meet the king of England. Sumter would go on to be a general in the American War of Independence, and Jefferson would write the document that formally declared it.

The sounds of the Cherokee language and the sight of the people assembling brought back for Jefferson childhood memories of the many times Ontasseté had visited his home while traveling from his Cherokee village to Williamsburg. Ontasseté liked to spend the night at the Shadwell, Virginia, farm of Peter Jefferson, and often Peter had invited his young son Thomas to join him and Ontasseté in conversations that stretched long into the evening. Peter Jefferson made friends instantly, had a lifelong fascination with native peoples and cultures, and had come to know dozens of Indian leaders as he mapped the Virginia colony 11 years earlier in 1751. (Thomas was eight the year his father mapped Virginia and met so many of the Indians; his father died five years later.)

"So much in answer to your inquiries concerning Indians," Thomas Jefferson wrote to John Adams in June 1812, "a people with whom, in the early part of my life, I was very familiar, and acquired impressions of attachment and commiseration for them which have never been obliterated. Before the Revolution, they were in the habit of coming often and in great numbers to the seat of government, where I was very much with them. I knew much the great Ontasseté, the warrior and orator of the Cherokees; he was always the guest of my father, on his journeys to and from Williamsburg."

(On June 19, 1754, when Jefferson was only eleven years old, Ben Franklin had introduced the Albany Plan of Union at a meeting attended by both his pre-Revolutionary compatriots and a delegation from the Iroquois Confederacy. Franklin had earlier attended an Iroquois Condolence Ceremony in 1753 and used Iroquois symbols both in his language and his design for early American currency. In 1770, Franklin wrote, "Happiness is more generally and equally diffus'd among Savages than in civilized societies. No European who has tasted savage life can afterwards bear to live in our societies."[21])

The heavy influence of Native American forms of democracy, particularly the Iroquois Confederacy, was a hot topic of conversation during Jefferson's childhood, and his father's close association with many Indians—particularly Ontasseté—brought to the now-teenage Jefferson an appreciation and understanding of the event he had been invited to witness.

The assembled Cherokee sat, as did Jefferson and Sumter, and Ontasseté began his farewell address. Although the Cherokee had signed their first treaty with England over 40 years earlier, colonists subject to the king had continued to encroach on Cherokee land and slaughter men, women, and children. Ontasseté had discussed this and similar matters many times with the king's men in Williamsburg and was now making an official visit to King George II himself—one head of state to another. Even though he would be the second representative of the Cherokee to cross the Atlantic in the giant ships, most operated by the East India Company, the crossings were always risky, and he didn't know if he'd ever see his family and friends again. He began his speech, as was the custom of his people, with thanks and prayers, speaking to the four sacred directions, to Mother Earth, and to Grandmother Moon.

"I was in his camp when he made his great farewell oration to his people the evening before his departure for England," Jefferson wrote in that letter to Adams many years later. "The moon was in full splendor, and to her he seemed to address himself in his prayers for his own safety on the voyage, and that of his people during his absence; his sounding voice, distinct articulation, animated action, and the solemn silence of his people at their several fires, filled me with awe and veneration, although I did not understand a word he uttered."

The Cherokee had suffered terribly, both from recurrent smallpox epidemics and from a series of betrayals by the British colonists with whom they'd aligned themselves during the French and Indian War. The treaties of 1721, 1754, and 1759 between the Cherokee and England had been repeatedly violated by British colonists, culminating in the atrocity of 1759 when Virginia colonists killed and mutilated 20 young Cherokee men, collecting a bounty on their scalps. This, and another land grab by the British in 1760, led to a bloody two-year war between England and the Cherokee.

Ontasseté, unaware that in just 11 years the British would be in an all-out shooting war with rebellious colonists, was hoping to make a final and lasting treaty of peace with King George II.

"That nation, consisting now of about 2,000 warriors, and the Creeks of about 3,000, are far advanced in civilization," Jefferson continued in his letter to Adams. At the time, the Cherokee had a written language of 86 letters, published their own newspaper called *The Phoenix,* and had adopted a constitution similar to that the Iroquois had held for centuries. "They have good cabins, enclosed fields, large herds of cattle and hogs, spin and weave their own clothes of cotton," Jefferson wrote, "have smiths and other of the most necessary tradesmen, write and read, are on the increase in numbers, and a branch of Cherokees is now instituting a regular representative government."

Adams replied to Jefferson's letter on June 28, 1813: "I have also felt an interest in the Indians, and a commiseration for them from my childhood. Aaron Pomham, the [Indian] priest, and Moses Pomham, the king of the Punkapang and Neponset tribes, were frequent visitors at my father's house, at least seventy years ago. I have a distinct remembrance of their forms and figures. They were very aged, and the tallest and stoutest Indians I have ever seen. The titles of king and priest, and the names of Moses and Aaron, were given them, no doubt, by our Massachusetts divines and statemen.

"There was a numerous family in this town, whose wigwam was within a mile of this house. This family were frequently at my father's house, and I, in my boyish rambles, used to call at their wigwam, where I never failed to be treated with whortleberries, blackberries, strawberries or apples, plums, peaches, etc., for they had planted a variety of fruit trees about them. But the girls went out to service, and the boys to sea, till not a soul is left. We scarcely see an Indian in a year."

Native Americans

Thus in May of 1776, as the war with Britain was already under way and a debate was ongoing in Philadelphia about a formal declaration of independence and the formation of a new nation, a delegation of 21 Iroquois arrived at the Continental Congress, which drafted the first document governing the nation birthed by the Declaration of Independence. A year earlier, at the Albany Conference, Iroquois attendees had openly raised questions with their friend Ben Franklin about a government with a chief executive, warning about the dangers of having a single elected official who might one day try to seize too much power for himself. They had been welcomed to the 1775 Continental Congress by John Hancock himself, who addressed a Delaware chief saying that "this council fire, [is] kindled for all the United Colonies."[22]

When the Iroquois arrived in Philadelphia, the president of the Continental Congress treated them as visiting dignitaries and wise elders and invited them to watch the debates. The second floor of Independence Hall (then the Pennsylvania State House) was given them to sleep in for over a month during the near-daily discussions, and Richard Henry Lee wrote that on May 17, 1776, the newly formed American army paraded over two thousand troops down the streets of Philadelphia for their review.[23] The *Pennsylvania Gazette* reported on the parade, saying that "the Members of Congress . . . and . . . the Indians . . . on business with the Congress" reviewed the troops along with General George Washington, General Mifflin, and General Gates.[24]

Three weeks later, after speeches were made expressing "friendship" that would "continue as long as the sun shall shine," an Onondaga chief gave Hancock the Iroquois name of "Karanduawn," meaning "Great Tree," a ceremony carefully recorded by attendee Charles Thompson. (The friendship struck up between the Onondaga and George Washington, apparently at this event, was so strong that an Onondaga woman accompanied Washington during most of the Revolutionary War as his cook, and the Onondaga saved Washington and his men from starvation during the bitter winter at Valley Forge by bringing them corn and other food.[25])

John Adams was there and noticed the events and discussions. In his book *Defence of the Constitutions of Government of the United States of America,*[26] written while the new Constitution for the United States of America was being hammered out, he noted how the ancient British and German tribesmen and many of the Native American tribes he knew represented branches of the human race who practiced the three-branches-of-government form of democracy that he and Jefferson advocated for the new United States of America. Adams pointed out that the Roman historian Tacitus thought a three-branch democracy was "laudable" but "doubted" its "practicability" and "duration," and that the great experiment America was about to undertake had never been done before successfully by those then thought of as "civilized people." But it was possible, and the Iroquois were living proof.

Adams wrote: "It would have been much to the purpose to have inserted a more accurate investigation of the form of government of the ancient Germans and modern [American] Indians; in both, the existence of the three divisions of power is marked with a precision that excludes all controversy. The democratical branch, especially, is so determined, that the real sovereignty resided in the body of the people . . ." and he added, "To collect together the legislation of the Indians, would take up much room, but would be well worth the pains. The sovereignty is in the nation, it is true, but the three powers are strong in every tribe."

Adams had asked Jefferson for more information on how Native American governments were organized, and Jefferson suggested that Adams read Joseph Lafitan. "Some scanty accounts of their traditions, but fuller of their customs and characters, are given us by most of the early travelers among them; these you know were mostly French. Lafitan, among them, and Adair an Englishman, have written on this subject."[27]

The Iroquois Confederacy

Lafitan wrote in 1724 about the Iroquois Confederacy, a group of five nations consisting of the Oneida, Mohawk, Onondaga, Cayuga, and Seneca. The Iroquois were particularly concerned with creating a lasting federation and knew that women were more in touch with the needs of future generations than men. Thus, the "head woman" of each family voted democratically to select (or remove) the sachems who represented families or clans to the confederation.[28]

Lafitan wrote fascinating accounts of Iroquois justice. These being tribes with neither police nor prisons, they depended on an extraordinarily high level of cultural pressure or what would have been called "civilization" during Jefferson's time to deal with people who committed crimes.[29]

Both Jefferson and Adams were wary of priests in all forms, as they both knew theocracies are enemies of democracy. Jefferson pointed out that the Indians shared their wariness: "You ask further, if the Indians have any order of priesthood among them, like the Druids, Bards or Minstrels of the Celtic nations? . . . The true line of distinction seems to be, that solemn ceremonies, whether public or private, addressed to the Great Spirit, are conducted by the worthies of the nation, men or matrons, while conjurers are resorted to only for the invocation of *evil* spirits. [Emphasis added.] The present state of the several Indian tribes, without any public order of priests, is proof sufficient that they never had such an order. . . . Indeed, so little idea have they of a regular order of priests, that they mistake ours for their conjurers, and call them by that name."

Jefferson was so impressed by the quality of some of the Native Americans he'd known, that he considered them at least the equals of whites. Several times in his personal letters he suggested that the best solution to the "Indian problem" was simply to have them all intermarry with whites until a single uniform race was created.

Tacitus on the natives of England

Jefferson also saw in the lives and stories of the Native Americans a strong parallel to his own tribal ancestors from the British Isles and an inspiration for the democracy he would help create.

One of the most famous writers who had encountered Jefferson's ancestors—the people of England—when they were still living tribally was the Roman senator Cornelius Tacitus (A.D. 56–117). Starting with an August 19, 1785, letter to Peter Carr and continuing to a January 15, 1825, letter to Joseph Coolidge Jr. just a year before Jefferson's death, we find dozens of references to Tacitus in the correspondences of Thomas Jefferson.

Jefferson wrote that from his childhood until well after his retirement from the presidency, he returned over and over again to Tacitus for inspiration and definition of his concept of the importance of standing up against tyranny, whether it be from another nation or from elites within his own country. As Jefferson wrote in a letter to David Howell the year he left the presidency, "I read one or two newspapers a week, but with reluctance give even that time from Tacitus."

Tacitus was a Roman orator of considerable fame who rose to be the Roman consul in A.D. 97 and the governor of Asia for two years beginning in 112. Pliny the Younger addressed some of his most famous letters to Tacitus, and although none of Tacitus's speeches survive, his histories of Germany and England—written in A.D. 98—are intact. Because Tacitus married the daughter of Agricola, the Roman emperor who conquered England, his account of his father-in-law Agricola's experience meeting the then-tribal English was particularly credible to Jefferson, who had first learned about the similarly tribal people of North America from his own father.

Tacitus discovers Jefferson's ancestors— and they're democratic.

To find what Tacitus had to say that left such a lasting impression on young Thomas Jefferson, and continued to inspire his vision of America right up to the time of his death, I found a book "Printed by W. Stark for J. Johnson, in St. Paul's Church-Yard, London" in 1777, titled A Treatise on the Situation, Manners, and Inhabitants of Germany and the Life of Agricola by C. Cornelius Tacitus with Copious Notes Translated into the English by John Aikin. The extensive commentary, missing from most modern publications that only translate and print the words of Tacitus, makes it clear that in 1777 even the translators believed Tacitus's entire account to be absolute fact.

While modern historians argue about the details of Tacitus's history, the prevailing notion at that time—clearly held by Jefferson, based on his letters and notes—was that Tacitus was a competent historian who reported the words and events of his time with brilliant accuracy.

The tribal English, before the Roman conquest during the first century, were, Agricola told his son-in-law Tacitus, a proud and fierce people who loved freedom. When the Romans confronted them, Tacitus writes, over 30,000 English tribesmen gathered to hear a speech by Galgachan, one of their leaders, prior to the battle that led to their defeat.[30] Agricola transcribed the speech, which was then published by Tacitus: "'When I reflect on the causes of the war and the circumstances of our situation,' said tribal leader Galgachan, 'I feel a strong persuasion that our united efforts on the present day will prove the beginning of universal liberty to Britain.'"

Although the Celts of continental Europe had been trading with the British tribesmen since between 800 and 500 B.C.E. and had conquered parts of what is now England, according to Tacitus, England was still populated by free tribal peoples when Agricola invaded with his Roman legions. Galgachan went on to say, "For none of us are hitherto debased by slavery; and there is no land behind us, nor is even the sea secure, whilst the Roman fleet hovers around. Thus the use of arms, which is at all times honourable to the brave, now offers the only safety even to cowards." Being lovers of freedom and democracy, Galgachan says, "even our eyes [are] unpolluted by the contact of subjugation."

The situation was bleak. As Galgachan continued, "There is no nation beyond us; nothing but waves and rocks, and the still more hostile Romans, whose arrogance we cannot escape by obsequiousness and submission."

Galgachan apparently thought of the Romans the same way Jefferson would often speak of the British 1,700 years later. "These plunderers of the world," Galgachan said, "after exhausting the land [of Italy] by their devastations, are riding the ocean:

stimulated by avarice, if their enemy be rich; by ambition, if poor; unsatiated by the East and by the West; the only people who behold wealth and indigence with equal avidity. To ravage, to slaughter, to usurp under false titles, they call empire; and where they make a desert, they call it peace."[31]

Jefferson, in his first draft of the Declaration of Independence, expressed a similar sentiment: "The history of the present King of Great Britain is a history of repeated injuries and usurpations, all having in direct object the establishment of an absolute Tyranny over these States.... in every stage of these oppressions we have petitioned for redress in the most humble terms: our repeated petitions have been answered only by repeated injury."

Paul de Rapin Thoyras on the history of England

Jefferson had two favorite histories of England: Tacitus and Paul de Rapin Thoyras. In an 1825 letter to an administrator at the University of Virginia, which he founded in 1817, Jefferson recommended Tacitus for ancient history and Paul de Rapin Thoyras as the single and absolutely best source of information on English history.

The reason Jefferson was so concerned that the university stock a copy of de Rapin's *History of England* was because history helped define people's views of politics. The Tory historian David Hume, for example, spread the idea that it was normal and natural for the mass of people to be subject to the authority of the few who were willing to grab or steal power, an idea Jefferson rejected.

The reason was that "Ludlow, Fox, Belsham, Hume, and Brodie" wrote history to please the royal family and, speaking of Hume in particular, Jefferson wrote "the object of his work was an apology for them. He spared nothing, therefore, to wash them white, and to palliate their misgovernment. For this purpose, he suppressed truths, advanced falsehoods, forged authorities, and falsified records. . . . But so bewitching was his style and manner, that his readers were unwilling to doubt anything, swallowed everything, and all England became Tories by the magic of his art."

On the other hand, "Of England," Jefferson wrote, "there is as yet no general history so faithful as Rapin's."

This was no small issue for Jefferson. In his letter to the university, he continued by pointing out how destructive to a nation a history could be that denied the truth of natural rights (granted by nature), as he believed the Saxons lived under, and instead substituted a belief that people should obtain their rights from government, rather than be firmly in control of government.

"The government of a nation may be usurped by the forcible intrusion of an individual into the throne," he wrote, "but to conquer its will, so as to rest the right on that, the only legitimate basis, requires long acquiescence and cessation of all opposition."

Jefferson even felt that reading the Tory history of Hume could make an American patriot acquiesce to the ideas of the American conservatives. "Hume," he added, "should be the last histories of England to be read. If first read, Hume makes an English Tory, from whence it is an easy step to American Toryism."

The best, though, was "the volume of Rapin, [that students] may read this first, and from this lay a first foundation in a basis of truth."

John Adams agreed, and wrote to Jefferson on July 15, 1813, that the conservative historian "David Hume had made himself so fashionable with the aid of the court and clergy . . . and by his elegant lies . . . that he had nearly laughed into contempt Rapin, Sydney, and even Locke."

The historian who influenced Jefferson is rediscovered.

In London, I tracked down a copy of *The History of England As Well Ecclesiastical As Civil* by Paul de Rapin Thoyras, printed in London in 1728, more than a decade before Jefferson was born. A similar edition was one of the first four books purchased from British booksellers for the newly created Library of Congress in 1802 during the presidency of and at the request of Thomas Jefferson.*

The book is one of the few to cover in detail the six-century period between the collapse of the Roman Empire and the Romans' departure from England in the fifth century, and the Norman invasion that led to the Battle of Hastings in 1066.

Jefferson believed the British Saxons had a better claim to the egalitarian, pre-Roman tribal values of his ancestors than did the French Normans (from Normandy) who defeated them in 1066 (and set up the kingdom that still rules England today). Life in England was quite different before 1066 than after.

The ancient history of England

In a chapter entitled "The Origin and Nature of the English Constitution," de Rapin points out that in the 1700s, "to put the King in a capacity to [rule] effectually, it is necessary he should have *great power* and a *revenue* large enough to live with splendor, in order to attract reverence and veneration from the people." De Rapin then lists the contemporary king's powers, including "Command of the armies . . . the pardoning of condemned criminals . . . the disposal of all places of trust or profit [regulating commerce] . . . and proclaiming peace and war," among others.†

The Saxons: a government controlled by its people

De Rapin says that the modern king of England (at that time George I) traces the legislative authority for his powers back to the traditions of the Saxon kings. "The King has great *prerogatives,* and they were the effect and consequence of the mutual agreement of the first *Anglo-Saxon* kings with their people."

But there were differences between the Saxon idea of government and that of George I's dynasty, and de Rapin bluntly

---

*Sadly, the book has been out of print for over a century.
†In transcribing this text, I've converted the f's to s's and dropped capitals but left the original italics intact.

points them out. "There were but two things the *Saxons* did not think convenient to entrust their kings with," he wrote, "for fear of the consequences attending the ill use of them; *the power of changing the laws that had been enacted by consent between the king and people;* and *the power of raising taxes by his own will and pleasure.*"

In these Saxon principles, we find the concept of taxation only by a democratically representative legislature, and of the laws and powers of a government coming solely from the consent of the governed.

De Rapin emphasizes this point: "These are two *important* articles, that branch themselves forth into numberless particulars relating to the *liberty* and *property* of the subjects, which the king can't meddle with, without breaking in upon the *Constitution.*" This is, he says, the foundational core of old Saxon law: "*The prerogatives of the Crown,* and *the rights and privileges of the people,* flowing from the two *articles* above, are the *ground-work* of all the laws that from time to time have been made by the *unanimous* consent of king and people."

And here we find in Saxon history and law the essence of the Revolutionary-era notion of the word "liberty" proclaimed in Jefferson's draft of the Declaration of Independence.

De Rapin continues in the next sentence: "The [Saxon] *English* government consists in an exact correspondence between the King's *prerogatives* and the people's *liberties.* So far are these from destroying, or running counter to one another, that they are the *strongest* cement of that *strict* Union so necessary between the prince and people."

This delicate balance between the power of government and the consent of the governed was the basis of Saxon civil society, including protections for the most vulnerable and in need. As de Rapin notes, "The King, by means of his *prerogatives,* is in a condition to protect his subjects, to see the laws duly executed, and justice impartially administered, to defend the weak from their powerful oppressors, to assist the unfortunate, and punish the disturbers of the society."

This promotes what our Constitution calls "domestic tranquility"—a people who are freed from worry and thus able to put
their time and efforts into building businesses, creating artistic
works, and doing other things of value to society. De Rapin
explicitly says this in the next sentence: "On the other hand, the
people, whilst in possession of their *liberties,* placing their whole
confidence in the laws and the king's care in duly executing them,
live securely without the least apprehension of losing their lives
or properties. They enjoy the fruits of their own labour and
industry. . . . If they make their court to the *nobles,* it is only when
their interest or assistance may be necessary, and not out of fear
of being oppress'd by them, since the *greatest* are equally subject to
the laws, with the *least.*"

This, the people of Jefferson's day believed, was the history of
pre-Norman-conquest England. In these words Washington,
Paine, Madison, and others found the archetype for an American
government that would last at least two centuries.

A warning about tyranny

But there was a warning in de Rapin's work, too. Continuing on
the same page, he gently notes the transition from Saxon values to
what Jefferson called a "system of tyranny" after the conquest of
1066: "It can't be denied but such a Government is extremely
well calculated to render both prince and people happy," de Rapin
writes, using language about "happiness" that would first appear
in any nation's founding history in the Declaration of Independence signed on July 4, 1776. "But when kings arose, as some
there were, that aim'd at *absolute power,* by changing the *old* and
making *new* laws at pleasure, and by imposing *illegal* and *arbitrary*
taxes on the people, this excellent government by these proceed-
ings being in some measure dissolved, *confusion* and *civil wars*
ensu'd, which some very *wrongfully* attributed to the *unsettled* tem-
per of the *English* nation."

De Rapin, being French, was able to write about the English

monarchy in a way that would have lost an Englishman his head. Nonetheless, he didn't want to offend the English, so he went to pains to point out that it was their monarchs and not their temperament that caused their problems. Interestingly, Jefferson often went to the same lengths, including one of the closing sentences in the Declaration of Independence that asserts the qualified friendship of Americans and the British.[32]

The origin of "civilized" representative government

De Rapin notes that a government that draws its power solely from the consent of the people didn't originate with the Saxons in the year 500, as some then believed.

Early precursors of democracies emerged and became widespread across Europe in the sixth century after the collapse of the Roman Empire. "If we look into the histories of the other *European* kingdoms founded by the *Northern* Nations," he writes, "we shall find like assemblies under different names, as *Dyets* in *Germany* and *Poland,* and *Cortez* in *Spain.* It is no wonder then the *Saxons* should establish in *England* the only form of government they knew any thing of."

In every case, there was an assembly representing the people, which chose the king by popular vote, passed laws that reflected the will of the people, and exclusively held the powers to tax and declare war.

"Now in order to preserve a perfect Union," de Rapin says, again presaging language used in the U.S. Constitution,[33] "it was necessary some way of communication and intercourse between them shou'd be established. This was done by the means of a Wittena-Gemot or *Assembly of Wise Men,* who were the *Representatives* of the whole Nation. This Method the *Saxons* brought with them from *Germany,* where all publick affairs were transacted in such like *conventions,* of which their Generals, chosen in the time of war, were Presidents." (His choice of words brings to mind the Constitutional Convention of 1774–1789 and General George Wash-

ington's unanimous election as president in 1789.[34] In all probability, the majority of the delegates to that Convention had read de
Rapin's *History of England.*)

The fall of representative government in England

With the final Battle of Hastings on October 14, 1066, cementing
the Norman conquest of the Saxons, everything changed. The
ruling Normans reinvented the old Roman story that the king
was king because God had ordained it: The "Divine Right of
Kings" replaced the "Natural Rights of Man." As a result, the
British experience of anything approximating a democratic
republic was put on hold until the modern era.

De Rapin says, "After the *conquest* these *assemblies* were called
Parliaments. If *William the Conqueror* continued them, which is a great
question, it was not with the same *rights* and *privileges* they enjoyed
under the *Saxon* Kings." It wasn't until the time of King Henry III
that Parliament came to play a role close to that of the "assembly
of wise men" that had elected previous kings under the Saxons,
and not until the great Reform of 1832 that England became a
modern democracy.

As the modern-day historical website www.battle1066.com
points out, "Our impression of a king today is of an aloof person
living in a luxurious castle or palace. Nothing could have been
further from the truth in those days." Kings were "elected" rather
than being warlords who had ruthlessly seized power, there were
many—dozens to hundreds—of elected "kings" all over the
British Isles, and they didn't enjoy the power of fealty or the
"right of the first night" or other bizarre royal customs introduced
after 1066. As the website points out, a king "was subject to the
same Saxon law as everybody else."

Thus, pre-1066 England was organized more along what
would today be called democratic tribal lines.

This commonly held view of history informed the colonists
who rose up like the ancient British tribal leader Galgachan—and
took on an empire.

The truth about the Tea Party

In elementary school we learned the story that the Revolutionary War was a struggle between the colonists and the king, but a larger story often goes untold until one reaches college history classes. That story is about the instrument of power the king wielded (or which wielded the king's power): a transnational corporation named the East India Company.

It turns out the Boston Tea Party wasn't about tax increases at all. It came about because a crony of the Crown, the East India Company, got a tax cut on its tea in the Tea Act of 1773, and this put all other small merchants at a disadvantage.

The East India Company got its way because it was so huge and powerful.

The early history of the times

We learned that the Pilgrims arrived in America in 1620 on a boat named the *Mayflower*, but few of us know that they'd chartered the boat from the East India Company, the world's largest and most powerful multinational corporation. The *Mayflower*, in fact, had already made the crossing between England to North America three times when the Pilgrims chartered it.

The East India Company was most responsible for the rise of England from a weak still-feudal state in the late 1500s to an international powerhouse by the mid-1600s. The Company was Queen Elizabeth I's second attempt to use a corporation to catch up with the other European seafaring powers.

Queen Elizabeth I was the largest shareholder and funder of the *Golden Hind*, Sir Francis Drake's ship that accidentally (he had planned to travel up the Nile) circumnavigated the globe between 1577 and 1580. Drake returned home with a mind-boggling array of treasures looted from various lands, including 26 tons of silver, so all of the investors, including the queen, saw a minimum 5,000 percent return on their investment.

Drake's success helped make Elizabeth willing to fund a new transnational trading company that—on behalf of the British Crown—would compete with the very successful Dutch trading companies. Thus, on December 31, 1600, she authorized a group of 218 noblemen and merchants from London (plus herself) to charter the East India Company.

A significant example of corporate cronyism is that in 1681, King Charles II and Parliament (nearly all of whom were stockholders) passed "An Act for the Restraining and Punishing Privateers & Pirates." This law required a license to import anything into the Americas (and other British-controlled parts of the world). The licenses were so expensive that they were rarely granted to anybody except the East India Company and other large British corporations. Anybody operating without a license was labeled a *privateer* and was subject to the death penalty "without the benefit of clergy."[35]

For the next 90 years, the trade provisions of the law were only spottily enforced, mostly because the offenders were usually small, entrepreneurial ships from America and the British navy didn't consider them worth chasing. The Company, facing British reluctance to enforce the law, created its own security force. The Company hired the infamous Captain Kidd to chase American private merchants, until the Company discovered that the good captain was secretly importing his seized tea, spices, and other goods into North America. They had him hanged in 1701, and for the next half-century drew more heavily on British irregulars to protect their interests.

The East India Company: history's first Wal-Mart

By the mid-1700s, the East India Company had become, to North America, the Wal-Mart of its day. It imported into North America vast quantities of products, including textiles, tools, steel, and tea, and exported to Europe tons of fur and tobacco, as well as many thousands of Native American slaves. Protesters and competitors were put down ruthlessly, and the Company worked so closely with the British military that they hired General Cornwallis after he lost the Battle of Yorktown in 1781 and put him in charge of much of its lucrative business in India (which they were beginning to rule as a corporate colonial power).

The late 1760s and early 1770s brought a crisis for the East India Company. Most of the easily found gold and other wealth around the world was now safely in Europe. The period between 1760 and 1773 brought a severe recession for both the American colonies and Britain, and demand for the Company's products went flat. Credit was tight, cash was tight, and as the colonies increasingly developed their own industries to manufacture things of steel, silver, and fabric, demand for imports from Europe slowed to a trickle, mostly of tea and spices.

The tea business with North America was still profitable, propping up many other sectors of the Company. As tea became more important, though, the Company also found itself facing increasing numbers of competitors.

Small entrepreneurs up and down the East Coast were building, buying, or chartering small private ships to sail to other parts of Europe or India to buy tea below the prices the Company was selling it for in North America. Nearly every block in most American cities had a teahouse, which dispensed the colonists' favorite drug of choice and also served as a local social center. Most of these teahouses were small businesses, and by the late 1760s the majority were buying their tea from local entrepreneurial "private" importers.

Fighting the privateers—even with the penalty of death as a weapon—had proved a waste of time. Rarely did the booty seized from a small entrepreneur's ship equal the cost to track, board, and seize the ship.

A legislative maneuver to quickly sell
17 million pounds of tea

Desperate for cash, the Company reached out to its stockholders—which included King George III and most of the members of the House of Lords—and asked them for an Enron-style tax cut that would allow them to undercut the prices of the small businesspeople of the colonies.

Parliament complied with the Tea Act of 1773, which not only cut the taxes on the East India Company's tea but also gave the Company a multimillion-pound rebate on taxes already paid on tea in inventory that would one day be shipped to North America.

American colonists, facing the destruction of their local small businesses by the East India Company, rebelled. The tax cut was so unfair that it revived the battle cry, "No taxation without representation."

As the *Encyclopaedia Britannica* notes in its 2001 online edition, the 1773 Tea Act was a "legislative maneuver by the British ministry of Lord North to make English tea marketable in America" by helping the East India Company quickly "sell 17 million pounds of tea stored in England."[36]

A new firsthand account of the Tea Party is discovered.

There are few books in print about the Boston Tea Party. Most are children's books, and the event is mentioned only briefly in many histories of the time. One of the reasons is that the men who participated swore a 50-year oath of silence, and few of them were alive 50 years later.

One, however, survived and went on to write a memoir that was published by a small New York press, S. S. Bliss, in 1834. To the best of my knowledge, it's the only existing account of the Boston Tea Party by an eyewitness, and it's been out of print for over 160 years. Discovering this, I set out on a search to find a copy and located one at a rare bookstore: I was thrilled to read this extraordinary first-person account.

The book is by George Robert Twelvetree Hewes and is titled *Retrospect of the Boston Tea Party with a Memoir of George R. T. Hewes, a Survivor of the Little Band of Patriots Who Drowned the Tea in Bos-*

ton Harbor in 1773. It was old, tattered, printed on a handpress with pages of slightly different sizes and hand-set type.

George Hewes was no stranger to scraps and fights on behalf of the colonists against the British in the 1770s. Originally a fisherman, he'd apprenticed as a shoemaker around the time of the Tea Party and appears repeatedly in Esther Forbes's classic 1942 biography of Paul Revere.[37] Forbes notes that when young Paul Revere went off to join the Continental army in 1756, Hewes tried to join him in Richard Gridley's regiment. But, she notes, "All must be able-bodied and between seventeen and forty-five, and must measure to a certain height. George Robert Twelvetree Hewes could not go. He was too short, and in vain did he get a shoemaker to build up the inside of his shoes."[38]

In anecdotes that recall how small the American communities were in that day (New York City had only 30,000 inhabitants at the time of the Revolutionary War), Forbes chronicles Hewes borrowing money from John Hancock and having dinner with George Washington. "Hewes says that, 'Madam Washington waited upon them at table at dinner-time and was remarkably social.' "[39]

Reading the hand-typeset brittle pages of Hewes's memoir brought the Boston Tea Party (a phrase which he apparently coined—prior to his book, it was referred to as "that incident in Boston harbor") and the struggle of the colonists against corporate rule fully to life. Hewes notes that weak enforcement of the Act for Restraining Privateers "rendered the smuggling of [tea] an object and was frequently practiced, and their resolutions against using it, although observed by many with little fidelity, had greatly diminished the importation into the colonies [by the East India Company] of this commodity. Meanwhile an immense quantity of it was accumulated in the warehouses of the East India Company in England. This company petitioned the king to suppress the duty of three pence per pound upon its introduction into America."[40]

Like Wal-Mart, the East India "super-ships" destroyed smaller competition.

Thus came about the Tea Act—a giant corporate tax cut—as Hewes notes: "The [East India] Company, however, received permission to transport tea, free of all duty, from Great Britain to America," allowing it to wipe out its small competitors and take over the tea business in all of America. "Hence," Hewes said, "it was no longer the small vessels of private merchants, who went to vend tea for their own account in the ports of the colonies, but, on the contrary, ships of an enormous burthen, that transported immense quantities of this commodity.... The colonies were now arrived at the decisive moment when they must cast the dye, and determine their course."

But it wasn't just the American tea merchants who were upset. England was filled with small businesspeople who wanted to import and sell their own tea, and they offered encouragement to the colonists in letters published in newspapers. "Even in England individuals were not wanting, who fanned this fire; some from a desire to baffle the government, others from motives of private interest, says the historian of the event, and jealousy at the opportunity offered the East India Company, to make immense profits to their prejudice."

Hewes continues: "These opposers of the measure in England [the Tea Act of 1773] wrote therefore to America, encouraging a strenuous resistance. They represented to the colonists that this would prove their last trial, and that if they should triumph now, their liberty was secured forever; but if they should yield, they must bow their necks to the yoke of slavery. The materials were so prepared and disposed that they could easily kindle."

The first confrontation between the colonists and the corporation appeared as if it would happen in Pennsylvania and New York.

"At Philadelphia," Hewes writes, "those to whom the teas of the [East India] Company were intended to be consigned, were induced by persuasion, or constrained by menaces, to promise, on no terms, to accept the proffered consignment.

"At New-York, Captain Sears and McDougal, daring and enterprising men, effected a concert of will [against the East India Company], between the smugglers, the merchants, and the sons of liberty [who had all joined forces and in most cases were the same people]. Pamphlets suited to the conjecture, were daily distributed, and nothing was left unattempted by popular leaders, to obtain their purpose."

The broad consensus was that boycotts and acts of civil disobedience would be enough to make the British rescind the tax breaks and rebates that were now allowing the East India Company to sell its tea below market value. But as newspapers began to expose the ways the East India Company had used monopoly control in other nations where it had put all the local small companies out of business, anger rose. Consider this pamphlet, which appeared on trees and buildings all over Philadelphia and Boston in the fall of 1773. It was titled *The Alarm* and signed by an enigmatic patriot who called himself only "Rusticus."[41]

Are we in like Manner to be given up to the Disposal of the East India Company, who have now the Assurance, to step forth in Aid of the Minister, to execute his Plan, of enslaving America? Their Conduct in Asia, for some Years past, has given simple Proof, how little they regard the Laws of Nations, the Rights, Liberties, or Lives of Men. They have levied War, excited Rebellions, dethroned lawful Princes, and sacrificed Millions for the Sake of Gain. The Revenues of Mighty Kingdoms have centered in their Coffers. And these not being sufficient to glut their Avarice, they have, by the most unparalleled Barbarities, Extortions, and Monopolies, stripped the miserable Inhabitants of their Property, and reduced whole Provinces to Indigence and Ruin. Fifteen hundred Thousands, it is said, perished by Famine in one Year, not because the Earth denied its Fruits; but [because] this Company and their Servants engulfed all the Necessaries of Life, and set them at so high a Rate that the poor could not purchase them.

The pamphlets and newspaper stories galvanized the populace, who succeeded in turning back the Company's ships when they tried to land in New York and Philadelphia harbors. "In Boston," Hewes wrote, "the general voice declared the time was come to face the storm. . . . Now is the time to prove our courage, or be disgraced with our brethren of the other colonies, who have their eyes fixed upon us, and will be prompt in their succor if we show ourselves faithful and firm."

Hewes adds, "This was the voice of the Bostonians in 1773. The factors who were to be the consignees of the tea, were urged to renounce their agency, but they refused and took refuge in the fortress. A guard was placed on Griffin's wharf, near where the tea ships were moored. It was agreed that a strict watch should be kept; that if any insult should be offered, the bell should be immediately rung; and some persons always ready to bear intelligence of what might happen, to the neighbouring towns, and to call in the assistance of the country people."

"Rusticus" added his voice in the May 27, 1773, pamphlet saying: "Resolve therefore, nobly resolve, and publish to the World your Resolutions, that no Man will receive the Tea, no Man will let his Stores, or suffer the Vessel that brings it to moor at his Wharf, and that if any Person assists at unloading, landing, or storing it, he shall ever after be deemed an Enemy to his Country, and never be employed by his Fellow Citizens."

A new edition of *The Alarm,* published on October 27, 1773, said, "It hath now been proved to you, That the East India Company, obtained the monopoly of that trade by bribery, and corruption. That the power thus obtained they have prostituted to extortion, and other the most cruel and horrible purposes, the Sun ever beheld."

But despite the protests, on a cold winter day the Company sailed its ships into the port of Boston.

"On the 28th of November, 1773," Hewes writes, "the ship Dartmouth with 112 chests arrived; and the next morning after, the following notice was widely circulated:

Friends, Brethren, Countrymen! That worst of plagues, the detested TEA, has arrived in this harbour. The hour of destruction, a manly opposition to the machinations of tyranny, stares you in the face. Every friend to his country, to himself, and to posterity, is now called upon to meet in Faneuil Hall, at nine o'clock, this day, at which time the bells will ring, to make a united and successful resistance to this last, worst, and most destructive measure of administration.

The pamphlet galvanized the citizens of Boston. Hewes writes, "Things thus appeared to be hastening to a disastrous issue. The people of the country arrived in great numbers, the inhabitants of the town assembled. This assembly which was on the 16th of December, 1773, was the most numerous ever known, there being more than 2000 from the country present."

Hewes continues: "This notification brought together a vast concourse of the people of Boston and the neighbouring towns, at the time and place appointed. Then it was resolved that the tea should be returned to the place from whence it came in all events, and no duty paid thereon. The arrival of other cargoes of tea soon after, increased the agitation of the public mind, already wrought up to a degree of desperation, and ready to break out into acts of violence, on every trivial occasion of offence. . . .

"Finding no measures were likely to be taken, either by the governor, or the commanders, or owners of the ships, to return their cargoes or prevent the landing of them, at 5 o'clock a vote was called for the dissolution of the meeting and obtained. But some of the more moderate and judicious members, fearing what might be the consequences, asked for a reconsideration of the vote, offering no other reason, than that they ought to do every thing in their power to send the tea back, according to their previous resolves. This, says the historian of that event,* touched the pride of the assembly, and they agreed to remain together one hour."

---

*Presumably Hewes is referring to himself in the third person, a form considered good manners in the eighteenth century.

During that hour, there was a strong and vigorous debate about whether or not they should take on the world's mightiest corporation, backed up by the greatest military force the planet had ever seen.

And then came a call for a vote: "The question was then immediately put whether the landing of the tea should be opposed, and carried in the affirmative unanimously. Rotch [a local tea seller], to whom the cargo of tea had been consigned, was then requested to demand of the governor to permit to pass the castle [return the ships to England]. The latter answered haughtily, that for the honor of the laws, and from duty towards the king, he could not grant the permit, until the vessel was regularly cleared.

"A violent commotion immediately ensued; and . . . a person disguised after the manner of the Indians, who was in the gallery, shouted at this juncture, the cry of war; and that the meeting dissolved in the twinkling of an eye, and the multitude rushed in a mass to Griffin's wharf."

What really happened at the Tea Party itself?

Much like some modern antiglobalization protesters, the group had voted to pass the point of no return and make a clear and unflinching statement, in this case a million-dollar act of vandalism. Hewes wrote:

> It was now evening, and I immediately dressed myself in the costume of an Indian, equipped with a small hatchet, which I and my associates denominated the tomahawk, with which, and a club, after having painted my face and hands with coal dust in the shop of a blacksmith, I repaired to Griffin's wharf, where the ships lay that contained the tea. When I first appeared in the street after being thus disguised, I fell in with many who were dressed, equipped and painted as I was, and who fell in with me and marched in order to the place of our destination.
>
> When we arrived at the wharf, there were three of our number who assumed an authority to direct our operations, to which

we readily submitted. They divided us into three parties, for the purpose of boarding the three ships which contained the tea at the same time. The name of him who commanded the division to which I was assigned was Leonard Pitt. The names of the other commanders I never knew.

We were immediately ordered by the respective commanders to board all the ships at the same time, which we promptly obeyed. The commander of the division to which I belonged, as soon as we were on board the ship appointed me boatswain, and ordered me to go to the captain and demand of him the keys to the hatches and a dozen candles. I made the demand accordingly, and the captain promptly replied, and delivered the articles; but requested me at the same time to do no damage to the ship or rigging.

We then were ordered by our commander to open the hatches and take out all the chests of tea and throw them overboard, and we immediately proceeded to execute his orders, first cutting and splitting the chests with our tomahawks, so as thoroughly to expose them to the effects of the water.

In about three hours from the time we went on board, we had thus broken and thrown overboard every tea chest to be found in the ship, while those in the other ships were disposing of the tea in the same way, at the same time. We were surrounded by British armed ships, but no attempt was made to resist us.

We then quietly retired to our several places of residence, without having any conversation with each other, or taking any measures to discover who were our associates; nor do I recollect of our having had the knowledge of the name of a single individual concerned in that affair, except that of Leonard Pitt, the commander of my division, whom I have mentioned. There appeared to be an understanding that each individual should volunteer his services, keep his own secret, and risk the consequence for himself. No disorder took place during that transaction, and it was observed at that time that the stillest night ensued that Boston had enjoyed for many months.

Hewes and his associates destroyed and threw overboard 342 chests of tea—enough to make 24 million cups of tea—worth over a million dollars in today's money. Instead of realizing that this was an uprising that could be handled by allowing the colonists to have their own small businesses, Parliament passed the Boston Port Act, which closed the port until Boston's citizens had repaid the Company for the tea. The colonists refused, leading to increasing tensions and leading, some say, directly to Paul Revere's April 18, 1775, ride that called out 77 Minutemen to face 700 British regulars (Redcoats) the next day on the Lexington Green.

The war was on, and a predatory multinational corporation had triggered it.

The cost to those who fought for democracy

The Declaration of Independence was the logical extension of the Revolution initiated by the Boston Tea Party, and was signed by a group bearing similar diversity to those in the various states who later ratified the Constitution.

A dozen of the 56 signers of the Declaration of Independence were politicians, physicians, or Protestant ministers; 11 were merchants; 9 were farmers. Ben Franklin was hard to define, although at the time he was referred to as a printer and Renaissance man; another was a musician, and one was a teacher. They ranged in age from their 20s to the octogenarian Franklin, although he was the only one who was truly elderly. Thomas Jefferson, at 33, represented the average age.

These men were the most idealistic and determined among the colonists. While the conservatives of the day argued that America should remain a colony of England forever, these liberal radicals believed in both individual liberty and societal obligations. A nation must care for the lives of its own, guarantee liberty, and ensure its citizens "happiness"—a radical concept that had never before appeared in any nation's founding documents.

The signers wrote in the Declaration, "We mutually pledge to each other our Lives, our Fortunes and our sacred Honor," and it was a simple statement of fact. The day they signed that document, each legally became a traitor and was sentenced to death for treason by the legal government that controlled their lands and their homes. As Ben Franklin pointed out, they stood at a point of no return, and, "Indeed we must all hang together, otherwise we shall most assuredly hang separately."

When Rhode Island's Stephen Hopkins signed the document, he remarked to his friend William Ellery that "My hand trembles, but my heart does not."[42] But Virginia's Benjamin Harrison, who weighed nearly 300 pounds, commented to Massachusetts's Elbridge Gerry, a short, thin man, "With me it [the hanging] will all be over in a minute, but you will be dancing on air an hour after I am gone."[43]

John Hancock, the wealthiest among them, signed his name large enough that the king "could read [Hancock's] name without glasses and could now double the reward," of 500 pounds that had already been put on his head for sedition.[44] Just six months later, Hancock would lose his newborn daughter to complications of childbirth arising from his wife's fleeing the oncoming British army. Although wealthy by the standards of the day, he would hardly qualify as "rich" by today's standards: he founded no dynasty, and no foundations today dispense his money; his legacy is our nation.

Another of the wealthiest of the signers was Thomas Nelson of Virginia, but a year after the signing the British had seized his home and lands. When he and George Washington attacked the British in Nelson's hometown, Nelson encouraged Washington to attack the Nelson homestead, which British General Cornwallis had taken as his headquarters, with cannons. The house was destroyed, and after the war Nelson, unable to repay loans he'd taken out against it to help finance the Revolution, lost his property and died in poverty at the age of 50.

The wealthy Philadelphia merchant Robert Morris lost 150 ships at sea in the war, wiping out his small fortune. Signer William Ellery of Rhode Island similarly lost everything, as did

Virginia's Carter Braxton and Benjamin Harrison, Pennsylvania's George Clymer, New York's Philip Livingston, Georgia's Lyman Hall, and New Jersey's Francis Hopkinson.

The British destroyed New York's Francis Lewis's property and threw his wife into such a hellhole of a jail that she died two years later. Three of South Carolina's four signers—Edward Rutledge, Thomas Heyward Jr., and Arthur Middleton—were captured by the British and held in a filthy, unheated prison and brutally tortured for over a year before George Washington freed them in a prisoner exchange.

New Jersey farmer John Hart's wife died shortly after he signed the Declaration, and his 13 children were scattered among sympathetic families to hide them from the British and conservative loyalists. He never saw them again, dying alone and wracked with grief three years later.

Altogether, 17 of the signers were wiped out by the war they declared.

New Jersey State Supreme Court justice Richard Stockton took his wife and children into hiding after he signed the Declaration, but conservatives loyal to the Crown turned them in. He was so badly beaten and starved in the British prison that he died before the war was over. His home was looted, and his wife and children lived the rest of their lives as paupers.

Altogether, nine of the men in that room died, and four lost their children as a direct result of putting their names to the Declaration of Independence. Every single one had to flee his home, and, after the war, twelve returned to find only rubble.

After the war was over and the conservatives had fled to Canada and England, the survivors of the new American nation met to put into final form the legal structure of the nation they had just birthed. It was not to be a nation of cynical, selfish libertarians who believed the highest value was individual freedom and independence from society, or that the greatest motivator was greed. It was not to be a kingdom, ruled by a warlord elite. It was not to be a theocracy, where religious leaders made the rules (as had been several of the states). And it was not to be a feudal nation, ruled by the rich.

As Benjamin Franklin told Philadelphia's Mrs. Powell after she asked him what sort of nation had been conceived in the Constitutional Convention, it was to be, "A republic, madam, if you can keep it."[45]

Although the Boston Tea Party ignited the forces for liberal democracy in what would become the United States, and the Declaration of Independence declared the war that birthed America, in some other nations democracy didn't survive an ultraconservative assault. Germany is a good example of how difficult and fragile democracy can be—particularly during its first generation—if a nation's own people don't fight to keep it.

4

WHEN DEMOCRACY FAILED

Many forms of Government have been tried, and will be tried in this world of sin and woe. No one pretends that democracy is perfect or all-wise. Indeed, it has been said that democracy is the worst form of government except all those other forms that have been tried from time to time.

—SIR WINSTON CHURCHILL (1874–1965),
November 11, 1947

For most of the twentieth century, Americans feared the greatest danger to our way of life was communism. We were wrong: fascism was a more potent external menace, and now may be our greatest internal threat. Consider this true story.

The 70th anniversary of February 27, 1933, wasn't noticed in the United States and was barely reported in the corporate media. But the Germans remembered well that fateful day in 1933. Many commemorated the anniversary by joining in demonstrations against the war in Iraq that had mobilized more millions of citizens all across the world than any in history.

The end of democracy started when the government, in the midst of a worldwide economic crisis, received reports of an imminent terrorist attack. A foreign ideologue had launched feeble

attacks on a few famous buildings, but the media largely ignored his efforts. The intelligence services knew, however, that
the odds were he would eventually succeed. (Historians are still
arguing whether or not rogue elements in the intelligence service
helped the terrorist; the most recent research implies that they
did not.)

But the warnings of investigators were ignored at the highest
levels, in part because the government was distracted; the man
who claimed to be the nation's leader had not been elected by a
majority vote, and many citizens claimed he had no right to the
powers he coveted. He was a simpleton, some said, a cartoon
character of a man who saw things in black-and-white terms and
didn't have the intellect to understand the subtleties of running a
nation in a complex and internationalist world. His coarse use of
language—reflecting his political roots in a southernmost state—
and his simplistic and often-inflammatory nationalistic rhetoric
offended aristocrats, foreign leaders, and the well-educated elite
in the government and media. As a young man, he'd joined a
secret society with an occult-sounding name and bizarre initia-
tion rituals that involved skulls and human bones.

Nonetheless, he knew the terrorist was going to strike
(although he didn't know where or when), and he had already
considered his response. When an aide brought him word that
the nation's most prestigious building was ablaze, he verified that
it was the terrorist who had struck and then rushed to the scene
and called a press conference.

"You are now witnessing the beginning of a great epoch in
history," he proclaimed, standing in front of the burned-out
building, surrounded by national media. "This fire," he said, his
voice trembling with emotion, "is the beginning." He used the
occasion—"a sign from God," he called it—to declare a war not on
another nation but on a tactic: terrorism. The terrorism his country was suffering from, he said, had to have originated with a
group of people of Middle Eastern origin who rationalized their
acts using religion.

Two weeks later, the first detention center for terrorists was built in Oranienberg to hold suspected allies of the infamous terrorist. In a national eruption of patriotism, the leader's flag was everywhere, even printed large in newspapers suitable for window display.

Within four weeks of the terrorist attack, the nation's now-popular leader had pushed through legislation—in the name of combating terrorism and fighting the philosophy he said spawned it—that suspended constitutional guarantees of free speech, privacy, and habeas corpus. Police could now intercept mail and wiretap phones; suspected terrorists could be imprisoned without specific charges and without access to their lawyers; police could sneak into people's homes without warrants if the cases involved terrorism.

Sunset provisions and gradual increases in terror

To get his patriotic "Decree on the Protection of People and State" passed over the objections of concerned legislators and civil libertarians, he agreed to put a four-year sunset provision on it: if the national emergency provoked by the terrorist attack was over by then, the freedoms and rights would be returned to the people, and the police agencies would be re-restrained. Legislators would later say they hadn't had time to read the bill before voting on it.

His federal police agencies stepped up their program of arresting suspicious persons and holding them without access to lawyers or courts. In the first year only a few hundred were imprisoned, and those who objected were largely ignored by the mainstream press, which was afraid to offend and thus lose access to a leader with such high popularity ratings. Citizens who protested the leader in public—and there were many—quickly found themselves confronting the newly empowered police's batons, gas, and jail cells, or fenced off in protest zones safely out of earshot of the leader's public speeches. (In the meantime, he was taking almost daily lessons in public speaking, learning to control his tonality, gestures, and facial expressions. He became a very competent orator.)

Within the first months after the attack, at the suggestion of a political adviser, he brought a formerly obscure word into common usage. He wanted to stir up "racial pride" among his countrymen, so, instead of referring to the nation by its name, he began to refer to it as "the homeland," a phrase publicly promoted by Rudolph Hess in a 1934 speech recorded in Leni Riefenstahl's famous propaganda movie *Triumph of the Will.* As hoped, people's hearts swelled with pride, and the beginning of an us-versus-them mentality was sown. Our land was "the" homeland, citizens thought: all others were simply foreign lands. We are the "true people," he suggested, the only ones worthy of our nation's concern; if bombs fall on others, or human rights are violated in other nations and it makes our lives better, it's of little concern to us.

Playing on this new nationalism, and exploiting a disagreement with the French over his increasing militarism, he argued that any international body that didn't act first and foremost in the best interest of his own nation was neither relevant nor useful. He withdrew his country from the League of Nations in October 1933 and then negotiated a separate naval armaments agreement with Secretary of State for Foreign Affairs Anthony Eden of the United Kingdom to create a worldwide military ruling elite.

His propaganda minister orchestrated a campaign to ensure the people that he was a deeply religious man and that his motivations were rooted in Christianity. He even proclaimed the need for a revival of the Christian faith across his nation, what he called "New Christianity." Every man in his rapidly growing army wore a belt buckle that declared "Gott mit uns"—God is with us—and most of them fervently believed it was true.

Creating a new homeland security bureau

Within a year of the attack, the nation's leader determined that
the various local police and federal agencies around the nation
were lacking the communication and coordinated administration
necessary to deal with the threat, particularly those citizens who
were of Middle Eastern ancestry and thus considered to be probably terrorist and communist sympathizers, and various trouble-
some "intellectuals" and "liberals." He proposed a national agency
to protect the security of the homeland, consolidating the actions
of dozens of previously independent police, border, and investigative agencies under a single leader. He appointed one of his
most trusted associates to be leader of this new agency, the Central Security Office for the homeland, and gave it a role in the
government equal to the other major departments.

His assistant who dealt with the press noted that since the
attack, "radio and press are at our disposal." Those voices questioning the legitimacy of their nation's leader, or raising questions
about his checkered past, had by now faded from the public's
recollection as his Central Security Office began advertising a
program encouraging people to phone in tips about suspicious
neighbors. This program was so successful that the names of
some of the people "denounced" were soon being broadcast on
radio stations. Those denounced often included opposition
politicians and celebrities who dared speak out—a favorite target
of his regime and the media he now controlled through intimida-
tion and ownership by corporate allies.

To consolidate his power, he concluded that government
alone wasn't enough. He reached out to industry and forged an
alliance, bringing former executives of the nation's largest corporations into high government positions. A flood of government
money poured into corporate coffers to fight the war against the
terrorists lurking within the homeland, and to prepare for wars
overseas. He encouraged large corporations friendly to him to

acquire media outlets and other industrial concerns across the nation, particularly those previously owned by "suspicious" people of Middle Eastern ancestry. He built powerful alliances with industry; one corporate ally got the lucrative contract worth millions to build the first large-scale detention center for enemies of the state. Soon more would follow. Industry flourished.

But after an interval of peace following the terrorist attack, voices of dissent arose again within and without the government. Students had started an active program opposing him (later known as the White Rose Society), and leaders of nearby nations were speaking out against his bellicose rhetoric. He needed a diversion, something to direct people away from the corporate cronyism being exposed in his own government, questions of his possibly illegitimate rise to power, and the oft-voiced concerns of civil libertarians about the people being held in detention without due process or access to attorneys or family.

The lies that convinced the people
war was necessary

With his number two man—a master at manipulating the media—the nation's leader began a campaign to convince the nation that a small, limited war was necessary. Another nation was harboring many of the "suspicious" Middle Eastern people, and even though its connection with the terrorist who had set afire the nation's most important building was tenuous at best, it held resources their nation badly needed if they were to have room to live and maintain their prosperity. He called a press conference and delivered an ultimatum to the leader of the other nation, provoking an international uproar. He claimed the right to strike preemptively in self-defense, and nations across Europe— at first—denounced him for it, pointing out that it was a doctrine claimed in the past only by nations seeking worldwide empire, like Caesar's Rome or Alexander's Greece.

It took a few months, and intense international debate and lobbying with European nations, but finally a deal was struck. Thus Adolf Hitler annexed Austria in a lightning move, riding a wave of popular support as leaders so often do in times of war. The Austrian government was unseated and replaced by a new leadership friendly to Germany, and German corporations began to take over Austrian resources.

In a speech responding to critics of the invasion, Hitler said, "Certain foreign newspapers have said that we fell on Austria with brutal methods. I can only say: even in death they cannot stop lying. I have in the course of my political struggle won much love from my people, but when I crossed the former frontier [into Austria] there met me such a stream of love as I have never experienced. Not as tyrants have we come, but as liberators."[46]

To deal with dissent, at the advice of his politically savvy advisers, Hitler and his "friends" in the press began a campaign to equate him and his policies with patriotism and the nation itself. In times of war, they said, there could be only "one people, one nation, and one commander in chief" ("Ein Volk, ein Reich, ein Führer"), and so began a nationwide campaign charging that critics of his policies were attacking the nation itself. Those questioning him were labeled unpatriotic, "anti-German," or "not good Germans," and it was suggested they were aiding the enemies of the state by failing in the patriotic necessity of supporting the nation's valiant men in uniform. It was one of his most effective ways to stifle dissent and pit wage-earning people (from whom most of the army came) against the "intellectuals and liberals" who were critical of his policies.

Nonetheless, once the annexation of Austria was complete and peace returned, voices of opposition were again raised in the homeland. The almost-daily release of news bulletins about the dangers of terrorist communist cells wasn't enough to rouse the populace and suppress dissent. An all-out war was necessary to divert public attention from the growing rumbles within the country about disappearing dissidents; violence against liberals, Jews, and union leaders; and the epidemic of crony capitalism that was producing empires of wealth in the corporate sector but threatening the middle class's way of life.

His increasing belligerence aroused concern all over the world, but after meeting with Hitler, Prime Minister Neville Chamberlain told the nervous British people that giving in to this leader's new first-strike doctrine for a second time would bring "peace for our time."

A year later, to the week, Hitler invaded Czechoslovakia; the nation was now fully at war, and all internal dissent was suppressed in the name of national security. It was the end of Germany's first experiment with democracy.

February 27, 2003, was the 70th anniversary of Dutch terrorist Marinus van der Lubbe's successful firebombing of the German Parliament (Reichstag) building, the terrorist act that catapulted Hitler to legitimacy and reshaped the German constitution. By the time of his successful and brief seizure of Austria, in which almost no German blood was shed, Hitler was the most beloved and popular leader in the history of his nation. Hailed around the world, he was later *Time* magazine's Man of the Year.

Most Americans remember his office for the security of the homeland, known as the Reichssicherheitshauptamt, and its Schutzstaffel, by its famous agency's initials: the SS.

Two nations take two different paths— in the 1930s.

Today, as we face financial and political crises, it's useful to remember that the ravages of the Great Depression hit Germany and the United States alike. Through the 1930s, however, Hitler and Roosevelt chose very different courses to bring their nations back to power and prosperity.

Germany's response was to use government to empower corporations and reward the society's richest individuals, privatize much of the commons, stifle dissent, strip people of constitutional rights, and create an illusion of prosperity through continual and ever-expanding war. America passed minimum-wage laws to raise the middle class, enforced antitrust laws to diminish the power of corporations, increased taxes on corporations and the wealthiest individuals, created Social Security, and through the WPA (Works Progress Administration) became the employer of last resort through programs to build national infrastructure, promote the arts, and replant forests.

To the extent that our Constitution is still intact, the choice is ours once more.

MYTHS ABOUT DEMOCRACY
IN AMERICA

Democracy extends the sphere of individual freedom, socialism restricts it. Democracy attaches all possible value to each man; socialism makes each man a mere agent, a mere number. Democracy and socialism have nothing in common but one word: equality. But notice the difference: while democracy seeks equality in liberty, socialism seeks equality in restraint and servitude.

—ALEXIS DE TOCQUEVILLE (1805–1859)

Myth: "Even our Founders knew democracies
eventually self-destruct."

Reality: Adams got it wrong. He thought people
could never rule themselves and democracy could
never survive.

President John Adams was skeptical about the survivability of democracy right up until the last days of his life. Agreeing with the conservative Federalist view that was then so prevalent, he felt that a benevolent autocracy wearing the mask of a democratic republic had the greatest chance of surviving, a belief that motivated him to pass laws allowing him to throw dissenting newspaper editors and legislators into prison. In the decade before his death, he wrote a letter to John Taylor and candidly noted, "Remember, democracy never lasts long. It soon wastes, exhausts, and murders itself. There never was a democracy yet that did not commit suicide."[47]

But the next two centuries have shown that Adams had failed to understand the new world that he had played a vital part in creating.

Jefferson understood that the key is to empower the people.

Jefferson, on the other hand, believed in the essential wisdom of democracy. While he knew a "pure democracy" could work only in a small setting like the local Saxon tribes of his family's England or the Indian tribes he'd personally observed, he also believed that a republic could be formed from a series of smaller democracies that would endure forever. Although the Greeks had never tried this (they kept their city-states separate from each other), and the Romans had failed at it when they didn't extend the vote franchise beyond the city of Rome, Jefferson had seen this system work very effectively in the Iroquois Confederacy.

Two years after Adams's bleak assessment, Jefferson wrote to Samuel Kercheval on September 5, 1816, stating that the key to making a democracy work was to continually reempower the people at a local level. "The article nearest my heart," he wrote about how governments should be organized, "is the division of counties into wards. These will be pure and elementary republics, the sum of all which, taken together, composes the State, and will make of the whole a true democracy as to the business of the wards, which is that of nearest and daily concern."

Jefferson might have smiled to learn that two hundred years later, House Speaker Tip O'Neill, one of the most successful legislators in America's history, would describe his success like this: "All politics is local."

Myth: "America was created by rich white men
to protect their wealth."

Reality: The Founders made enormous sacrifices.

This is perhaps the most unfortunate and destructive of the widespread American myths.

People on the extreme ends of both the Left and the Right in contemporary American debate say the nation was founded exclusively of, by, and for "rich white men," and the Constitution had, as its primary purpose, the protection of the wealth of this class of men against all others (particularly "the commoners"). They would have us believe that the signers didn't really mean all that flowery talk about liberal democracy; they were just putting up a good front while they set up a nation for their private benefit.

But the signers didn't send other people's kids to war, as we do today when we wage war; the Founders themselves gave up everything, even risking (and losing) their families' lives, giving up their life's savings, and losing their own homes and families. While many of the conservative Tory families still have considerable wealth and power (in Canada and England), not a single Founder's family persists today as a wealthy or politically dominant entity.

Where the myth of the greedy Founders came from

This myth/theory was first widely advanced by Columbia University professor of history Charles Beard, who published in 1913 a book titled *An Economic Interpretation of the Constitution of the United States*. Numerous historians and economists—on both the right and the left—have since cited his work as evidence that America was founded solely for the purpose of protecting wealthy interests. His myth helps conservatives advance the notion that their prowealth and procorporate agenda is simply a continuation of the intent of the nation's Founders and Framers, and feeds liberal cynicism.

But, recent research proves, Beard was wrong. The majority of the signers of the Constitution were acting against their own best economic interests when they put their signatures on that document, just as had the majority of the signers of the Declaration of Independence. The story of how Beard's myth took such deep root in American popular culture and has come to be so widely believed by contemporary historians is fascinating, and the story of the actual actions and goals of the Constitution's signers is inspiring.

Beard imagined the present gave him clues to the past.

In many ways, there were significant parallels between Beard's time and the constitutional era. Twenty years before Beard wrote his book, America had been wracked by economic crisis and such a broad explosion of poverty—in the midst of the conspicuous wealth of the robber barons—that it spawned an era of populism during which old assumptions of governance were challenged.

Similarly, two decades before the Constitution was signed, Charles Beard noted in *The Rise of American Civilization* (coauthored with his wife, Mary Beard), America had faced a similar economic crisis.

"A widespread business depression had just set in," the Beards wrote about the late 1760s and early 1770s. "During the nine years of the French and Indian War [1754–1763], American merchants, planters, and farmers had been unusually prosperous . . . ," but the bubble of this prosperity burst when "the swift reaction that followed inflated prices collapsed, business languished, workmen in the towns were thrown out of employment, farmers and planters, burdened by falling prices, found the difficulties of securing specie [cash] steadily growing."[48]

And it wasn't just a depression among the big businesses in New York and Boston that led, in part, to the American Revolution, according to the Beards: "Moreover, all the colonies, not merely the commercial North, were now thrown into distress; all classes, too, disenfranchised and unemployed workmen of the towns as well as farmers, planters and merchants. This is signifi-cant; it was the workmen of the commercial centers who fur-nished the muscle and the courage necessary to carry the protests of the merchants into the open violence that astounded the friends of law and order in England and America and threatened to kindle the flames of war."

Although America wasn't facing a revolutionary or civil war during Beard's era, it was facing an eerily similar time of great social upheaval, which ultimately brought about sweeping changes in our form of government. After the Seventeenth Amendment was ratified in 1913, citizens directly elected the U.S. Senate, which had previously been appointed in backroom deals by pro-fessional politicians in the states. Liquor was banned nationwide in 1919. Women gained the right to vote with the ratification of the Nineteenth Amendment on August 18, 1920. In 1921 the U.S. Supreme Court nearly broke the back of the Ameri-can labor movement in the *Truax v. Corrigan* case by ruling that unions couldn't picket or distribute handbills about employers, and in several different cases during the early 1920s, the Court declared both minimum-wage laws and maximum-hour laws unconstitutional.

Just as during the Revolutionary era, when people studied the writings of John Locke, Charles de Montesquieu, and Jean-Jacques Rousseau to gain an understanding of how an ideal democratic government might work, in the first few decades of the twentieth century, people read the works of Beard and other Progressive thinkers to understand the basis of American history.

Thus, Charles Beard cast his gaze back to September 17, 1787, a cool day in Philadelphia that had broken an unusually hot sum-mer, when James Madison noted in his diary of the Constitu-tional Convention: "The Constitution being signed by all the Members except Mr. Randolph, Mr. Mason, and Mr. Gerry who declined giving it the sanction of their names, the Convention dissolved itself by an Adjournment *sine die.*" Of the original 55 del-egates, 14 had previously walked out, many to attend to homes, families, or businesses, and a few in disagreement. But now the deed was done, and in need only of ratification by the states.

There were no robber barons among the Founders in the colonial era—just among conservative loyalists.

Beard, writing as the great financial robber baron empires of Rockefeller, Gould, Morgan, and Carnegie were being solidified, looked back at the Framers of the Constitution and imagined he was seeing an earlier, albeit smaller, version of his own day's history.

Beard wrote: "The whole theory of the economic interpretation of history rests upon the concept that social progress in general is the result of contending interests in society . . . ," and we can only understand the Constitution when we realize that it was "an economic document drawn with superb skill by men whose property interests were immediately at stake; and as such it appealed directly and unerringly to identical interests in the country at large."

And those interests weren't insignificant. In *The Rise of American Civilization,* Beard's most famous work, he notes that on the banks of the Hudson River, "From mansions that were castles, the Johnsons ruled in the Upper Mohawk Valley with a sway that was half feudal and half barbaric, relying on numerous kinsmen, armed Negro slaves, trained bands of Gaelic retainers, and savage allies from the dread Iroquois to maintain their sovereignty over forest and plain."

What Beard fails to mention is that the Johnsons were squarely in the middle of several wars against the Indians in the 1760s on behalf of England, were loyalists to the Crown throughout the Revolutionary War, and most eventually fled to Canada.

By the time of the constitutional era, Beard noted in *Civilization,* the wealthy of America who were closest to the Crown were reinventing the old British caste system. "In all the colonies the ruling orders, in English fashion, demanded from the masses the obedience to which they considered themselves entitled by wealth, talents, and general preeminence. At Harvard and Yale, authority, houses, lands, and chattels determined the rank of students in the academic roll. In churches, Puritan and Anglican alike, congregations were seated according to age, social position, and estate. One old Virginia family displayed its regard for the commoners of the vicinity every Sunday by requiring them to wait outside the church until the superiors were duly seated in the large pew especially provided for them."

These rich families, he suggests, in 1787 pushed on the American people a constitution grounded "upon the concept that the fundamental private rights of property are anterior to government and morally beyond the reach of popular majorities."

What he overlooks is that it was generally the wealthiest families of the colonies who most strongly opposed both the Revolutionary War and the Constitution, because both endangered the stability of their fortunes, most of which were grounded in trade or relationships with England. Thousands of these families fled the colonies after the Revolutionary War, both to England and Canada.

Beard thought he saw his own era's robber barons among the colonial economic elite. And, had the Revolution not have happened, he might have been right. But the great fortunes loyal to the Crown were dispersed or fled, and while we still have the financial empires of Beard's day with us, nobody can point to a Rockefeller dynasty equivalent that survived colonial times.

How rich is rich?

Although among the Founders and Framers in America, some had amassed great land holdings and what was perceived then as a patrician lifestyle, Pulitzer Prize–winning author Bernard Bailyn suggests in his brilliant 2003 book, *To Begin the World Anew: The Genius and Ambiguities of the American Founders,* that they couldn't hold a candle to the true aristocrats of England.[49] With page after page of photographs and old paintings of the homes of the Founders and Framers, Bailyn shows that none of those who created this nation were rich by European standards.

After an artful and thoughtful comparison of American and British estates, Bailyn concludes bluntly: "There is no possible correspondence, no remote connection, between these provincial dwellings and the magnificent showplaces of the English nobility." After showing and describing to his readers the mansions of the families of power in eighteenth-century Europe, Bailyn writes: "There is nothing in the American World to compare with this."

While the Founders and Framers had achieved a level of literacy, creativity, and a depth of thinking that rivaled that of any European state or era, nonetheless, Bailyn notes, "The Founders were provincials, alive to the values of a greater world, but not, they knew, of it—comfortable in a lesser world but aware of its limitations."

As Kevin Phillips documents in his masterpiece book *Wealth and Democracy: A Political History of the American Rich,* "George Washington, one of the richest Americans, was no more than a wealthy squire in British terms."[50] Phillips says that it wasn't until the 1790s—a generation after the War of Independence—that the first American accumulated a fortune that would be worth one million of today's dollars.* The Founders and Framers were, at best, what today would be called the upper middle class in terms of lifestyle, assets, and disposable income.

Even Charles and Mary Beard noted that wealth and land ownership, which in many states defined who could vote, was diffuse. Land, after all, didn't have the scarcity it does today, and thus didn't have the same value. Just about any free man could find land to settle, where Native Americans had either been decimated by disease or displaced by war.

Some histories posit George Washington as one of the

---

*Shipowner Elias Hasket Derby of Salem, Massachusetts.

wealthiest men among the Revolutionaries, which is true. But Washington, when he wrote his will and freed his slaves, didn't have enough assets to buy the slaves his wife had inherited and free them as well. Like Jefferson, who died in bankruptcy, Washington was "rich" in land but poor in cash.

The "rich white guys" hypothesis crumbles.

In 1958, one of America's great professors of history, Forrest McDonald, published an extraordinary book debunking Charles Beard's 1913 hypothesis that the Constitution was created of, by, and for rich white men. McDonald's book, titled *We the People: The Economic Origins of the Constitution,* bluntly states, "Economic interpretation of the Constitution does not work."[51]

Over the course of more than four hundred meticulously researched pages, McDonald goes back to original historical records and reveals who was promoting and who was opposing the new Constitution, and why. So far as I can tell, he is the first and only historian to do this type of original-source research, and his conclusions are startling.

McDonald notes that a quarter of all the delegates to the Constitutional Convention had voted in their own state legislatures for laws that would have helped debtors and the poor and thus harmed the interests of the rich. "These [debt relief laws] were the very kinds of laws which, according to Beard's hypothesis, the delegates had convened to prevent," says McDonald. He adds: "Another fourth of the delegates had important economic interests that were adversely affected, directly and immediately, by the Constitution they helped write."

Whereas Beard theorizes that the Framers were largely drawn from the class of wealthy bankers and businessmen, McDonald shows that "the most common and by far the most important property holdings of the delegates were not, as Beard has asserted, mercantile, manufacturing, and public security investments, but agricultural property." Most were farmers or plantation owners and, as noted earlier, owning a lot of land did not always make one rich in those days, particularly compared with the bankers and mercantilists of New York and Boston.

"Finally," McDonald concludes, "it is abundantly evident that the delegates, once inside the convention, behaved as anything but a consolidated economic group."

After dissecting the means and motivations of the Framers who wrote the Constitution, McDonald goes into an exhaustive and detailed state-by-state analysis of the constitutional ratifying conventions that finally brought the U.S. Constitution into law. For example, in the state of Delaware, which voted for ratification, "almost 77 percent of the delegates were farmers, more than two-thirds of them small farmers with incomes ranging from 75 cents to $5.00 a week. Slightly more than 23 percent of the delegates were professional men—doctors, judges, and lawyers. None of the delegates was a merchant, manufacturer, banker, or speculator in western lands."

In other states, similar numbers showed up. Of the New Jersey delegates supporting ratification, 64.1 percent were farmers. In Maryland, "the opponents of ratification included from three to six times as large a proportion of merchants, lawyers, and investors in shipping, confiscated estates, and manufacturing as did the delegates who favored ratification." In South Carolina it was those in economic distress who carried the day: "No fewer than 82 percent of the debtors and borrowers of paper money in the convention voted for ratification." In New Hampshire, "of the known farmers in the convention 68.7 percent favored ratification."

The Constitution wasn't primarily written to protect its authors' wealth.

But did farmers support the Constitution because they were slave owners or the wealthiest of the landowners, as Beard had guessed back in 1913? McDonald shows that this certainly wasn't the case in northern states like New Hampshire or New Jersey, which were not slave states.

But what about Virginia and North Carolina, the two largest slaveholding states, asks McDonald rhetorically. Were their plantation owners favoring the Constitution because it protected their economic and slaveholding interests?

"The opposite is true," writes McDonald. "In both states the wealthy planters—those with personality interests [wealth] as well as those without personality interests—were divided approximately equally on the issue of ratification. In North Carolina small farmers and debtors were likewise equally divided, and in Virginia the great mass of the small farmers and a large majority of the debtors favored ratification."

After dissecting the results of the ratification votes state by state—the first author in history to do so, as far as I can determine—McDonald sums up: "Beard's thesis—that the line of cleavage as regards the Constitution was between substantial personality interests [wealth] on the one hand and small farming and debtor interests on the other—is entirely incompatible with the facts."

So what did motivate the Framers of the Constitution?
Along with the answer to this question, we may also find the answer to the question historians have asked for two centuries about why the Constitutional Convention was held in secret behind locked doors, and why James Madison didn't publish his own notes of the Convention until 1840, just after the last of the other participants had died.

As with any political body, a few of the delegates, "a dozen at the outside," according to McDonald, "clearly acted according to the dictates of their personal economic interests."

But there were larger issues at stake. The men who hammered out the Constitution had such a strong feeling of history and destiny that it at times overwhelmed them. They realized that in the seven-thousand-year history of what they called civilization, only once before—in Athens, and then only for a brief flicker of a few centuries—had anything like a democracy ever been brought into existence and survived more than a generation.

Their writings show that they truly believed they were doing sacred work, something greater than themselves, their personal interests, or even the narrow interests of their constituents back in their home states. They believed they were altering the course of world history, and that if they got it right it would truly create a better world.

Thus the secrecy, the hurry, the intensity. And thus the willingness to set aside economic interest to produce a document— admittedly imperfect—that would establish an enduring beacon of liberty for the world.

George Washington, who presided over the Constitutional Convention, wrote to the nation on September 17, 1787, when "transmitting the Constitution" to the people of the new nation: "In all our deliberations on this subject we kept steadily in our view, that which appears to us the greatest interest of every true American, the consolidation of our Union, in which is involved our prosperity, felicity, safety, perhaps our national existence."[52]

Washington noted that many compromises were made, and many in the Convention had acted in a far more noble and altruistic way than political cynics might think. "This important consideration," he wrote, "seriously and deeply impressed on our minds, led each state in the Convention to be less rigid on points of inferior magnitude, than might have been otherwise expected." He concluded with his "most ardent wish"—that the Constitution "may promote the lasting welfare of that country so dear to us all, and secure her freedom and happiness."[53]

Myth: "The Founders wrote slavery into
the Constitution."

———————

Reality: The compromise necessary to get the
Constitution ratified prevented a ban on slavery,
but Jefferson and many other Founders believed
slavery would be ended in their lifetimes.

A recent correspondent, hearing me discuss this topic on the radio, wrote to say, "Nobody can credibly assert that the Constitution originally intended to include the rights of women, Blacks, Native Americans, or others than rich, white land-owning men!" He went on to point out that "Blacks were identified as only three-fifths human in the Constitution!" In these, the writer was echoing the most common myths about the Constitution and the Framers.

When trying to pull together a nation after the Revolutionary War, the Framers knew that if they couldn't bring in the southern states, heavily dependent on slave labor for their agricultural prosperity, they wouldn't be able to create a nation that would hold together. Even many of the Founders who had inherited slaves and slavery-based estates were concerned about the future damage slavery could do to the new nation they were birthing.

Jefferson's thoughts on slavery

Consider, for example, the slaveholding Founder Thomas Jefferson. In 1781, he wrote a collection of answers to questions posed by "a Foreigner of Distinction, then residing among us," which was published on February 27, 1787, as his *Notes on Virginia.* In one of the most brilliant short essays written by any of the Founders on the issue of slavery, Jefferson reveals an extraordinary insight into the nature and problem of slavery and honestly lays out his fears for the damage slavery may wreak on the nation he helped birth:

"There must doubtless be an unhappy influence on the manners of our people produced by the existence of slavery among us. The whole commerce between master and slave is a perpetual exercise of the most boisterous passions, the most unremitting despotism on the one part, and degrading submissions on the other. Our children see this, and learn to imitate it; for man is an imitative animal."

In this, Jefferson saw slavery as an institution that was train-

ing future generations of Americans to submit to slavery by foreign or domestic governments or corporations run wild, just as it
oppressed slaves in the process. He continued:

"This quality is the germ of all education in him. From his
cradle to his grave he is learning to do what he sees others do. If a
parent could find no motive either in his philanthropy or his self-
love, for restraint in the intemperance of passion towards his
slave, it should always be a sufficient one that his child is present.
But generally it is not sufficient. The parent storms, the child
looks on, catches the lineaments of wrath, puts on the same airs in
the circle of smaller slaves, gives a loose to the worst of passions,
and thus nursed, educated, and daily exercised in tyranny, cannot
but be stamped by it with odious peculiarities."

Nobody, Jefferson said, except the most rare of individuals
could remain uncorrupted by slavery existing in a free society.
"The man must be a prodigy who can retain his manners and
morals undepraved by such circumstances. And with what exe-
cration should the statesman be loaded, who, permitting one half
the citizens thus to trample on the rights of the other, transforms
those into despots, and these into enemies, destroys the morals
of the one part, and the amor patrice of the other."

Thus, Jefferson suggested, slavery would ultimately corrupt
the entire nation, both morally and economically. "With the
morals of the people, their industry also is destroyed. For in a
warm climate, no man will labor for himself who can make
another labor for him. This is so true, that of the proprietors of
slaves a very small proportion indeed are ever seen to labor."

Jefferson fears slavery's consequences.

At this point in his letter, Jefferson reflected on the theological
implications of the issue, writing words that are repeated on the
walls of the Jefferson Memorial in Washington, D.C.: "And can the
liberties of a nation be thought secure when we have removed
their only firm basis, a conviction in the minds of the people that
these liberties are of the gift of God? That they are not to be vio-

lated but with His wrath? Indeed I tremble for my country when I reflect that God is just; that his justice cannot sleep forever; that considering numbers, nature and natural means only, a revolution of the wheel of fortune, an exchange of situation is among possible events; that it may become probable by supernatural interference!

"The Almighty has no attribute which can take side with us in such a contest."

Jefferson was also hopeful that he would see the ending of slavery in America, perhaps even in his own lifetime. He ended his thoughts on slavery in this 1781 letter by writing, "I think a change already perceptible, since the origin of the present revolution. The spirit of the master is abating, that of the slave rising from the dust, his condition mollifying, the way I hope preparing, under the auspices of heaven, for a total emancipation, and that this is disposed, in the order of events to be with the consent of the masters, rather than by their extirpation."

In fact, as Fawn M. Brodie points out in what is one of the finest biographies of Jefferson ever written (*Thomas Jefferson: An Intimate History*), "It deserves notice that his phrase 'all men are born free,' which appeared six years later in his Declaration of Independence, and which has been traced with such zealous scholarship to men of the Enlightenment, first came to his lips publicly in the legal defense of a black man."[54]

Jefferson fights slavery.

In April of 1770, Jefferson was practicing law and defended a slave who was requesting his freedom (*Howell v. Netherland*). In his arguments on behalf of the slave, Jefferson said that "under the law of nature, all men are born free, and every one comes into the world with the right to his own person, which includes the liberty of moving and using it at his own will."

The year before, 1769, as a legislator in Virginia, he had written a bill to abolish the importation of slaves into that state. It was unsuccessful, and even brought down the wrath of many of his peers on him and his relative, Richard Bland, who Jefferson had asked to introduce the proposed legislation.

In his 1774 booklet *A Summary View of the Rights of British America,* Jefferson attacked King George III for forcing slavery on the colonies, a charge that was repeated in his first draft of the Declaration of Independence in 1776 but deleted from the final draft in order to keep the representatives of South Carolina and Georgia willing to sign the document. That same year, Jefferson tried to write into the constitution of the state of Virginia a provision that would gradually but totally eliminate slavery, starting in 1800; and in 1778 he presented an even more radical bill that would have abolished slavery altogether in Virginia. Although these attempts failed, he was successful in passing a Virginia law that year preventing any more slaves from being imported into the state.

In 1783, he again unsuccessfully attempted to amend Virginia's constitution, proposing language that said: "The general assembly shall not . . . permit the introduction of any more slaves to reside in this State, or the continuance of slavery beyond the generation which shall be living on the thirty-first day of December, 1800; all persons born after that day being hereby declared free."

The next year, he proposed at a national level a law banning slavery in the "Northwest Territories"—the Midwest and western states—and stating that any state admitted to the union would have to declare any person of any race born in that state after 1800 to be a free person. His proposal lost by a single vote, although parts of his proposed legislation were lifted and inserted into the Northwest Ordinance, which became law when Jefferson was in Paris in 1787.

Nonetheless, Jefferson, like most of the Founders, confronted the terrible balancing act of trying to hold together a nation that included slave states while still laying down an archetypal foundation of liberty that he believed would eventually encompass all persons. The conflict he faced is evident in a letter he wrote from

Paris in 1788 to J. P. Brissot de Warville, the leader of a French abolitionist society:

"Sir, I am very sensible of the honor you propose to me, of becoming a member of the society for the abolition of the slave trade. You know that nobody wishes more ardently to see an abolition, not only of the trade, but of the condition of slavery; and certainly, nobody will be more willing to encounter every sacrifice for that object.

"But the influence and information of the friends to this proposition in France will be far above the need of my association. I am here as a public servant, and those whom I serve, having never yet been able to give their voice against the practice, it is decent for me to avoid too public a demonstration of my wishes to see it abolished. Without serving the cause here, it might render me less able to serve it beyond the water."

The year after the signing of the Declaration of Independence, Vermont—which was then a sovereign nation—modified its constitution to ban slavery. Pennsylvania passed a law initiating the emancipation of slaves in that state in 1780. New Hampshire and Massachusetts followed Vermont's lead in 1783, although by court rulings in both states, and the process spread down the eastern seaboard to New York and New Jersey by the turn of the century.

In Thomas G. West's seminal book *Vindicating the Founders: Race, Sex, Class, and Justice in the Origins of America,* he notes that the southward movement of the abolition movement had achieved tidal wave proportions during Jefferson's lifetime: "Delaware owners freed their slaves in such large numbers that it amounted to a near abolition. By 1810, 76 percent of Delaware blacks were free; in Maryland, free blacks numbered a substantial 23 percent."[55]

African Americans and the three-fifths argument

Even the argument that the Constitution condoned slavery and defined African Americans as "three-fifths human" is inaccurate.

Slavery was the hottest issue debated at the Constitutional Convention of 1787, and—to keep the Union together—ultimately led to several compromises. One was that the importation of slaves would be phased out by 1807 (Article I, Section 9 of the Constitution still reads: "The migration or importation of such persons as any of the states now existing shall think proper to admit, shall not be prohibited by the Congress prior to the year one thousand eight hundred and eight . . ."), and the other being an effort to prevent the southern states from using their large slave populations to gain such influence in the House of Representatives that they might be able to keep legislating in favor of slavery.

The southern representatives argued that, since it was agreed that their slaves would eventually be free (even if it was in future generations), the slaves should be considered part of the census that determined the number of representatives a state could send to Congress. The northern states argued that because the slaves were not allowed to vote in the South (free blacks did in the North), they should not be counted in the census at all. This would have dramatically reduced the power of the southern states, because they didn't have large cities like New York or Boston but were instead mostly rural and agrarian. Without their slaves being counted toward their census numbers, they'd have so few representatives that, they suggested, they would be wasting their time joining the republic that was being forged in Philadelphia that summer of 1787.

Because this issue was a deal breaker that could have ended the nation before it began, a compromise was reached. The South could count three-fifths of its slaves toward the census, even though they couldn't vote, and thus have a bit more power in Congress, but it couldn't count any more African Americans than that until they were freed.

The language, as written into Section 2 of the U.S. Constitution, lays this out: "Representatives and direct taxes shall be apportioned among the several states which may be included within this union, according to their respective numbers, which shall be determined by adding to the whole number of free persons, including those bound to service for a term of years, and excluding Indians not taxed, three fifths of all other Persons."

As West notes in *Vindicating the Founders,* the Constitution, while it allowed slavery, also allowed freedom for slaves. Millions of African Americans exercised the right to vote and other civil rights long before the Civil War, and, "The rest won their liberty through a [Civil] war fought under its authority."[56]

The South fights to keep slavery.

Nonetheless, the Founders who believed that they would see the end of slavery within a few years after the founding of the nation—or at least by 1808—were devastated by the forcefulness with which the southern states held on to the manpower that made their agricultural enterprises profitable. The Virginia legislature made it impossible for any slave owner to free his slaves and still maintain contact with them: On May 1, 1806, while Jefferson was president but held no power in Virginia, the Virginia Assembly passed a law that any slave freed in the state had to leave the state forever or would be arrested by the state itself and sold back into slavery.[57]

Virginia slave owners like Jefferson were also haunted by an earlier 1691 Virginia law that specified that slaves who were freed and stayed in the state risked being "hung, burned at the stake, dismembered, castrated and branded" as well as the ordinary punishment of whippings.[58]

The practical consequence of this was that upon arriving in any other state, a newly freed Virginia slave with no right of return and no recourse to Virginia could easily be "captured" and impressed back into slavery. This probably accounts for why Jefferson was unwilling to free his own slaves during his lifetime or in his will (he couldn't afford, as Washington did with some of his slaves, to pay for their safe resettlement). He was also haunted by a 1662 Virginia law that said if the authorities of Virginia ever determined he had fathered children by Sally Hemmings, she would be given to "churchwardens of the parish" for two years of "hard Christian labor" and then sold into the general slavery market along with her children.[59]

Thus, slavery was still an issue long after 1808, when the Framers of the Constitution had assumed they had mandated it would end.

In 1820, for example, Missouri and Maine were being admitted as states to the Union, and a fierce debate had erupted over whether Missouri should be allowed to join the nation if it continued to allow slavery (Maine was free of slavery). In the ultimate compromise, which was passed by Congress, Missouri was admitted to the Union as a slave state.

Congressman John Holmes of Massachusetts wrote to an elderly Thomas Jefferson to inform him of the compromise, and on April 22, 1820, just six years before his death, writing with a quill pen, his hands cramped by arthritis, Jefferson candidly expressed his despair in his response to his old friend and colleague. In it, he foresaw the day when the nation would be torn apart across a "geographical line" over the issue of human beings being considered "that kind of property."

"I thank you, dear Sir," Jefferson wrote, "for the copy you have been so kind as to send me of the letter to your constituents on the Missouri question. It is a perfect justification to them. I had for a long time ceased to read newspapers, or pay any attention to public affairs, confident they were in good hands, and content to be a passenger in our bark to the shore from which I am not distant.

"But this momentous question, like a fire-bell in the night, awakened and filled me with terror. I considered it at once as the knell of the Union.

"It is hushed, indeed, for the moment. But this is a reprieve only, not a final sentence. A geographical line, coinciding with a marked principle, moral and political, once conceived and held up to the angry passions of men, will never be obliterated; and every new irritation will mark it deeper and deeper.

"I can say, with conscious truth, that there is not a man on earth who would sacrifice more than I would to relieve us from this heavy reproach, in any practicable way. The cession of that kind of property, for so it is misnamed, is a bagatelle [a small issue, a trifle] which would not cost me a second thought, if, in that way, a general emancipation and expatriation could be effected; and, gradually, and with due sacrifices, I think it might be.

"But as it is, we have the wolf by the ears, and we can neither hold him, nor safely let him go. Justice is in one scale, and self-preservation in the other."

Jefferson's despair in his last days

After pondering the legal issues involved, Jefferson—who, as president, had signed into law an 1808 act banning the slave trade with Africa—finally poured out his anguish in this private letter to Holmes, again foreseeing the unthinkable possibility of a civil war over slavery, which gave the lie to freedom in America and was thus a "treason against the hopes of the world" that looked to America as a beacon of liberty:

"I regret that I am now to die in the belief that the useless sacrifice of themselves by the generation of 1776, to acquire self-government and happiness to their country, is to be thrown away by the unwise and unworthy passions of their sons, and that my only consolation is to be, that I live not to weep over it. If they would but dispassionately weigh the blessings they will throw away, against an abstract principle more likely to be effected by union than by scission, they would pause before they would perpetrate this act of suicide on themselves, and of treason against the hopes of the world."

The Founders and Framers, who thought they could take the wolf of slavery by the ears and dance with it to a just conclusion in their lifetimes, were wrong. But it wasn't for want of trying, and the 620,000 Americans who died in the Civil War paid the ultimate price of their failure.

Then and now

It's easy for us, in this day and age, to look back two hundred years ago and criticize Jefferson for all of this. He used the cheap labor resource of his slaves to maintain his lifestyle, and the consequence of the failure of his efforts to abolish slavery was a bloody Civil War followed by a hundred years of legal apartheid.

Although he rationalized his slaveholding by keeping them in a style that exceeded that of most poor whites of the day (both were grim by today's standards), it was, nonetheless, a rationalization of slavery. Jefferson's lifestyle was made possible by slave labor, and there is no other way to say it. Recognizing that fact, many Americans are righteously indignant and quick to judge him harshly.

Yet how many of us would willingly free our slaves?

I'm typing these words on a computer containing many parts made in countries where laborers are held with less freedom and in conditions worse than those of Jefferson's slaves. My rationalization is that no companies in America or any other developed nation make many of those components any longer, and without parts from China and Malaysia I would have no computer. But it's just a rationalization, and no less hypocritical than Jefferson's.

Sitting here at my keyboard, I notice that the shirt I'm wearing was made by modern-day slaves, and that the lamp that is lighting my room (the sun is just beginning to rise) was manufactured in China, where workers who try to organize are imprisoned. Since Levi Strauss just closed their last American jeans factory this year, odds are the pants I'm wearing were made in a slaveholding nation as well.

I can rationalize all the products of distant slaves that I use—after all, I don't have to look into their faces as Jefferson did (which may account for why biographer Fawn Brodie notes that whenever Jefferson returned to Monticello from any trip he brought gifts for his slaves, and his household ledgers show evidence that he smuggled significant sums to Sally Hemmings over the years)—but it's still just a rationalization.

The stark reality is that we in America didn't "end" slavery. We simply exported it.

And it's so much more comfortable for us to criticize Jefferson for agonizing over—but still using—slave labor two hundred years ago when we don't have to look into the faces of today's slaves who are toiling and dying at this very moment to sustain our lifestyles.

Myth: "A woman's place is in the home, and the Founders knew it."

Reality: The Constitution was gender neutral, and women voted and had property rights in many states.

Another widely held misperception about the Constitution is that it explicitly forbade women from voting. In fact, the words "male" and "female" appear nowhere in the Constitution: its language is entirely gender neutral, referring to "electors" and "persons." Thomas G. West points out in *Vindicating the Founders*: "As was the case with blacks, not one word of the Constitution had to be changed for women to obtain the vote. Indeed, also as with blacks, some women were already voting at the time the Constitution was adopted. Large numbers of women were voting in several states before the Nineteenth Amendment was finally approved in 1920."

The problem was that the Constitution—written by men fiercely in favor of states having strong rights—leaves to each state the ability to define who it shall allow to vote. Many of the states chose to exclude women.

(Some states also had property ownership requirements to

vote in the early years of this nation, causing some historians to assert that "only property-owning white males" were empowered to vote by the Constitution. In fact, the Constitution makes no such provisions or prohibitions, and in many states women and blacks—and whites—who owned no property whatsoever were voting the year after the ratification of the Constitution.)

To compound the situation, however, after the Civil War, the Thirteenth, Fourteenth, and Fifteenth Amendments to the Constitution were proposed to impose federal power to free the slaves in all the former slave states. The Fourteenth Amendment, for the first time, included the word "male," an event that brought into collision the suffragette movement (which opposed the amendment) and the abolition movement (which supported it).

While the Fourteenth Amendment's first article guaranteed due process of law to all "persons," its second article regarding the makeup of the House of Representatives included the phrase "the proportion which the number of such male citizens shall bear to the whole number of male citizens."

Elizabeth Cady Stanton echoed the suffragettes' alarm when she wrote in 1866, "If the word male be inserted [in this Constitution] it will take a century to get it out again."[60] Nonetheless, the amendment passed both houses of Congress and was ratified by enough states to become law on July 28, 1868.

Four years later, Susan B. Anthony cast a ballot on November 1, 1872, to test the Fourteenth Amendment's use of the word "male," which, she said, contradicted the previously gender-neutral language of the rest of the Constitution. Two weeks after she voted, on November 12, 1872, she wrote, "All persons are citizens—and no state shall deny or abridge the citizen rights."[61]

Six days later, however, she was arrested for voting illegally, and a state court ruled that the issue of women's right to vote had now been taken away from the states and enshrined in federal law. It wasn't until 1920 that the Constitution was amended to reverse the male-only language of the Fourteenth Amendment and overrule any state laws that forbade women from voting.

Myth: "The Republican Party has always been the party of
big business and cheap labor."

Reality: By the 1850s the Democratic Party had been
corrupted by slavery, and the Republican Party first
emerged as a party of reform.

Just as, in the last years of his life, Jefferson wrote anguished letters about how he feared his failure to eliminate slavery—which
he had thought would have been ended well before his death—
would irredeemably harm democracy, Abraham Lincoln, before
he ran for the presidency, saw the rising up of a wealthy class of
"crowned heads" as threatening the nation.

On April 6, 1859, Lincoln had been invited to address a Republican Party festival in Boston honoring the birthday of Jefferson, but he was unable to attend. Instead, he wrote a poignant
letter, to be read to the crowd, suggesting that the Democratic
Party of Jefferson had been captured by wealthy corporate and
special interests that were putting democracy in grave danger. His
own newly formed Republican Party was a party of democracy, he
believed, and it largely held that position until 1872, when the
Progressives split off from it to form their own movement.

Lincoln opened his speech by noting the irony of the Republicans gathering to celebrate the birthday of Jefferson, who had
founded the Democratic Party.

Yet, Lincoln wrote, it was a good thing that if the Democrats
had degenerated into support of wealth and slavery, at least the
Republicans were there to pick up Jefferson's ideals. "Remember-
ing, too, that the Jefferson party formed upon the supposed superior devotion to the personal rights of men, holding the rights of
property to be secondary only and greatly inferior, and assuming
that the so called Democracy of today are the Jefferson [party],
and their opponents the anti-Jefferson party, it will be equally
interesting to note how completely the two have changed hands
as to the principle upon which they were originally supposed to

be divided. The Democracy [Democrats] of today hold the liberty of one man to be absolutely nothing, when in conflict with
another man's right of property; Republicans, on the contrary, are
for both the man and the dollar, but in case of conflict the man
before the dollar."[62]

Lincoln couldn't resist, at that point, telling a joke. "I remember being very much amused at seeing two partially intoxicated
men engaged in a fight with their great-coats on, which fight,
after a long and rather harmless contest, ended in each having
fought himself out of his own coat and into that of the other. If
the two leading parties of this day are really identical with the two
in the days of Jefferson and Adams they have performed the same
feat as the two drunken men.

"But soberly, it is now no child's play to save the principles of
Jefferson from total overthrow in this nation. . . .

"The principles of Jefferson are the definitions and axioms of
free society and yet they are denied and evaded, with no small
show of success."

Lincoln pointed out that the Democrats had abandoned
Jefferson's ideals and were turning the country in what he considered the direction of a caste system, a new aristocracy. The
Democrats, Lincoln said, were "supplanting the principles of free
government, and restoring those of classification, caste, and legitimacy. They would delight a convocation of crowned heads plot-
ting against the people. They are the vanguard, the miners and
sappers of returning despotism. We must repulse them, or they
will subjugate us."

Bringing his speech back to Jefferson's ideals—Jefferson being
the slave owner who had proposed one of America's first antislav-
ery laws—Lincoln closed his letter by writing: "This is a world of
compensation; and he who would be no slave must consent to
have no slave. Those who deny freedom to others deserve it not
for themselves, and, under a just God, cannot long retain it. All
honor to Jefferson—to the man, who in the concrete pressure of a

struggle for national independence by a single people, had the coolness, forecast, and sagacity to introduce into a merely revolutionary document an abstract truth, applicable to all men and all times, and so embalm it there that today and in all coming days it shall be a rebuke and a stumbling-block to the very harbingers of reappearing tyranny and oppression."

Ironically, the two drunken men started fighting again just a dozen years after Lincoln's speech, and by the Gilded Age of the late nineteenth century the Republicans had become the party representing caste and wealth while the Democrats were beginning to move in the direction that ultimately led to FDR's helping America recover from disastrous Republican fiscal policies (like Hoover's huge tax cuts for the wealthy) of the 1920s.

Myth: "The Founders thought the Constitution was perfect and should never change."

Reality: It was the beginning of a work in progress, designed to change with the times.

A common thread among those who consider the U.S. Constitution (or any democratic instrument) infallible is the suggestion that the world in which the Founders and Framers lived should define the limits of our world. If they didn't have welfare, we shouldn't. If they didn't have Social Security, we shouldn't. If they didn't have limits on weaponry, we shouldn't, and so on.

This argument begins to break down quickly when you look at it over the arc of time. The Founders didn't outlaw people owning surface-to-air missiles because missiles hadn't yet been invented, but they certainly would have stopped anybody from building up a private army or a personal warship. They didn't outlaw abortion, and in fact during that era both surgical and herbal abortion were available. They grew hemp (both Jefferson and Washington did, among others), and opium and cocaine were sold in retail stores. In several states women and minorities couldn't vote, although there were no federal laws prohibiting this until the next century.

There were, on the other hand, strong laws that are now gone, regulating corporate behavior, limiting the power of individual wealth, and providing for the establishment and protection of the commons. If a corporation or wealthy man were to offer politicians money, he would be thrown in jail or the corporation dissolved. If somebody spoiled a common area, he would immediately be held accountable. And in most states if a family built a huge fortune in one generation, it would be heavily taxed upon the founder's death to avoid the rise of dynastic families in this new republic. The Founders were just as wary of the corporate aristocracy of the East India Company as they were of the family aristocracy of King George III, and they fought the Revolutionary War against both.

But the Founders also knew that times change. They didn't intend their system to be inflexible, although they did intend that the principles upon which it was established should remain strong.

Eight years after he had retired to Monticello, Thomas Jefferson wrote to Samuel Kercheval in a July 12, 1816, letter his thoughts on the idealism of 40 years earlier when he had drafted the Declaration of Independence and the lessons he had learned since.

"Some men look at constitutions with sanctimonious reverence, and deem them like the Ark of the Covenant, too sacred to be touched," Jefferson wrote. "They ascribe to the men of the preceding age a wisdom more than human, and suppose what they did to be beyond amendment. I knew that age well; I belonged to it, and labored with it. It deserved well of its country. It was very like the present, but without the experience of the present; and forty years of experience in government is worth a century of book reading; and this they would say themselves, were they to rise from the dead.

"I am certainly not an advocate for frequent and untried

changes in laws and constitutions. I think moderate imperfections had better be borne with; because, when once known, we accommodate ourselves to them, and find practical means of correcting their ill effects.

"But I know also, that laws and institutions must go hand in hand with the progress of the human mind. As that becomes more developed, more enlightened, as new discoveries are made, new truths disclosed, and manners and opinions change with the change of circumstances, institutions must advance also, and keep pace with the times.

"We might as well require a man to wear still the coat which fitted him when a boy, as civilized society to remain ever under the regimen of their barbarous ancestors."

But how often should the laws of the land be revisited? Jefferson gave a candid and somewhat startling answer to the question: "What these periods should be, nature herself indicates. By the European tables of mortality, of the adults living at any one moment of time, a majority will be dead in about nineteen years. At the end of that period then, a new majority is come into place; or, in other words, a new generation. Each generation is as independent of the one preceding, as that was of all which had gone before. It has then, like them, a right to choose for itself the form of government it believes most promotive of its own happiness."

While the previous generation made laws for their own time, Jefferson wrote, they were now dead and gone. Some would say their laws should stay on the books because thoughtful people put them there or the laws served the people well. "But," Jefferson wrote, "the dead have no rights. They are nothing; and nothing cannot own something. Where there is no substance, there can be no accident. This corporeal globe, and everything upon it, belongs to its present corporeal inhabitants, during their generation. They alone have a right to direct what is the concern of themselves alone, and to declare the law of that direction; and this declaration can only be made by their majority."

So long as the principles were held true, Jefferson believed, times would change and laws would change but a democratic republic would survive.

On the other hand, "If this avenue be shut to the call of sufferance, it will make itself heard through that of force, and we shall go on, as other nations are doing, in the endless circle of oppression, rebellion, reformation; and oppression, rebellion, reformation, again; and so on forever. These, Sir," Jefferson summarized to Kercheval, "are my opinions of the governments we see among men, and of the principles by which alone we may prevent our own from falling into the same dreadful track."

Myth: "Government is an evil entity that's against the people."

Reality: Government *is* us.

Conservatives love to attack the government as if it's the enemy of freedom, liberty, and commerce. Although this may be true of despotic governments and kingdoms, the major innovation of the Founders was the idea that *the government is us.* It's owned by us, run by us for the benefit of us, exists solely because we continue to approve of it, and is 100 percent answerable to us.

This was an idea that the anti-Revolution conservatives of 1776 strongly opposed. Many of them were among the richest men in America, and to protect their wealth, they wanted the colonies to remain part of Great Britain. But the liberals of 1776 had the new idea that instead of people getting their rights from a king, they, themselves, were the sole legitimate holders of rights. And they could confer privileges on a government they could create, so long as it behaved in a fashion that supported "We the People."

Of course, there have been some hiccups along the way. In 1886, conservatives tried to take control of the government by claiming that corporations should have equal rights with humans, and it seemed that the Supreme Court had gone along with it. Later, corporations began to claim human rights against discrimination, and giant chain stores fought communities that don't want them wiping out local merchants by claiming that laws that guarantee rights for African Americans should also protect them. A giant chemical company claimed Fourth Amendment privacy rights to block the EPA from doing surprise inspections looking for cancer-causing poison emissions. And corporations even asserted the First Amendment human right of free speech, including the right to give politicians campaign cash (formerly a felony in most U.S. states) and the right to lie in advertising and PR (ditto); and in a celebrated case, a so-called fair and balanced media corporation even claimed the right to lie in newscasts and defended it up through the courts, calling it a "vindication" when a federal court ruled that FCC regulations requiring truth in news reporting were only "guidelines."

But the bottom line in America is that the government is us.

Conservatives, however, don't much like this idea of democracy. From trying to overturn elections by judicial process to using the power of corporations and corporate money, they consistently laugh at the notion of "the will of the people" or "the good of the people." Instead, they suggest, government should provide huge breaks and welfare for corporations.

Myth: "The Founders and Framers were impractical, idealistic Enlightenment-era dreamers."

Reality: Democracy is the most practical, stable, and normal form of governance for both nature and humans.

The Founders and Framers of American democracy weren't just experimenters and dreamers. They were grounded in the realities of the most fundamental and visceral science of biology. They knew that Gilgamesh's eruption of despotism had caused humanity to lose its way.

They were returning us to a form of governance both functional and ancient, which they saw working in tribes all around them and that they knew from the history of Athens could be made to work among technologically advanced and literate societies as well as among indigenous peoples. As you'll learn in chapter 7, in "The biology of democracy" section, even in nuance, like requiring different voting thresholds for different types of decisions, the Framers of our Constitution perfectly modeled the behavior of the rest of nature, and the true historic behavior of humans.

The most recent peer-reviewed scientific research gives the lie to the now-fashionable trend among conservative historians to characterize democracy advocates like Thomas Jefferson and James Madison as out of touch with reality, while they suggest that those like John Adams, who favored a more oligarchic form of government, had a more realistic view of how democracy could best survive.

When Joseph Ellis wrote in his biography of Jefferson (*American Sphinx*[63]) that "the Jeffersonian magic works because we permit it to function at a rarefied region where real-life choices do not have to be made,"[64] he was echoing the conservative belief that democracy is both magic and rarefied. Nature and a broad view of human history tell us otherwise.

As John Locke wrote in 1690, in the sixth chapter of his *Second Treatise of Civil Government* (a work widely read during Jefferson's day): "The State of Nature has a Law of Nature to govern it. . . . Reason teaches all Mankind . . . that being all equal and independent, no one ought to harm another in his Life, Health, Liberty, or Possessions."

Myth: "The Constitution offers no right to privacy."

Reality: "Privacy" had a very different meaning two
hundred years ago.

Today conservatives claim the power to invade citizens' private lives (even their bedrooms) and tell them what to do in private—

because, they say, there is no "right to privacy" in the United States. As evidence, they point to the fact that the word "privacy" doesn't occur even a single time in the Constitution or the Bill of Rights.

Troubled radio commentator Rush Limbaugh said on his program on June 27, 2003: "There is no right to privacy specifically enumerated in the Constitution." Jerry Falwell (the same reverend who felt God punished America on 9/11 for tolerating gays) agreed on Fox News. They could just as well point out that the Constitution doesn't grant a right to marry, or eat, or read, or have children.

There are two egregious errors in such statements: they're wrong about the Constitution, and the English language has changed in two hundred years.

The Fifth Amendment protects liberty, and the Ninth Amendment protects other rights.

There are two substantial errors in the assertion that the issue of privacy doesn't appear in the Constitution:

▶   The Fifth Amendment does protect people's liberty to do as they wish, saying, "No person shall be . . . deprived of . . . liberty . . . without due process of law."

▶   The Ninth Amendment says the Constitution is not intended to list all the rights held by We the People: "The enumeration in the Constitution, of certain rights, shall not be construed to deny or disparage others retained by the people." Thus, Limbaugh's argument has no meaning in the first place. And a substantial body of correspondence during the creation of the Bill of Rights makes this abundantly clear.

Additionally, there's good reason to believe that the Founders and Framers did write a right to privacy into the Constitution. However, living in the eighteenth century, they would never have used the word "privacy." A search, for example, of all of the more than ten thousand of Thomas Jefferson's letters and writings produces not a single use of the word "privacy." Nor does Adams use the word in his writings or any of the other Founders, so far as I can find.

The issue of the privy

The reason is simple: "privacy" in 1776 was a code word for toilet functions.

A person would say, "I need a moment of privacy" as a way of excusing themselves to use the "privy" or outhouse. The chamber pots around the house, into which people relieved themselves during the evening and which were emptied in the morning, were referred to as "the privates," along with another meaning that continues today.

"Privacy," in short, was a word that wasn't generally used in political discourse or polite company.

It wasn't until 1898 that Thomas Crapper began marketing the flush toilet and discussion of toilet functions became relatively acceptable. Prior to then, saying somebody had a "right to privacy" would have meant "a right to excrete"—which is obvious but is certainly not something that would have been enumerated in the Constitution.

Our best defense against today's pervasive ignorance about American history and human rights is education, a task that Jefferson undertook in starting the University of Virginia to provide a comprehensive and free public education to all capable students. A well-informed populace will always preserve liberty better than a powerful government, a philosophy that led the University of California and others to once offer free education to its state's citizens. We must ensure that when politicians of any stripe misquote the Constitution, our children and their children will be prepared to stand up and say "Wrong!"

Myth: "Jefferson said it's wrong for the rich
to pay more in taxes."

Reality: What he opposed was double taxation.

Jefferson is often quoted as saying: "If the overgrown wealth of an individual be deemed dangerous to the State, the best corrective is the law of equal inheritance to all in equal degree; and the better, as this enforces a law of nature, while extra-taxation violates it."

This seems like a straightforward statement that taking "extra" taxes from rich people in order to provide services to poor people is a bad thing.

The reality, however, is quite different.

That quote came from a letter that Thomas Jefferson wrote to Joseph Milligan on April 6, 1816. A week later, in a letter to Albert Gallatin, Jefferson explains why he had been corresponding with Milligan. He describes a book on the relationship between politics and economics by Messier Destutt Tracy (Antoine Louis Claude Destutt, Comte de Tracy, 1754–1836), "the ablest writer in France in the moral line."

Jefferson explained that the original translation of Tracy's book was so bad that he had offered to retranslate it. Jefferson "worked on it four or five hours a day for three months"—while he was president—until it was finished.

What was it that Jefferson thought was so important that he'd give it so much attention while running the new country?

Liberal economics

Tracy was the founder of what is today called the French Liberal School, a line of thinkers who brought us modern liberal democracies as we see in most of modern Europe. He challenged Adam Smith's cost theory of value and was a major inspiration for the famous British economist David Ricardo (1772–1823). Tracy even invented the word "ideology," although his definition of the word was "the science of ideas."

Tracy was vigorously opposed to monopolies and would look upon today's anticompetitive corporate behemoths with horror. Monopolies that were controlled by the government were doubly evil, as was then the case in much of Europe.

In Jefferson's translation, Tracy wrote: "Monopoly . . . is odious, tyrannical, contrary to the natural right which every one has of buying and selling as he pleases, and it necessitates a multitude of violent measures."[65]

But nations had the power to narrow or broaden competition by allowing corporations to become so large as to become monopolistic, or preventing them (with measures like the later Sherman Anti-Trust Act) from seizing control of entire commercial sectors.

The greatest sin, in Tracy's mind, was when a corporation became big enough to get government to use the force of law to help it accomplish its aims. (Today we call the process "lobbying"; back then it was called "bribery and influencing.") In speaking of how powerful men (at the time there were only a handful of corporations in America) would try to use government regulation or deregulation to allow them to form monopolies, Tracy wrote: ". . . every one fears competition in his own way, and would wish to be alone in order to be master. If you pursue further the complication of these different interests, in the progress of society, and the action of the passions which they produce, you will soon see all these men implore the assistance of force in favour of the idea with which they are prepossessed; or, at least, under different pretexts, provoke prohibitive laws, to constrain those who obstruct them in this universal contention."[66]

Because he was what was then called a liberal, Tracy was banned by Napoleon from publishing his works in France. Thus, he turned to the president of the United States, through their mutual friend the Marquis de Lafayette, to ask for help getting his work *Commentaires* published.

Jefferson was, however, sensitive to the impact it could have on international relations if an American president was known to be writing the translation of a banned French liberal.

"My name must in nowise appear connected with the work," he wrote, even though ". . . I should be happy to see it in the hands of every American citizen."

Jefferson points out that another topic of the book is potentially explosive. "Taxation is in fact the most difficult function of government—and that against which their citizens are most apt to be refractory."[67]

Jefferson: Don't double-tax.

Jefferson wrote that taxes "class themselves readily" into: "1. Capital. 2. Income. 3. Consumption."

Having defined these three types of taxes, Jefferson notes: "A government may select either of these bases for the establishment of its system of taxation . . . and, if this be correctly obtained, it is the perfection of the function of taxation."

Thus, Jefferson suggests (as did Tracy), a government could tax people three ways.

The first is to place a tax on the wealth people own. The main forms of this in the United States are property taxes on real estate and estate taxes when a person dies. It was, during Jefferson's time, a common form of taxation in Europe: each person's or each family's wealth was determined every year, and a tax was levied on the overall total of their assets. Some nations taxed only real estate, as we do in the United States (although most states now also tax the value of automobiles by rating the license fee on the cost of the car), whereas others considered the totality of a person's wealth.

The second form of taxation is to charge a tax only on what people earn, regardless of what they own or what they consume. This, today, is called an income tax.

The third form of taxation is to charge a tax only on consumption—typically a sales tax.

"Once a government has assumed" the basic form of taxation it's going to use, Jefferson wrote, if it also hits people "from either of the other classes" of taxes, that "is double taxation." Using the example of a person buying whiskey, broadcloth, or a coach, Jefferson noted that "for that portion of income with which these articles are purchased, having already paid its tax as income, to pay another tax on the thing it purchased, is paying twice for the same thing." This, he said, "is an aggrievance on the citizens who use these articles" and "contrary to the most sacred of the duties of a government, to do equal and impartial justice to all its citizens."

There are, however, times when it may be important to pay a double tax "on the importation of certain articles, in order to encourage their manufacture at home, or an excise on others injurious to the morals or health of the citizens."

Most important, Jefferson agreed with Tracy that the poor shouldn't be hit as hard as the wealthy by taxation, be the taxes based on wealth, consumption, or income.

Thus, in the writings of Tracy and Jefferson we find the basis of progressive taxation: poor and middle-class people, who spend all or much of their income on food, shelter, clothing, transportation, medical care, and other necessities, should not pay taxes on that portion of their income or wealth that meets life's necessities.

On the other hand, those with wealth or income high enough to extend beyond the necessities should be taxed at levels necessary to support the functions of government and reflecting the disproportionate "blessings" they have derived from the commons, the infrastructure of government, and the nation as a whole.

Which brings us to the final paragraph of Jefferson's 1816 letter to Joseph Milligan, so often quoted by conservatives, which opened with this passage. "Whether property alone, and the whole of what each citizen possesses, shall be subject to contribution, or only its surplus after satisfying his first wants, or whether the faculties of body and mind shall contribute also from their annual earnings, is a question to be decided. But, when decided, and the principle settled, it is to be equally and fairly applied to all."

In context, we realize Jefferson was urging his day's politicians to come up with a way of taxing people and applying it to everybody equally, with the exception of taxing a person only "after satisfying his first wants" are purchased. This is the core principle of "progressive taxation."

Jefferson urged inheritance taxes, to prevent dynasties.

Jefferson explicitly suggested that if individuals became so rich that their wealth could influence or challenge government, then their wealth should be decreased upon their death.

This is one reason why until the Republicans rose up during the robber baron era of the mid- to late nineteenth century there were no American dynastic families. We don't see fortunes left over from the Revolutionary era; all of America's wealthy elite gained their status during and after the Civil War.

Jefferson was not arguing against taxes, or even against higher taxes on the rich, and particularly not against inheritance taxes. He was arguing that a tax system must be fair, uniform, and predictable, consistent with the prime concepts of the liberal school of thought, that government must not produce or allow monopolies in commerce, and that no person (or business, he notes elsewhere) must be allowed to become so wealthy as to be "dangerous to the State."

In this, he was making the same argument that the Framers of Pennsylvania tried to make when writing their constitution in 1776. A Sixteenth Article to a Pennsylvania Bill of Rights declared: "An enormous proportion of property vested in a few individuals is dangerous to the rights, and destructive of the common happiness of mankind, and, therefore, every free state hath a right by its laws to discourage the possession of such property."[68]

Myth: "Working women are responsible for the loss of good-paying jobs."

Reality: Procorporate, antilabor policies such as unregulated "free trade" globalization are devastating our middle class.

In the third week of December 2003, Rush Limbaugh declared psychological war on the working white males of America, although most of them probably didn't realize it. That week Limbaugh rolled out a "funny" faux advertisement for the "Hillary Clinton Testicle Lock Box" that now any woman can use to clamp down on men's testicles just as he implied Hillary does.

Ask most men "Who are you?" or "What do you do?" and you won't hear, "I'm my wife's husband" or "I'm my son's dad." Men typically answer such questions by describing what they do for a living. Men do this because they're so conditioned to think of themselves as breadwinners, and they generally derive most of their social status from their occupation.

That's why, in this day and age, men who work for a living are a troubled bunch. Jobs are moving overseas in record numbers, conservatives have declared war on organized labor, and insecurity in the workplace is at a peak not seen since the Great Depression. And the change from a generation earlier—when men were most often sole breadwinners (because a good union job could easily support an entire family)—to 2003, when fully 32 percent of women earned more than their husbands, has been dizzying for "traditional" males.[69] Add to this the fact that most men feel their masculinity is defined in part by their ability to be successful breadwinners, and you have a potent formula for psychological manipulation.

Today's working-poor and middle-class men, living with job insecurity and a declining standard of living, feel emasculated. Their ability to earn a living is eroding, and, with it, their sense of their own potency, their ability to project themselves onto the world and "conquer" it in a way that meets the needs of their family. The result is that working men are getting angry or falling into despair.

Suicide increases under conservative rule around the world.

The despair of working men is reflected in suicide statistics. As the BBC reported on July, 29, 2003, "Suicide is the single biggest cause of accidental or violent death among men in England and Wales," even exceeding deaths in car accidents, traditionally the largest killer. Suicide among men in England, the BBC noted, "accounted for more than one third (34%) of the total number of male accidental or violent deaths during the year."[70] It's a particular problem, another BBC report noted, for men in areas of high unemployment, such as Britain's suicide capital, Manchester. In that community, the suicide rate among working-age men has doubled over what it was twenty years ago when jobs were more secure and pay relatively higher.[71]

The problem has spread throughout the developed world, where good jobs are being lost in droves. In Japan, for example, Japan Update news service reported that in the working-class prefecture of Okinawa, "The male suicide rate per 100,000 people has increased 1.5 times compared to 20 years ago." It added bluntly, "The suicide rate in the 50–60 age group is especially high and the reason for the dramatic increase is thought to be a combination of low income and high unemployment."

Two recent exhaustive and thorough epidemiological studies done in Australia and the United Kingdom show that when conservative parties take power, suicides increase dramatically, whereas when the liberal "Labour" parties rule, suicides drop.[72]

As Kendall Powell noted in his article "Suicide Rises Under Conservative Rule" in the journal *Nature,* "The researchers accounted for the effects of drought, both world wars, and the availability of sedatives. Even so, men and women were 17 and 40 per cent more likely to take their own lives, respectively, with conservatives in power."[73] *Nature* quotes University of Manchester psychologist Cary Cooper as confirming that "poorer social support and higher job insecurity may drive more to suicide under conservative regimes."

The British study, which looked at suicide in England and Wales from 1901 to 2000, was so compelling that a BBC report noted, "The figures suggest that 35,000 people would not have died had the Conservatives not been in power."[74]

Given the preceding, is it any wonder that when policies favor concentration of power, ordinary citizens are more likely to despair?

Instead of getting sad, some get mad.
The majority of unemployed or underemployed men don't kill themselves, however. Instead, they get angry. And most, not being particularly well informed about the details of social and economic policy, look in other places for the sources of their pain. And this is where the conservatives are working hard to perform an elegant smoke-and-mirrors switch of attention.

Conservatives have figured out how crucial it is to make sure that the working-class "NASCAR Dad" demographic—so important to conservatives that NASCAR drivers were invited to place their cars on the White House lawn for a Bush photo op—don't connect their sense of lost masculinity with this conservative administration's procorporate, antiemployee policies.

Thus Rush's Hillary Clinton Testicle Lock Box. And Bush's Phallic Projection Force War Against Iraq. And the Big Bulge Strut on the Aircraft Carrier Deck.

This is psychological warfare of the first order and will be successful if advocates of liberal democracy fail to respond properly. Conservatives like George W. Bush and Karl Rove have effectively used 9/11 as a substitute for job anxiety, and Bush's various wars as an opportunity for men to feel personal power via their stand-in, the macho-acting man in the White House.

At the same time, Limbaugh and the vast conservative talk

machine are working overtime to assure the underemployed and threatened men of America that the target of their rage should not be conservative policies but, instead, "castrating women": they say we should blame Hillary Clinton and those damn liberals for all the ills that have befallen the working class.

The simple reality is that "cheap labor" conservative policies are responsible for the thinning out of the middle class in America, not women who aspire to work in the labor force or to rise in political power.

Myth: "Liberals wrote child labor laws to create a shortage and drive up wages."

Reality: Banning child labor produced more educated citizens and helped create a middle class to buy goods.

In the 1900 census, more than 18 percent of the labor force was between ten and fifteen years old. Those children never finished school and rarely became economically productive consumers.

But today, conservatives love to complain that the only reason liberals pushed through child labor laws in 1916 was to drive up the cost of labor by denying factory owners access to all that labor. Indeed, when child labor was banned, the cost of labor increased.

What the conservatives never cite is that this helped create the American middle class.

And that's not to mention the fact that child labor had kept children out of school, which kept them from becoming the informed thinking citizens that Jefferson envisioned. This led to a particularly harmful form of circular thinking on the part of pseudoconservatives: child labor resulted in uneducated adults, which conservative leaders said proved their case that some people (the rich) were simply better than others.

One wonders what conservative philosopher Edmund Burke, who suggested hairdressers and candle makers should never be given political power, would have thought about hairdressers who got college educations, perhaps even trained in free public universities.

The benefits of realistic regulation of business

Child or immigrant labor laws are sometimes cited as an example of "overregulation of business"—something that stifles economic growth. The same is sometimes said about regulations for worker safety and consumer safety. For instance, the Occupational Safety and Health Administration (OSHA) is a favorite target.

On one level there may be something to that argument— something that illustrates how twisted our judgments can become if we look only at numbers and forget about the humans. Here's why.

The first substance regulated by OSHA when it came into being in 1970 was asbestos, a substance that causes a terrible form of cancer. And every time someone gets cancer in the United States, it's great for the economy: it causes a miniboom of about a quarter-million dollars, because the average patient gets expensive treatments, nursing and doctor care, and, often, a funeral.

So there's no question that asbestos is good for economic growth. Indeed, every cancer avoided is a quarter-million dollars lost to the medical services part of our economy—which is today about one-seventh of the entire U.S. economy.

Similarly, economic activity is reduced by regulations that reduce cancer-causing arsenic in drinking water, or soot from power plants and auto exhaust, or emissions of chemicals from factories, exposures to pesticides and other agricultural chemicals by farm workers and consumers.

However, it keeps more of us—We the People—alive and well.

Or—best of all—our "socialist military," with its strict rules that the highest paid may not make more than twenty times the salary of the lowest paid, its comprehensive free health-care system, and its subsidized housing? Indeed, the military might qualify as the most "socialist" institution in our government (though I doubt they'd like to be called that, by conservatives or anyone else).

So why do conservatives incessantly apply this label to programs that don't match the definition? It's because the word has such a negative reputation. Socialist and communist nations have for the most part been conspicuous failures, killing tens of millions of dissenters in the process.

Modern democracy is not collective ownership, but a political system in which the voice of the people is not only heard in government but *is* the government.

The means of production and distribution of goods and services (except those in the commons like police, fire, etc.) should continue to be privately owned. But just as certainly, We the People must take back ownership of our government. This will remove us from Benito Mussolini's vision of a corporate state and adequately protect us from the possibility of socialism. It will leave us in the "radical middle" place of a constitutionally limited democratic republic: a modern liberal democracy.

Myth: "Free markets are nature's way of making the winner fit and strong (it's Darwin)."

Reality: Darwin's method led to more diversity, not less.

Conservative activists love to complain about the dangers associated with the concentrated power of government. Indeed, anybody who's ever spent time in most of the Third World, in dictatorships like the old Soviet Union, or in a repressive communist state like modern-day China (I've worked in all three) understands how dangerous concentrated and unrestrained government power can be.

The real problem, however, arises when there are gross inequities in the size and power of different entities in a culture. This is true whether the giant party is a powerful government, a powerful corporation, or a vastly powerful individual: in any case, ordinary people can find themselves in trouble, without a thing they can do about it, no matter how great the injustice.

For that reason, the conservatives' answer is just as bad as the problem. They suggest ceding more authority to very large corporations while reducing the power of a democratic government that might constrain them to balance their power with that of the nation's citizens.

The result of this, every time it's been tried in the United States (most conspicuously during the era of the robber barons, and under the administrations of Reagan/Bush, Clinton/Gore, and Bush/Cheney), has been to bring about a new feudalism, "rule by the rich," which in every case led quickly to so much abuse that it was overthrown—but not before great damage was done to many individuals.

This is a vitally important point when evaluating the arguments of conservatives who claim to represent our Founders. The Founders explicitly rejected a government dominated by corporations when they started the American Revolution by throwing the East India Company's tea into Boston Harbor in 1773.

Where is the real power held?

Although any form of government has the potential to be oppressive, one of the biggest things the conservatives miss is that in a liberal democracy like the United States, the government is ultimately answerable to We the People. We have both the right and the power (and, according to the Declaration of Independence, the duty) to restrain or even change our government when it overreaches.

Corporations, however, are not answerable to We the People in any sort of democratic way. Their internal structure is more like a kingdom or a feudal state, and their position within society is more often similar to that of a feudal lord than to a citizen.

Ah, but we can choose not to buy from corporations, the conservatives will say. If you don't like the way they do business, go elsewhere! Vote with your feet—this is democracy that involves corporations!

But, as is so often the case, real-world experience shows that conservative theories are more religion than science. When a large, predatory corporation like Wal-Mart comes into a community and wipes out all the smaller businesses, citizens no longer have the option of voting with their feet.

But doesn't that mean that Wal-Mart has "won" in the free market competition? That the people have "voted" for them over the smaller, local businesses? Isn't that how democracy and the free market are supposed to work?

Fortunately, the answer is no.

The real law of the jungle

The core of this logic is that unrestrained competition is the "law of the jungle," the way all of nature works, and that economic systems are just imitating natural systems. Only the fit survive; the weak are consumed or destroyed.

Certainly there are dimensions of nature that are competitive. We've been well sensitized to them, ever since Darwin first adapted Victorian-era economics to biology. But—as Darwin himself pointed out—the key survival element of nature is not raw win/lose competition, but a "struggle for existence" that leads to greater rather than less diversity. In this regard, Wal-Mart is anti-Darwinian, as is the entire conservative idea that unrestrained "free" market behavior enhances democracy and improves the quality of people's lives in a "natural" way.

Consider Darwin's own words, from his landmark book *The Origin of Species*. "We will now discuss in a little more detail the struggle for existence," he wrote to open his chapter titled "The

Struggle for Existence." "Nothing is easier than to admit in words [than] the truth of the universal struggle for life."

But in referring to the struggle for existence, Darwin didn't mean what the conservatives think when they support one individual company (species) getting bigger and bigger while consuming all the small ones in its path. In fact, he contemplated that with horror.

"I should premise that I use the term 'Struggle for Existence' in a large and metaphorical sense, including the dependence of one being on another," Darwin said, laying it out clearly. Darwin then supplied examples of how the *goal* of the "struggle for existence" is to enhance variety—as all the little shops in a town center would do—and not to reduce diversity as a Wal-Mart or other big out-of-town predatory company does.

Nature's balancing systems are like democracies balancing the power of corporations.

So not only is Darwin *not* saying that only the strongest survive against all others, he is explicitly saying that nature has put specific caps and checks into the system—just as good government does in economic systems—to keep the struggle going while at the same time keeping even the smallest and most fragile parts of the system alive.

And any person, Darwin suggested, who thought "survival of the fittest" or "to the victor go the spoils" was a natural law was profoundly ignorant of how such delicately balanced systems work. In fact, we'd even create stories of great floods or lost continents, or commonsense-defying "laws" (like "trickle-down economics"), to try to explain what should be obvious. "Nevertheless so profound is our ignorance," he wrote, "and so high our presumption, that we marvel when we hear of the extinction of an organic being; and as we do not see the cause, we invoke cataclysms to desolate the world, or invent laws on the duration of the forms of life!"

Thus, we see that the free market is never free—as life exists on the earth's crust, business exists on the substrate of a government court system to enforce its contracts, a government monetary system to ensure the stability of its means of commerce and exchange (currency and banking), and a government system of regulation and controls to prevent profits from being held in higher esteem than human health or quality of life.

Similarly, unconstrained capitalism makes no more sense in the ecology of nations than an unconstrained cell within your body. Every cell must act in concert with those around it, regulated by a system that looks out for the common good, and when a single cell decides to grow without limits, we call that cancer. In business and economy, it is necessary for government to provide a basis for the existence and function of small and medium-sized businesses, and to prevent large businesses from becoming cancerlike, subsuming everything in their path.

"Business" and "big business" are different animals.

President Theodore Roosevelt said in Columbus, Ohio, in 1912, "The great mass of business is of course done by men whose business is either small or of moderate size." These businesspeople, he said, "are satisfied with a legitimate profit" and an entrepreneur, as a rule, is "in no sense dangerous to his community, just because he is an integral part of his community, bone of its bone and flesh of its flesh. His life fibers are intertwined with the life fibers of his fellow citizens."[77]

From that praise of the organic elegance of small and medium-sized businesses in the life of America, Roosevelt turned his attention to the handful of large corporations that, even then, were trying to get lobbying and antitrust laws changed so they could grow ever bigger.

"So much for the small business man and the middle-sized business man. Now for big business," Roosevelt said.

"A wicked big interest is necessarily more dangerous to the community than a wicked little interest. 'Big business' in the past has been responsible for much of the special privilege which must be unsparingly cut out of our national life." While he did "not believe in making mere size of and by itself criminal," Roosevelt said that because big business had so much potential power, "there should be by law provision made for the strict supervision and regulation of these great industrial concerns."

The challenge was to prevent corporations from growing so large and powerful that they destroyed the ability of entrepreneurs—the jobs-creating powerhouse of America from its founding—to succeed. It should "be not only possible but easy for an ambitious man, whose character has so impressed itself upon his neighbors that they are willing to give him capital and credit, to start in business for himself, and, if his superior efficiency deserves it, to triumph over the biggest organization that may happen to exist in his particular field. Whatever practices upon the part of large combinations may threaten to discourage such a man, or deny to him that which in the judgment of the community is a square deal, should be specifically defined by the statutes as crimes."

Myth: "Taxes are an unfair burden and a waste of money."

Reality: The commons—including the commons of government—are necessary for our survival and quality of life.

When you woke up this morning, the odds are you used a shower and toilet that wouldn't function if it weren't for taxpayer-funded water supplies and sewage treatment systems. Your bathroom was lighted with power carried across public rights-of-way, built and maintained with tax dollars. When you stepped out of your home or apartment, looters or muggers didn't attack you because the taxpayer-funded police are on their jobs. If you'd had a fire, the taxpayer-funded fire department would have been there within minutes.

Your streets and sidewalks were put there with tax dollars,

and if you drove to work, your car was as safe as the state of the art allows because of tax-funded research and tax-funded agencies that required airbags and other safety standards. (If you took public transportation, it was created with tax dollars.) The air you breathed on the road today was cleaner than our parents' air because of tax-funded research and tax-funded agencies that require clean air from our cars, power plants, and other past polluters.

If you work for a company, it owes its existence to tax dollars: only state governments can authorize the creation of a corporation, and taxpayer-funded courts provide the legal infrastructure and stability necessary to do business. The taxpayer-funded federal government authorizes the creation of the money your corporation uses to conduct business, and it works to keep stable both the value of our currency and the banking system through which it flows.

Companies use telephone and Internet systems that were developed with taxpayer dollars and depend on taxpayer-maintained rights-of-way. When your company's employees travel, they do so on a taxpayer-funded highway, rail, or air traffic control system, knowing these are safe because of taxpayer-funded government standards and inspectors. And your business couldn't exist without a competent workforce educated in public schools at taxpayer expense.

Conservatives who protest paying taxes want to use all the benefits of a free society, but let others—particularly average wage earners—pay the expenses through payroll taxes, sales taxes, property taxes, and user fees.

They complain almost exclusively about "income taxes," which are paid only by people making over roughly $20,000 a year, and they completely ignore payroll taxes paid by *all* workers on the first $81,000 of their income (but not paid by wealthy people on anything after that first $81,000).

The core concept of taxation in a free society is one the Founders well understood—if the government is to administer the commons, then we all, by virtue of agreeing to remain citizens of this nation, are voluntarily entering into a social contract to pay for them.

"But I didn't sign any social contract!" say some conservatives. The simple answer is that this is a free society and our outbound borders are not closed—if they don't like the social contract, they have the option to change it through the electoral process, or go elsewhere. But denying that it exists won't work.

During the 2003 tax-cut debate, I was driving on a tax-funded public road to visit our tax-funded public library. Turning on the radio, I was just in time to hear Sean Hannity squeal at a guest something to the effect of, "You don't want the government to let you keep your own money? It's your money! You earned it!"

George W. Bush proposed in 2003 that the federal government borrow over $1.2 trillion and hand it over to people in America who earn more than $150,000 per year. (Some "tax cuts" went to people earning less, but I'm not including them in the $1.2 trillion figure, as they would raise it slightly.) Running a country into debt to give cash to wealthy taxpayers is not a tax cut; it's a tax postponement. Eventually that money will have to be repaid—most of the Treasuries (IOUs) sold to fund the debt will come due in either ten, twenty, or thirty years—and will be repaid (with interest) by taxes, pure and simple.

That American citizens (particularly those who speak on our nation's airwaves) could be so ignorant—or willing to blatantly lie—about the nature of the social contract our Founders put into place, and think that borrowing money and giving it to the wealthy was a "tax cut," is an indication of the damage conservatives have done with thirty years of relentless attacks on the funding and functioning of our public education system, and the consolidation of our media keeping out nonconservative voices.

The last two American presidents to submit balanced budgets were Jimmy Carter and Bill Clinton. In the meantime, the so-called conservative Reagan/Bush, Bush/Quayle, and Bush/Cheney administrations have supervised the handing over of more than

$6 trillion to America's wealthiest citizens and most powerful corporations—all of it borrowed in the name of you and me, and due and payable in the future by us, our children, and their children.

Myth: "Social programs are the liberals' way of buying votes."

Reality: Democratic government is *supposed* to respond to the needs and desires of the majority of its citizens, while protecting the rights of its minorities.

This myth betrays either an ignorance of or disregard for the system of representative democracy.

When elected officials do what the majority of the people want, that's called democracy. When they do something that serves only the interests of a narrow part of the electorate, that's antidemocratic.

"But," the conservatives say, "what if most people (and their representatives) vote in a system where most never work at all and the minority who work and are wealthy have to support them?"

It won't happen. It never has in a democracy.

The reality is that most people want to work. Work defines us and gives our lives purpose. Even people who are fabulously wealthy search for meaningful work to do, and those who don't work often end up depressed and self-destructive. This is why in all the two-hundred-plus years of various nations experimenting with constitutionally limited democratic republics, none has ever voted for a system where the majority of the people don't work and the minority who work have to support them.

As Ben Franklin pointed out, it is true that poorly constructed "welfare" systems can train people in dependence and multigenerational poverty. It's similarly true that the police don't capture all of our criminals, and our fire departments don't stop all fires. These are all arguments for improving the way our social protective systems work, not discarding them.

It makes no sense whatsoever to destroy a social safety net for all of us to prevent a few of us from scamming the system. That would be like eliminating highways to prevent some people from speeding.

Why, then, do conservative leaders say we should dismantle the social safety net?

Why did Ronald Reagan produce an epidemic of homelessness in America by refusing the chronically long-term mentally ill housing in state mental hospitals?

Why did George W. Bush's Treasury secretary call for the total elimination of Social Security, Medicaid, and Medicare in May 2001?

Greed: a sociopathic mental illness?

Conservative social critics are right in noting that a few lazy people will always try to "game the system," being interested only in their own comfort regardless of what it costs others. But they should equally acknowledge the flip side: there are also greedy people, who are similarly gaming the system, interested only in their own personal comfort regardless of who it harms or how it damages society. Both are ways of getting something for nothing.

The difference is that people who are unhealthy with laziness usually end up powerless, but those mentally ill with greed often end up very wealthy and thus powerful—even though they may have destroyed many lives in the process.

It only takes a handful of people with severe greed to seize control of a political party and wreak havoc on a nation, particularly if they believe the end justifies the means and they're willing to lie to We the People to reach their goals.

A well-thought-out social system, as in most of the advanced democratic republics of Europe, protects society from both: from the small damages that can be inflicted on it by the lazy, and the huge damages that can be caused by the greedy.

And it realizes that when elected representatives propose systems that are broadly popular, that's not called "vote buying"—it's called "democracy."

Myth: "Unlimited growth and concentration of power is nature's way and it's good for us."

Reality: Absolute power corrupts absolutely; only allowing voters—and not institutions—to influence politics is our protection as people.

Combining political power with the economic power of great wealth was a danger to democracy, and one of the reasons why Thomas Jefferson suggested amending the Constitution to "ban monopolies in commerce."

As Jefferson pointed out in a December 26, 1825, letter to William Giles, economic powers will always seek to gain political power and thus threaten to create "a single and splendid government of an aristocracy, founded on banking institutions, and moneyed incorporations under the guise and cloak of their favored branches of manufactures, commerce and navigation, riding and ruling over the plundered ploughman and beggared yeomanry [working class]."

Every past tyrannical government in the history of civilization had oppressed its citizens because it had combined political power with one or more of the other three categories, and the Founders were determined to prevent America from repeating the mistakes of previous nations.

Thus, political power would be held only by We the People and never again shared with military, corporate, or religious agencies.

Myth: "Media conglomerates are just nature
taking its course."

Reality: Without a free, independent, nonmonopolized
press, democracy is at risk.

In a January 28, 1786, letter to James Currie, Jefferson noted:
"Our liberty depends on the freedom of the press, and that cannot be limited without being lost."

Echoing a similar sentiment in 1835, Alexis de Tocqueville
closed *Democracy in America* with a prescient chapter titled "What
Sort of Despotism Democratic Nations Have to Fear." He noted:
"I think that men living in aristocracies may, strictly speaking, do
without the liberty of the press: but such is not the case with
those who live in democratic countries. . . . Servitude cannot be
complete if the press is free: the press is the chief democratic
instrument of freedom."

In the past few decades, conservatives have taken the archetypal ideas carried by all Americans and twisted "freedom of the
press" around to mean "freedom of one to own all the presses."
This is, in fact, the opposite of what Jefferson and de Tocqueville
were championing.

Freedom of the press means the freedom of media to speak
what it perceives as truth and to offer its opinions. For years, the
television networks and TV and radio stations across the nation
were so aware of the critical importance of unbiased and clearly
presented news to democracy that their news operations were
separate from all other divisions of the corporation and were not
required to make a profit. Producing news was part of the "giving
back," fulfilling the obligation of electronic media that uses public
airwaves or public rights-of-way (in the case of cable) to "serve
the public good."

But since the Reagan era, the ascendancy of conservative corporate values has changed the equation. News divisions are now
answerable to the bottom line, and the result is that many net-

works have closed foreign bureaus. News operations have become ratings-driven and are often used to advance—or at least to not hurt—the profit agendas of their corporate owners.

It's time to break up our media monopolies and return to local ownership and a diversity of voices.

Myth: "The media have a liberal bias."

Reality: Most of America's media is now in the hands of large, generally conservative corporations who strive for "truth."

It's a good thing that Fox News has a conservative bias. It's in the finest tradition of American journalism for a media outlet to state the position through which they filter the news, to be up front about their bias, and to invite in like-minded people to read or listen or watch.

Through nearly the entire history of America, most towns had several newspapers and those papers each took a different political position. From the days of Jefferson, when it was Federalist-leaning newspapers against Democratic-Republican-leaning newspapers, to the 1920–1970s era, when it was Republican-leaning versus Democratic-leaning newspapers, everybody knew where everybody stood.

The simple reality is that truly fair and balanced reporting is impossible. Every reporter, every news organization, and every corporation involved in the business of the news brings their own bias to the table. At least Fox is (relatively) honest about its bias.

The problem is that our local media have been wiped out, replaced by large corporations who offer most communities only one single newspaper and only a few nationally affiliated corporate-owned radio and TV outlets. For these corporations, homogeneity is the name of the game—play everything right down the middle. The result is pabulum news, hyperfocus on celebrity and sex scandals, and the death of investigative reporting.

Let's give up on the charade of "neutrality," "truth," and "fair and balanced reporting." We need more media with a liberal bias, and we need more media with conservative bias. Both locally owned, reflecting the passions and concerns of the local community. Only then will serious debate and discussion of the real issues of our time return to the stage of American life.

Myth: "There's too much regulation: Get government off the backs of big companies."

Reality: Big companies *create* regulations, which protect them from lawsuits.

Successful lies are always built on a germ of truth, and everybody who has ever filled out government forms or stood in line at the Department of Motor Vehicles knows how frustrating it can be to deal with government bureaucrats. But notice how the word "bureaucrat" is always preceded in conservative rhetoric with the word "government," and never the word "corporate."

Corporate bureaucracies create far more pain and hassle for Americans than government bureaucracies, as anybody who has ever tried to get an insurance company to pay for a claim or to deal with a problem in telephone or credit billing can tell you.

Nonetheless, this myth is phrased in such a way that the average person imagines big business dealing with government bureaucrats in the same exasperated fashion as we deal with the DMV or the IRS.

The reality is that the larger and more toxic the business, the more it may welcome—indeed, may even demand—regulation by government. The reasons for this are simple: regulations legalize activity that would otherwise subject the business to consumer lawsuits, and highly regulated environments can make it easy for big corporations to keep out smaller competitors.

Corporate lobbyists routinely press lawmakers to increase favorable regulations on their industries. For example, when

George H. W. Bush was vice president in 1986, Monsanto approached him about creating regulations for genetically modified organisms (GMOs), which at the time were not in production. One of the Monsanto executives at the meeting, Leonard Guarraia, told the *New York Times* in 2001: "There were no [GMO] products at the time, but we bugged him for regulation. We told him that we have to be regulated." And so, the *Times* reported, "the White House complied," and Monsanto got the regulations they wanted with the EPA, USDA, and FDA.[78]

The reason regulations can be so important to big corporations that manufacture products that may be dangerous is because the regulations serve to shield them from prosecution or financial liability. If a corporation is selling soft drinks that contain 10 parts per billion (ppb) arsenic—which can cause cancer—then consumers who get cancer could sue them. But if there are regulations in place that say a corporation may sell a product that contains up to but not above 10 ppb, then that 10 ppb becomes legal, and there is no recourse for consumers.

The secondary benefit of such regulation is that a huge commercial concern can easily spread out the cost of complying with regulations over a large budget. But smaller companies and new entrepreneurial start-ups often can't afford the cost of complying with some regulations. Thus, some companies in regulated industries (like pharmaceuticals) actually lobby for the government not to perform tests on their products but for they themselves to be required to bear the costs of testing and performance reviews. This isn't so they can cook the books on the tests, but to make the cost of bringing a product to market too high for anybody but a very large corporation.

This can also bring the regulatory agency under the effective control of the industry it is supposed to be regulating. As Robert Monks and Nell Minow, who worked with the Presidential Task Force on Regulatory Relief during the Reagan administration, wrote in their 1991 book *Power and Accountability*, "We found that business representatives continually sought more rather than less regulation, particularly when [the new regulations] would limit their liability or protect them from competition." They added: "The ultimate commercial accomplishment is to achieve regulation under law that is purported to be comprehensive and pre-empting and is administered by an agency that is in fact captive to the industry."[79]

The other types of regulations that industry seeks are those that limit government protection of consumers. On May 26, 1992, Vice President Dan Quayle said, "We will ensure that biotech products will receive the same oversight as other products, instead of being hampered by unnecessary regulation."[80] What he meant was that regulations were being promulgated that would limit the ability of consumers to know what was in their foods.

Under regulations proposed by the GMO industry, the dangers of genetically modified foods would be determined by the manufacturers, not the government, and testing would occur only when the companies wanted it to. And consumers were not to be notified if their food contained GMOs. "Labeling was ruled out as potentially misleading to the consumer, since it might suggest that there was reason for concern," noted *Times* reporter Kurt Eichenwald.[81] And, "the new policy strictly limited the regulatory reach of the F.D.A."[82]

There are regulations, however, that industry specifically objects to, and these are usually the ones that corporate-jet conservatives complain about when they discuss "excessive government regulation." Those are the rules that We the People have put into place to protect us from the products and processes of industry.

As Paul Hawken wrote in 1994 in *The Ecology of Commerce,* industry launched such a huge lobbying effort to fight back regulations on toxic chemicals after passage of the 1970 Clean Air Act that by 1990 "the agency has been able to muster regulations for exactly 7 of the 191 toxins that fell under the original legislation."[83]

In the years since 1990, things have only gotten worse. The last year for which EPA statistics are available on the release of toxic chemicals into the environment by industry is 1999, and in that year 7.7 billion pounds of toxics were released directly into our air and water, most with unknown short- or long-term effect.

Corporate lobbyists have succeeded in defining EPA regulations so that now only 650 of the more than 80,000 chemicals being used in industry have to be reported (so the 7.7 billion pound total represents only 1 percent of the possible chemicals in use). And those figures include only accidents and spills. As Worldwatch Institute's Anne Platt McGinn noted in a commentary entitled "Detoxifying Terrorism" on November 16, 2001, "releases during routine use are not included" in that 7.7 billion pound figure.[84] Platt goes on to add that we don't yet even know how dangerous or carcinogenic are "over 71 percent of the most widely used chemicals in the United States today" because the data simply doesn't exist or hasn't been released by industry.

Conservatives suggest that even though the corporations producing these toxins are using taxpayer-financed infrastructure like roads, water, septic, and electricity, with a taxpayer-educated workforce, and the taxpayer-funded treasury, banking, and legal systems, the consequences of their actions are none of the taxpayers' business.

Myth: "NAFTA/GATT/WTO 'free trade' is good for all nations."

Reality: "Free trade" is only free for multinational corporations, and they are its prime beneficiaries.

Nations differ in many respects. Some are richer than others in natural resources like minerals, oil, or timber, whereas others have large pools of potential laborers. The optimal state for every nation is to achieve an internal balance or homeostasis, relative self-sufficiency, with the means of production and distribution (mostly the businesses) locally owned and operated, producing an economy appropriate to local conditions.

Over history, the result of this has been that population-heavy and natural-resource-light nations have developed economies where people live well using less fuel and fewer resources, while those in nations that have lower populations and higher resource bases have had higher levels of resource consumption. (Americans consume, for example, about 30 times the resources of people in India.)

While a middle-class person in Bombay is paid the U.S. equivalent of $5,000 a year, because he or she lives in India, that person can still buy a comfortable home, clothes, groceries, a car, and put children through school, pay for health care, and even save for retirement. Internal stabilities are achieved, and local economies flourish. One of the things that keeps national economies relatively stable is that national borders are barriers to the movement of people.

Into this milieu have stepped multinational corporations, asserting that while people can't easily and quickly move from nation to nation, they should have the "right" to roam the world searching for the cheapest sources of all sorts of materials, including human labor. In doing so, they pit the middle class of India against the middle class of America (for example) and the result benefits only the corporation.

The reason the middle class of India isn't truly benefited by this is because in competing with America's middle class it will have its own level of income raised, and eventually it will begin to cost the multinational corporation more than similar labor would cost in some other developing nation. As soon as the corporation finds cheaper labor elsewhere, it will depart India, leaving behind a wake of social and economic devastation.

This pattern has repeated itself over and over again since corporate "free trade" really began to spread across the globe in the 1980s. When the Taiwanese, Thais, and South Koreans raised the average income of their middle class by manufacturing products previously made in Japan, Europe, and the United States, corporations pulled out and moved to China. Today the former "Asian tigers" are still struggling with the consequences of this. A similar pattern has happened in Mexico, which got many American jobs in the late 1990s and saw an explosion of factory building, but now has seen so many jobs go to China and other slave-labor nations that poverty is actually worse in Mexico now than before NAFTA and GATT were signed.

Myth: "Unions harm economies by driving up
wage expenses."

Reality: A rising tide from the bottom up lifts all boats.

Thirteen million Americans are members of unions today, but another 40 million say they would join a union if they could. It's not hard to figure out why: unionized employees earn 26 percent more than nonunionized employees and generally enjoy better benefits and more job security.

Conservatives argue that the higher labor costs drive up the cost of goods and services, and to some extent that's true. But at the same time, unionization increases the disposable income of the middle class, making those slightly-more-expensive goods and services more easily purchasable.

If labor were 100 percent of the cost of a product, it would be a zero-sum game. But because labor is usually only a small fraction of a product's cost, increasing labor costs increases product and service costs only slightly.

The result of widespread well-paid workers and "more expensive" goods is a strong middle class and a healthy local and national economy, as America had during the 40 years before radical conservatives took the White House and Congress in the 1980s. The result of the loss of good-paying jobs may have meant cheaper goods at Wal-Mart, but it hasn't led to healthier communities or an expansion of the middle class. To the contrary, the Wal-Martization of America has driven up the number of people falling out of the middle class and into the category of the working poor, the largest percentage of adults in poverty.

It's time to set aside the myths.

While conservatives want to "get government off the back of business" so business can fasten itself firmly onto your back, the rest of us are interested in seeing healthy and profitable businesses that are not controlling us and are not controlling the government.

Democracy depends on the sole political power of a nation residing in, of, by, and with We the People—not in an invasive supergovernment (think John Ashcroft), not one-sided corporate power (consider how your health insurance company, phone company, or credit card company treats you when there's a problem), or in church power (do you really want somebody telling you that you should live a particular way because *their* god said so?).

Three generations ago Franklin D. Roosevelt made the point that hungry or fearful people are not free people. It doesn't mean that the state should subsidize people who are capable of working: that, too, can be a form of tyranny. But it does mean that the government ought to concern itself with whether people have jobs—even people who've been out of work for 18 months and are no longer counted in the statistics.

And it means government has an important role to play in defining the rules by which business plays, so people don't work hard and still go hungry—as is the case with so many of the "new jobs" being created by big-box retailers and other parts of the service and retail industries.

A hockey game without rules or referees is anarchy, and history shows that the same is true of unregulated capitalism: it inevitably becomes predatory, dominated by bullies, and destructive to democracy.

By defining the terms of the game—"Pay a livable wage and don't threaten the environment or hurt people; in exchange we will provide you with an educated workforce, a stable currency, a reliable court system, transportation systems and other parts of the commons, and international agreements to protect your business and your workers"—government of, by, and for We the People can play a vital and important role in retaining freedom and democracy in America.

WHAT BECAME OF REAL AMERICAN CONSERVATIVES?

The occupation of a hair-dresser, or of a tallowman [candle maker], cannot be a matter of honor to any person—to say nothing of a number of other more servile employments. Such description of men ought not to suffer oppression from the state, but the state suffers oppression if such as they, either individually or collectively, are permitted to rule.

—Conservative English philosopher
EDMUND BURKE (1729–1797)

*T*oday's so-called conservative agenda is about ownership, and the power that comes from it. Specifically, it's about ownership of the assets of the United States of America—things that the Founders intended would be owned by We the People. Ultimately, it's about having effective control of the U.S. government itself, and keeping the majority of Americans in a state of perpetual economic fear, a variation on what in feudal times was called serfdom.

Those who are not independently wealthy yet support this

so-called conservative agenda are pushing for their own children to become slaves.

The modern conservative movement: Russell Kirk

In many ways the modern conservative movement is the heir to Alexander Hamilton's ideas of a small federal government under aristocratic control. It was reinvented in large part in 1953 with the publication of the original edition of Russell Kirk's book *The Conservative Mind.*[85] In this book, Kirk laid out six basic tenets of modern conservatism:

1. A divine intent, as well as personal conscience, rules society.
2. Traditional life is filled with variety and mystery while most radical systems [the opposite of conservative systems] are characterized by narrowing uniformity.
3. Civilized society requires orders and classes.
4. Property and freedom are inseparably connected.
5. Man must control his will and his appetite, knowing that he is governed more by emotion than by reason.
6. Society must alter slowly.

When closely examined, these tenets fail to hold water.

Kirk's "divine intent" is an updated version of "the divine right of kings" and other conservative arguments that our rights were solely granted to us by a benevolent (but sometimes angry) God and therefore must be exclusively interpreted by those ordained by God. It's the beginning of the slippery slope to theocracy, a fact that makes "conservative" religious leaders with political aspirations, such as onetime presidential candidate Pat Robertson, very happy.

Kirk's "traditional life" argument falls flat when you consider America's Founders. They were radicals, rejecting the traditional life of royal Britain, but few would suggest their lives lacked variety or mystery, or that they or the nation they created were "characterized by a narrowing uniformity." If anything, experience indicates that "narrowing uniformity" best characterizes those who call themselves conservatives.

The heart of conservative thinking throughout history, as Kirk points out, is found in his argument that "civilized society requires orders and classes." This was the same argument made by conservatives like Hamilton at the Constitutional Convention of 1787 and was largely rejected (other than in the selection of the Senate). It's also the attitude shown by John Adams, as he regally traveled through towns and demanded that those who disagreed with him be imprisoned.

History shows that democracy and this element of conservative thought are incompatible. Democracy requires the involvement of all, not just particular orders and classes. Conservatives have been animated for centuries by conservative philosopher Edmund Burke, who wrote that the "state suffers" if such rabble as "a hair-dresser" or a candle maker "are permitted to rule."

If you believe that property and freedom are inseparable, then logic suggests that the less property one owns, the less free one is. It's hard to understand how a society built on "orders and classes," with those who own the most property having the most freedom, is compatible with either democracy or American values.

Kirk's argument about will, appetites, emotion, and reason assumes that the normal state of humans is evil and dominating. In fact, the past century of steady movement worldwide toward more liberal democracies shows the error of this thinking. Another problem is that this idea leads naturally to a police state—as we've seen with archconservative U.S. Attorney General John Ashcroft—because those in power assume "the governed" are inherently evil and must be controlled.

And, while the slaveholders of the Old South agreed with

Kirk that "society must alter slowly," the worldwide history of rapid improvements in peacefulness and standards of life when nations make an abrupt transition from dictatorship to democracy proves this to be another destructive conservative myth.

Kirk's book, however, lit the fuse on what has exploded as the modern conservative movement. Wealthy Republicans like William F. Buckley Jr. and Barry Goldwater heartily endorsed his concepts, and wealthy plutocrats like Joseph Coors, Rupert Murdoch, and Sun Myung Moon saw in the philosophy a palatable way to retain and build their influence and power.

The shift to pseudoconservative values

Through the 1960s, the conservative movement grew rapidly among the most affluent in America and by the 1970s and 1980s had think tanks and newspapers in its fold. The 1990s saw giant media outlets like Fox News, the *Washington Times,* and Clear Channel embracing and promoting conservatism, while the movement's most well-known spokesman, Rush Limbaugh, grew in national fame and fortune.

Today, largely as a result of the pseudopopulist rhetoric of conservatives like Limbaugh and Patrick Buchanan, the majority of average Americans who call themselves conservative have no idea what the term means or where it came from. Most think "conservative" means a strong national defense and a call for religious and moral values. Experience has shown that conservative belligerence has not strengthened America's defenses* and that bringing religion into government moves the nation toward a Taliban-like state and away from freedom and democracy.

---

*The Soviet Union was already crumbling under internal rot and the pressure of an internal democracy movement long before Reagan borrowed trillions from future taxpayers and gave the money to his campaign donors to develop Star Wars: conservative mythology aside, its collapse had almost nothing to do

Indeed, if the government of the United States represents a democracy, the conservatives explicitly claim to be against democracy. As a leading spokesman for the conservative agenda, Grover Norquist told National Public Radio's Mara Liasson in a May 25, 2001, *Morning Edition* interview, "I don't want to abolish government. I simply want to reduce it to the size where I can drag it into the bathroom and drown it in the bathtub."

Awakening to the antidemocratic conservative damage

It's now more than 20 years since Ronald Reagan, the first president who was a true believer in the modern cult of conservatism, came to power. A generation later seems an appropriate time to evaluate the damage done to America by Reagan and Bush II's conservative deficits, Gingrich's conservative power politics, Cheney's conservative foreign policy, the rise of conservative corporate monopoly media, and the sustained, two-decades-long conservative assault on the quality of the environment and the rights of organized labor.

In each case, the results are chilling.

Conservative "supply-side" economics (called "Voodoo Economics" by George H. W. Bush) have brought us the largest national debt in the history of the United States—so severe that recently the World Bank warned that we were treading the path already walked by Argentina and other nations who had slipped beyond their ability to repay their own debt.

---

with increased American defense spending. The bottom line is simply that dictatorship doesn't work, whether it's a dictatorship by a hereditary lineage of kings, wealthy corporate barons, or bureaucrats who have seized power and pretend to operate in the name of the people but only perpetuate their own power (the cautionary tale from the USSR).

Jefferson predicted it.

It's a testimony to the power of the American democratic republic our Founders created that it took 227 years before a president succeeded in inflicting such a potentially mortal wound on America. But, although they did everything they could to prevent it, the Founders still worried that the day would come.

In a letter to Samuel Kercheval, Jefferson noted the temptation of governments to spend money they don't have in order to produce a temporary feel-good boom in the economy, just in time for an election. But a true statesman wouldn't resort to such tactics to buy votes, Jefferson wrote: "We must not let our rulers load us with perpetual debt. We must make our election [choice] between economy and liberty, or profusion and servitude."

But Reagan, and then his spiritual heir George W. Bush, suggested that perpetual debt and the short-term profusion it would bring were just fine. Many of us have already forgotten it, but in just eight years, Reagan's budgets doubled the entire national debt that the country had accumulated since its founding. This debt used to produce the "Reagan recovery," on which we are still paying interest, is particularly bizarre, considering that traditional American conservative values call for thrift and being responsible for oneself.

Reagan and both Bushes spent trillions of borrowed money, producing the same sort of stage-prop prosperity you or I could have if we had a credit card with a million-dollar credit limit that we knew somebody else would have to pay. But the debt they ran up was and is real, and it will have to be repaid by the generation today coming of age and their children.

Yet even beyond this real economic harm, the main damage conservative raw power politics has produced is the epidemic of cynicism across America, as people simply take on the attitude of "Why should I bother? I can't make a difference." Although it's fashionable to say that increasing numbers of Americans don't vote, the reality is that increasing numbers have been abstaining as their only way of saying "none of the above." Negative ads and scorched-earth politics, like those played by Newt Gingrich and Tom DeLay, produce a revulsion that propels people away from the political arena.

Back in 1988, Lee Atwater, the campaign consultant to George H. W. Bush who developed the infamous Willie Horton commercials, brought attack politics and "the perpetual campaign"—the cornerstones of the younger Bush's presidency—into vogue. In a way that would make George Orwell shiver, the younger Bush's "brain" and adviser Karl Rove has run the most poll-driven, image-conscious White House in the history of America, with every issue and every word carefully parsed, tested, and rehearsed—thus denying the American people the kind of honest interchange and candid answers that Britons get when their prime minister must publicly respond to the "Prime Minister's Questions" put to him by the House of Commons. To compound this loss of accountability, we also see a press corps totally cowed by threats of loss of access and punishments such as that meted out by Bush to the elder stateswoman of journalism, Helen Thomas, for daring to ask him a tough question.

Once again, the factors at work here are eternal: when power is concentrated in too much wealth, instead of ordinary people, abuse results. Back in 1781, after unsuccessfully submitting a bill to the Virginia legislature to outlaw slavery, Thomas Jefferson wrote in his *Notes on Virginia* about his frustration with a legislature taken over by wealthy conservatives. He said that he expected "a time, and that not a distant one, when a corruption in this country" would become rampant.

"The time to guard against corruption and tyranny," he concluded, "is before they shall have gotten hold of us. It is better to keep the wolf out of the fold, than to trust to drawing his teeth and claws after he shall have entered."

———

Today, conservatives often assert that it's natural for "the strong to survive," and for one dominant winner to emerge. They point to the dominant or "alpha" animal in a pack—snarls and all—as clear evidence. But is that true? It turns out that the latest science says no. Let's examine the relevance of these new findings, because they hold the key to understanding why democracy is such a driving force in the human spirit.

7

DEMOCRACY, NOT DOMINANCE, IS THE WAY OF NATURE

Whenever a new discovery is reported to the scientific world, they say first, "It is probably not true." Then after, when the truth of the new proposition has been demonstrated beyond question, they say, "Yes, it may be true, but it is not important." Finally, when sufficient time has elapsed to fully evidence its importance, they say, "Yes, surely it is important, but it is no longer new."

—MICHEL DE MONTAIGNE,
French Renaissance philosopher (1533–1592)

*U*ntil very recently, many believed that the normal state of humankind was to be forcibly ruled by others, rather than to live in a democratic state of self-rule. After all, apart from a few centuries of Athenian and modern democracy, the whole multi-millennial sweep of human history seems to indicate that humans are most often—and most stably—ruled by warlord kings (wielding violence), or by popes and mullahs (wielding threats of violence or eternal damnation), or feudal lords and plutocrats keeping people in line by threat of unemployment and poverty.

Additionally, our science—from Aristotle to political science texts published as recently as 2002—has suggested that the dominance and hierarchy we've seen in our history is nature at work. It's the way all of nature is, the argument goes; it's natural that humans would be that way.

The argument continues: it's animal nature to be dominant and savage, so it's natural for humans to treat one another that way, too.

Entire civilizations—and the religions that support or reflect them—have been built on this simple premise over the past six to seven thousand years.

But now the most recent science is proving both assumptions false. The new evidence leads us to these conclusions:

▸ Without exception, the natural state of group-living animals is to cooperate, not dominate. Democracy, it turns out, is hardwired into the DNA of species from ants to zebras. And it includes all of the hominids, from the great apes to *Homo sapiens*.

▸ Our view of history has been terribly one-sided. We've forgotten how people (your and my ancestors) actually lived in tribal "precivilized" times. Instead of what we now know is actual history, we've filled our past with Hobbesian* stories of life being short, brutish, and nasty.

The result is that outside of the community of cultural anthropologists, few people know that democracy is the natural state of humans, a way of life for the majority of cultures on the planet both today and for all of human history.

---

*Thomas Hobbes was an English philosopher who asserted that life is hard (he was born in an impoverished clerical family) and people have a fundamental right to selfishness, but they'll relinquish those rights to a more powerful authority (an absolute monarch) for the common safety. He lived and died a century before the modern democratic era began (1588–1679).

The biology of democracy

Dominance-based political and economic systems have been the exception, not the rule, in the arc of human history (as we'll see in detail in a few pages), and empires have a nasty habit of imploding every century or so, as a succession of European, African, South American, and Asian empires show.

This led biologists Tim Roper and L. Conradt at the School of Biological Sciences, University of Sussex, England, to propose a study of democracy versus despotism in animals. The prevailing assumption has always been that because there are identifiable "alpha" members of animal groups—from alpha males among gorillas to alpha females among wolves—that these alpha members exercise despotic rule over the others in the tribe, pack, or community.

In this, Roper and Conradt's research shows, we're projecting our own vision of the value of despotism onto animals. Part of the problem is that nobody has thought to challenge our cultural assumptions and actually model or study animal decision-making and governance behaviors. We've simply assumed that there are "kings" and "queens" throughout the animal world, and that's that. As Conradt and Roper point out in a paper titled "Group Decision-Making in Animals," published in the January 9, 2003, edition of the prestigious scientific journal *Nature,* "group decision-making processes have been largely neglected from a theoretical point of view."[86]

When animals—or people—move together to do something, that's called *synchronization* by biologists. Whether it's a nation's decision to engage in war or a herd's decision to finish grazing and move to the water hole, synchronization has both benefits and costs. With the water hole, for example, moving too quickly may mean that many of the members of the herd aren't fully grazed and thus become nutritionally deficient. On the other hand, if they stay too long grazing, they may become a more appetizing target for a predator or their bodies may become dehydrated.

Because we assume that despotism is the natural state, we've always assumed that the alpha or leader animal of the herd or group makes the decision, and the others follow. The leader knows best: he or she is prepared for that genetically by generations of Darwinian natural selection.

But could it be that animals act democratically? That there's a system for voting among animals, from honeybees to primates, that we've just never noticed because we weren't looking for it?

Prior to Conradt and Roper's research, nobody knew whether or not animals could act democratically and, if so, whether democracy was an aberration or a norm in the animal world. "Many authors have assumed despotism without testing [for democracy]," they note in their *Nature* article, "because the feasibility of democracy, which requires the ability to vote and to count votes, is not immediately obvious in non-humans."

Stepping into this vacuum of knowledge, the two scientists decided to create a testable model that "compares the synchronization costs of despotic and democratic groups."

Conradt and Roper discovered that democracy always trumps despotism, both over the short and the long term. When a single leader (despot) or small group of leaders (oligarchy) makes the choices, the swings into extremes of behavior tend to be greater and more dangerous to the long-term survival of the group. Because in a despotic model the overall needs of the entire group are measured only by the leader's needs, wrong decisions would be made often enough to put the survival of the group at risk.

With democratic decision making, however, the overall knowledge and wisdom of the entire group, as well as the needs of the entire group, come into play. The outcome is less likely to harm anybody, and the group's probability of survival is enhanced. "Democratic decisions are more beneficial primarily because they tend to produce less extreme decisions," they note in the abstract to their paper.

Democracy in nature

Britain's leading mass-circulation science journal, *New Scientist,* looked at how Conradt and Roper's model actually played out in the real world. Researchers modeled the behavior on red deer, which are social animals with alpha "leaders."

What they found was startling: red deer always behave democratically.

If any individuals want to move on, they're ignored until a particular critical mass is reached. "In the case of real red deer," James Randerson noted in his *New Scientist* article titled "Democracy Beats Despotism in the Animal World," "the animals do indeed vote with their feet by standing up. Likewise, with groups of African buffalo, individuals decide where to go by pointing in their preferred direction. The group takes the average and heads that way."[87]

But what happens when the alpha animal is older, wiser, and more experienced? Our cultural myth is that such a leader will always make better decisions than a group, but research demonstrates that nature rejects the idea. As Randerson noted, "surprisingly, democracy was favoured even if the dominant individual is an experienced individual that makes fewer errors in its decisions than the subordinates."

So why have an alpha male or female if they're not going to lead? The answer appears to be grounded back in Darwin—to create a sexual pecking order, which helps ensure the most fit individuals produce the most offspring. But being sexually dominant has nothing to do, it turns out, with leadership of those who are already alive in the community. The alpha individual—across the broad spectrum of species—is usually merely one more voter among the group when animals democratically decide how to behave. (Among predators, the alpha animal is often also the hunt leader, but as with human tribal "chiefs," instead of that being a position of power over others it simply carries more of a burden and a greater chance of injury or death.)

Conradt and Roper found not only that animals will always choose democracy over despotism, but that the nature of the vote will vary from situation to situation, depending on the importance of the decision. In some situations, it takes only half the animals "voting" for the herd to make a decision; in others it may take more. They note: "Modified democratic decision-making mechanisms are comparable to the tradition, in many human societies, of using a two-thirds majority rather than a 50 percent majority for decisions that are potentially more costly if taken than if not taken (for example, constitutional changes for Germany)."

When I called Dr. Tim Roper, he told me, "Quite a lot of people have said, 'My gorillas do that, or my animals do that.' On an informal, anecdotal basis it [the article] seems to have triggered an, 'Oh, yes, that's quite true' reaction in field workers." But it takes years for good research to be done, compiled, analyzed, and printed, so, "apart from that [feedback], no [follow-up research has yet been published]."

I asked him if his theory that animals—and, by inference, humans in their "natural state"—operate democratically contradicted Darwin. He was emphatic. "I don't think it is [at variance with Darwin]. I see this as essentially a mechanistic model. It's not the group selection model because each individual is doing what is best for it. So the point about this model is that democratic decision making is best for all the individuals in the group, as opposed to following a leader, a dominant individual [which can harm individuals in the group]. So we see it as an individual selection model, and so it's not incompatible with Darwin at all."

Is democracy the same thing as enlightened self-interest?

But in modern society, the libertarian idea of "self over all" has taken considerable root, being the animating theme of the conservative movement. How could it be, I asked Roper, that democracy—where individuals often don't get what they personally want—is best for them? The answer, he said, is that democracy always supports the survival of the group over the long term, and, because the individual is a part of the group, it therefore benefits the individual as well.

"For the kinds of animals we're talking about," he said, "and for humans as well, it is in every individual animal's best interest to be a part of the group. You see that at its most extreme in the social insects where you can't imagine a worker bee or a single queen bee surviving on its own. You can't imagine a chimpanzee surviving on its own, because it needs social companions to help protect it from predators, to tell it where the food is, and all the rest of it, so in these kinds of societies, individuals are highly dependent on being a member of a social group."

But what about the American ideal of the noble woodsman, the rugged individualist, the man who looks out for himself first in all cases? Such a mythos, Roper pointed out, sounds nice but would ultimately lead to chaos and perhaps even species extinction. "The idea of individuals going it alone is simply not viable for most intensely social creatures because if they left the group they would get knocked off by a predator in five minutes, or starve . . . , [or not make it through a winter]. Being a member of a group is a sort of survival necessity in individual terms. And therefore it's in every individual's selfish interest that the group remains a coherent unit. That's the sort of logic that our model is based on, the logic that the group must remain a coherent unit. You can't have one individual deciding that it's time to sleep and going to sleep while all the others are going on their way, because then that individual would cease to become a part of the group and be susceptible to predation and so on."

Roper believes democracy is so wired into us and our behavior that we don't even notice it in everyday situations.

"We think of the analogy," he said, "as, suppose you've got a dozen people in a committee room, and eventually somebody will start shuffling around and shuffling their papers and then others do, and eventually somehow a collective decision gets made. That's the sort of situation we're talking about."

Thoughtfully, he added, "Maybe that's where [modern political] democracy came from in an evolutionary context."

But what about "survival of the fittest"?

In *Darwinism, Dominance, and Democracy: The Biological Bases of Authoritarianism,*[88] political scientists Albert Somit and Steven A. Peterson start their book with the simple mantra of civilized people around the world: "Throughout human history, the overwhelming majority of political societies have been characterized by the rule of the few over the many, by dominance and submission, by command and obedience."

They add, "No matter the century or era, we see the same pattern—authoritarian regimes are notable by their presence and persistence, democracies by their infrequency and impermanence."

Like Darwin, they say that humans have "a genetic bias toward hierarchy, dominance, and submission." Autocratic regimes exist more frequently than do democracies because "evolution has endowed our species, as it has other primates, with a predisposition for hierarchically structured social and political systems."

In this, as both anthropology and biology show, they are quite simply wrong.

Tribal democracy

Democracy is actually far more ancient and far more pervasive than some political scientists think. Up until a century or so ago, more than half the humans in the world lived in societies that were essentially democratic, and from the dawn of humanity until a thousand years ago, as many as 90 percent of all humans lived in various types of democracies. We just didn't (and don't) call them that: we call them tribes.

Democracy isn't a cultural, social, and political experiment: it's as old as humanity itself. The experiment—which has yet to prove itself viable—is rule by special interest and brute force; government by the wealthy and powerful for the wealthy and powerful; kingdoms and corporate estates.

In the late 1990s, I was invited by the premier of the Northwest Territories, Don Morin, to Yellowknife and Fort Resolution to address a group of elders and representatives of tribes from all across northern Canada. The next day, Morin took me to a meeting of the legislative assembly, where I met and spoke with the members of that province's legislature—a body that makes decisions by consensus. Following a tribal tradition that is so ancient its origin is lost in the mists of antiquity, they make decisions by talking around a circular meeting area and if any single member casts a veto, the issue is turned down.

I've met and worked with tribal people or tribal remnants on every populated continent and have always encountered the same thing—an ancient history of governance and decision making that is far different from what Hobbes and Darwin hallucinated, but, rather, is familiar to any student of democracy.

Many of the groups I visited had chiefs, and one even had what they called a king. In every case, though, this leadership position was considered a burden and an obligation of service, not an opportunity for self-enrichment or lording it over others. While history does show that some Native American tribes had authoritarian governance, those groups tended to be younger in culture and history and were often ostracized by other tribes.

And tribal governance was neither power based nor rudely simple, as Darwin imagined. The late Dr. Peter Farb describes with startling and forceful eloquence in his landmark work *Man's Rise to Civilization, As Shown by the Indians of North America from Primeval Times to the Coming of the Industrial State* how the nuance and depths of typical Native American tribal cultures were, as he said of Shoshone rituals, "every bit as complex as those of the Vatican or the Court of Versailles."[89]

The end of war

Neither were they generally warlike, Farb notes: "Much of the warfare carried on by American Indians stemmed directly from contact with Europeans. Indian groups were early set into conflict with one another because of the loss of their lands, the increasing dependence upon Whites for trade items, and the necessity of sharing traditional hunting areas with alien groups that had been pushed westward by advancing Whites."

Prior to this contact, there were Indian wars, but they were rare. Instead, nearby communities practiced a form of competition and score-settling that whites call lacrosse: the object, instead of killing each other, was to score a goal. Occasionally this was played for entertainment, and sometimes even to determine the outcome of a dispute such as a territorial boundary. Even in actual combat, often a "war" was declared as "won" when the first blood was drawn. "Counting coup" is a translation of an old Indian phrase for touching an opponent or drawing his blood, but it was rarely associated with death in battle.

The Shoshone tribe that occupied much of what is Nevada today had achieved a singular accomplishment that was not uncommon among tribal people. As Farb attests: "They did not engage in warfare."

Farb points out that their reason for refusing to participate in wars was more practical than anything else. "The Shoshone did not wage war because it served no purpose. They had no desire to gain military honors, for these were meaningless in their kind of society. They had no territories to defend, for a territory is valuable only at those times when it is producing food, and those were precisely the times when the Shoshone cooperated rather than made war."

The fate of the Stinkards—to marry royalty

Some tribes—particularly the agricultural ones—had hierarchical-appearing forms of social and governmental organization. For example, the Natchez of the Northwest Coast had a four-tiered caste system with the Suns at the top, followed by the Nobles and the Honored People. At the bottom were the Stinkards.

But, Farb notes, while the Natchez did have a caste system, it was quite the opposite of the rigid systems in India or the rarely changing European and American systems created by family dynasties of great wealth versus multigenerational families living in great poverty. Instead, when a young man or woman became eligible for marriage, "Every member of the three noble classes had to marry a Stinkard."

Because caste affiliation was matrilineal, children were always a different caste from their fathers. The offspring of ruling Great Suns fathers were always dropped a notch to Nobles because their mother was a Stinkard. When the Noble male child of this pairing married a Stinkard, as was required, their children (now the grandchildren of the Great Sun) were Honored People. And when that grandson married a Stinkard and produced a child, the now-great-grandchildren of the Great Sun were automatically Stinkards.

"To us familiar with the rules of succession to European thrones, this complex system might seem preposterous," Farb writes. But it provided a remarkable level of social mobility, which ensured social and political stability. Everybody—no matter their class in society—was related by marriage to one of the rulers, and everybody was equally related to, or wanting to marry, a Stinkard.

The Natchez had survived along the Pacific Coast for millennia, perhaps as much as 20,000 years, with relative stability, until they met representatives of the French dictatorship headed by Louise XIV (ironically known as the Sun King). "Exactly thirty years after the first missionary visited them in 1699," Farb chronicles, "the Natchez made their final desperate attempt to fight back against the encroaching French." The French (now under Louis XV) slaughtered them, and "the four hundred survivors of the attack, including the Great Sun, were sold into slavery in the West Indies."

The natural state of things

The French slaughter of the Natchez was the sort of thing Darwin had often observed. It led him to conclude that the power-based, war-driven, dictator-led technological culture of Europeans was superior to that of "savages" because it was the one that usually prevailed. The typical Indian warrior was, in defense of home and family, "ready to sacrifice his life, as many a savage has been."

Thus, Darwin noted, "it is extremely doubtful whether the offspring of the more sympathetic and benevolent parents, or of those who were the most faithful to their comrades, would be reared in greater numbers than the children of selfish and treacherous parents belonging to the same tribe." They were weeded out by the process, he said, "of natural selection."[90] And the fact that tribes continued to produce altruistic individuals was simply a matter that couldn't be accounted for and so was safely ignored.

Warlords and democracies

With this new view of the ways cultures develop, emerge, and change, the early European reports suggesting that some Native American tribes were kind and peaceful and others were violent warriors begin to make sense.

Many Native American tribes had been in one place for

10,000 years or more when Europeans first arrived here—adequate time for them to figure out how to create democracy.

Others violated the laws of nature and began consuming excessively, storing up surplus food as did the slaveholding Stseélis and Skaúlits near Vancouver Island, or were provoked to prey on others' lands because of changes in their local environment (such as drought or extensive wildfire). Some tribes had been forced to abandon the democracy they had worked out by trial and error over thousands of years and invaded the lands of democratic people, provoking pain and distress.

In most cases, there was enough memory of democracy even among the nondemocratic people that they didn't try to wipe out the people whose lands they wanted part of. Thus, when eight hundred or so years ago a group of Athabaskan-speaking people from what is now Canada traveled south and invaded the territories of the Pueblo-speaking people in the American West and Southwest, eventually an uneasy truce was defined. Over time, the Navaho (Athabaskan) and the Hopi (Pueblo) learned to live together, because even the nondemocratic Navaho invaders still remembered and carried many of the basic core democratic values, and they eventually rebuilt them into their culture once they had finally settled in among the more southern lands.

When Europeans began the westward march across North America, they claimed to carry the democratic values laid out in the words of Jesus' Sermon on the Mount. But while many tribes were living those words, they had not been realized even in part by "civilized" people since the fall of Athens. Europe had been under the control of antidemocratic warlords, popes, and wealthy feudal lords so long that by 1600, European leaders only gave lip service to the possibility that Jesus might have been speaking practical, daily livable, essentially democratic truths.

It's important to remember, too, that none of the Native American tribes started out as stable and sustainable democratic indigenous cultures, since they arrived in North America from

Asia as itinerant hunter-gatherers. Evidence of the arrival of people from Asia corresponds with the wiping out of dozens of species of large, edible land animals in North and South America. Many of those now-extinct animals' bones have been uncovered with marks showing spears or arrows killed them, and their bones carry meat-cutting marks.

The first Americans were making the same mistakes the explorer Melanesians did in New Zealand, the Europeans did when warlords conquered their tribes, and the first people to visit Australia did when they wiped out many indigenous species. There is no shortage of ancient Native American graveyard finds showing evidence of widespread Indian warfare following the extinction of the easy-to-kill animals.

But overall, Native American tribes in different parts of the two continents figured out how to live in peace with each other and in balance with their environment and all other life. Although some were still ruled by warlords, kleptocrats, or cult-like theocrats, most Native American tribes at the time of European contact were living in peace and had democratic forms of governance. They had successfully made the inevitable transition toward democracy.

Democracy always wins.

Darwin's contemporaries mistakenly believed that democracy was merely an experiment, and one that is only tenuously held together by the unique human power of intellect. They incorrectly believed the natural human state—and, indeed, that of all animals—is despotism.

In this worldview, economists and politicians from Gilgamesh to George W. Bush echoed Darwin: the largesse of the most powerful and wealthy in society was the result of an inherent superiority, be it genetic, spiritual, or moral, and the most appropriate way to hold society stable while preventing the poor from rioting was to let some benefits trickle down to them in a controlled fashion.

During Darwin's time influence peddlers roamed the halls of the British House of Commons, and lords inherited their titles and power just as today the son of a president is entitled to become a president and the most powerful and wealthy interests in our society are represented by more than 20 lobbyists for every member of Congress, while the working poor (the largest segment of the poor in America) typically cannot take time off work to vote.

But democracy is our natural state, and if American democracy is to reawaken, it will take a populace awake and aware of the threats that face it.

8

WARLORDS, THEOCRATS, AND ARISTOCRATS RISE AGAIN

As nightfall does not come at once, neither does oppression. In both instances, there's a twilight where everything remains seemingly unchanged, and it is in such twilight that we must be aware of change in the air, however slight, lest we become unwitting victims of the darkness.

—WILLIAM O. DOUGLAS, U.S. Supreme Court Justice
(1939–1975)

The peculiar evil of silencing the expression of an opinion is that it is robbing the human race; posterity as well as the existing generation; those who dissent from the opinion, still more than those who hold it. If the opinion is right, they are deprived of the opportunity of exchanging error for truth: if wrong, they lose, what is almost as great a benefit, the clearer perception and livelier impression of truth, produced by its collision with error.

—JOHN STUART MILL, *On Liberty* (1869)

*I*n the Bill of Rights there is an interesting—and startling—difference between one category of rights and another.

The rights regarding property and freedom to move about have conditions. These are the rights where society's interest might be at stake: for instance, the Fourth Amendment allows searching your possessions when there's good reason to suspect a crime.

But there is one area where the rights are absolutely unconditional: *the rights to hold and express any opinion.* These rights were put at the very start of the Bill of Rights, with wording so strong that the government itself is explicitly forbidden from passing any laws that may restrict them:

> Congress shall make no law respecting an establishment of religion, or prohibiting the free exercise thereof, or abridging the freedom of speech, or of the press; or the right of the people peaceably to assemble, and to petition the government for a redress of grievances.

Indeed, without absolute freedom to hold and express an opinion, how could there possibly be a democracy? How could it be possible for the voice of the people to be heard?

It wouldn't be possible. And that is why curtailing freedom of opinion should be a matter of the gravest concern in a democracy.

Yet that is exactly what's happening in America.

Warlord presidents use "national security" to grab power.

In war, the discretionary power of the Executive [President] is extended. Its influence in dealing out offices, honors, and emoluments is multiplied; and all the means of seducing the minds, are added to those of subduing the force of the people. The same malignant aspect in republicanism may be traced in the inequality of fortunes, and the opportunities of fraud, growing out of a state of war . . . and in the degeneracy of manners and morals, engendered by both. No nation could preserve its freedom in the midst of continual warfare.

—PRESIDENT JAMES MADISON (1809–1817)

Since 9/11 many civil libertarians have expressed concern about the reduction of liberties by the government. Our history shows that there is both reason for concern, and hope for the pendulum to swing back toward liberty. But many Americans are unaware of how bad it's gotten at times in America's past.

Adams, the war president

One of John Adams's main rationales for promoting the Alien and Sedition Acts—which banned dissent against government policies or speaking ill of the president—was a series of conflicts the United States was having with France. In the last year of the Washington administration, the new "Directory at Paris" (the French executive branch) refused to receive an American minister. It then went on to suggest that even though Washington had put forth a "Proclamation of Neutrality" with regard to France's conflict with England, the United States had no intention of keeping to it. French military vessels began boarding American merchant ships carrying British goods, and French privateers* attacked American merchant ships in the West Indies.

Anti-French passions ran high in the United States as John Adams assumed the presidency, and he knew how to use them to his advantage. When the French didn't receive an American representative appropriately, Adams wrote to the House of Representatives on June 21, 1798, "I will never send another minister to France without assurances that he will be received, respected, and honored as the representative of a great, free, powerful, and independent nation."

Then, in a series of over 70 short messages, many reprinted in newspapers or on handbills, Adams whipped up a patriotic frenzy among Americans. The missives "bristled with combativeness," according to historian and author John Ferling in his book *A Leap in the Dark: The Struggle to Create the American Republic*: "National dishonor was a greater evil than a just war! It was cowardice to

---

*Government-authorized pirates.

shrink from war! The national character would be ruined if the populace failed to resist tyranny! This generation would betray its colonial forefathers if it proved to be spineless!"[91]

The result was a huge surge in popularity for Adams's party, the Federalists. So intense was the publicity that Anti-Federalists (today's Democrats) not only agreed with Adams about the danger of the French, but they were increasingly afraid to criticize him for anything else.

As Ferling notes: "As the Quasi-War heated up, he [Adams] was esteemed by the public as never before. By mid-1798 he was proclaimed for his 'manly fortitude,' 'manly spirited' actions, and 'manly independence.'"[92] The result was that the Federalists gained more power in various elections held in late 1798 and early 1799.

On June 15, 1815, when both Jefferson and Adams were old men and had reconciled, Jefferson sent Adams a letter in which he referenced two memoirs of the time that highlighted the conflicts between Jefferson and Adams in 1798: "Whether the character of the times is justly portrayed or not, posterity will decide. But on one feature of them they can never decide, the sensations excited in free yet firm minds by the terrorism of the day."

The "terrorism" that Jefferson was speaking of, however, wasn't that of the French privateers. It was the terrorism inflicted by Adams and his Federalists against Jefferson and his Anti-Federalist Democratic-Republicans.

"None can conceive who did not witness them," Jefferson wrote in the next sentence, "and they were felt by one party only. This letter exhibits their side of the medal. The Federalists, no doubt, have presented the other in their private correspondences as well as open action."

Alien and Sedition Acts: A regal president stifles dissent.

When Congress let out in July of 1798, John and Abigail Adams made the trip home to Braintree, Massachusetts, in their customary fashion—in fancy carriages as part of a parade, with each city they passed through firing cannons and ringing church bells. (The Federalists were, after all, as Jefferson said, the party of "the rich and the well born." Although Adams wasn't one of the super-rich, he basked in their approval and adopted royal-like trappings for the presidency, which were later discarded by Jefferson.)

As the Adams entourage, full of pomp and ceremony, passed through Newark, New Jersey, a man named Luther Baldwin was sitting in a tavern, probably quite unaware that he was about to make a fateful comment that would help change history.

As Adams rode by, soldiers manning the Newark cannons loudly shouted the Adams-mandated chant, "Behold the chief who now commands!" and fired their salutes. In a moment of drunken candor Luther Baldwin said, "There goes the President and they are firing at his arse." Baldwin further compounded his sin by adding that, "I do not care if they fire thro' his arse!"[93]

The tavern's owner, a Federalist named John Burnet, overheard the remark and turned Baldwin in to Adams's thought police. The hapless drunk was arrested, convicted, and imprisoned for uttering "seditious words tending to defame the President and Government of the United States."

Imprisonment for merely expressing an opinion seems unthinkable today; it's clearly unconstitutional. But under Adams, it became law.

The Alien and Sedition Acts reflected the new attitude Adams and his wife had brought to Washington, D.C., in 1796, a take-no-prisoners type of politics in which no opposition was tolerated.

In sharp contrast to his predecessor George Washington, America's second president (John Adams) had succeeded in creating an atmosphere of fear and division in the new republic, and it brought out the worst in his conservative supporters. Across the new nation, Federalist mobs and Federalist-controlled police and militia attacked Democratic-Republican newspapers and shouted down or threatened individuals who dared speak out in public against John Adams.

A Vermont congressman dares defy Adams—
and pays the price.

For example, on January 30, 1798, when Vermont's congressman Matthew Lyon charged on the floor of the House of Representatives that Adams and the Federalists served only the interests of the rich and had "acted in opposition to the interests and opinions of nine-tenths of their constituents," he was beaten with a cane by conservative Connecticut congressman Roger Griswold: "Mr. Griswald [sic] [was] laying on blows with all his might upon Mr. Lyon. Griswald continued his blows on the head, shoulder, & arms of Lyon, [who was] protecting his head & face as well as he could. Griswald tripped Lyon & threw him on the floor & gave him one or two [more] blows in the face."[94]

When Lyon later wrote an article pointing out Adams's "continual grasp for power" and that Adams had an "unbounded thirst for ridiculous pomp, foolish adulation, and selfish avarice," Adams's political allies indicted Congressman Lyon for bringing "the President and government of the United States into contempt."

Lyon, who had fought with George Washington's troops to free his nation from Britain, was paraded in shackles through his hometown of Vergennes, Vermont. He ran for reelection from his 12-by-16-foot Vergennes jail cell and handily won his seat. "It is quite a new kind of jargon," Lyon wrote from jail to his constituents, "to call a Representative of the People an Opposer of the Government because he does not, as a legislator, advocate and acquiesce in every proposition that comes from the Executive."

Similarly, Adams used his new law to arrest and imprison the majority of the newspaper publishers and editors who had editorialized against him, so effectively stifling dissent in the mainstream press that he put many of them out of business, drove one into hiding, and another out of the country.

But Adams's embrace of the 1798 version of today's conservative crackdown on dissent was well noted by Americans. Thomas Jefferson, then vice president, left town in protest the day Adams signed the laws. The laws passed through Congress on the slimmest of majorities and carried a sunset provision that they'd expire on the last day of Adams's presidency. Americans of all political persuasions were so horrified by Adams's naked abuse of the First Amendment through the Alien and Sedition Acts that they didn't reelect him, as they had done with Washington—they turned him out of office in 1800 after only four years.

When Thomas Jefferson then took the presidency in 1801, one of his first official acts was to repeal the Alien and Sedition Acts, release from prison the newspaper editors Adams had locked up, and reimburse them for their losses and legal expenses with an official apology. This so infuriated Adams that it was decades before he'd again speak to Jefferson, and then only by correspondence.

Clearly, despite the revisionist history books that praise him today, John Adams was not the least bit interested in freedom of expression. In fact, it apparently scared him enough that he used the power of the government to stifle it.

And this was not the last time this would happen.

Sedition Acts, version 2: 1918

More than a century later, the U.S. government again tried to stifle free speech, when Republicans gained control of both the House and the Senate and passed the Sedition Act of 1918 despite the concerns of conservative Democratic president Woodrow Wilson. World War I had ended, but this law radically amplified the 1917 Espionage Act, making it a crime to speak out against corporations producing materials for use in World War I, or to make negative statements about the U.S. Constitution or flag, or to discourage young men from joining the army.

Under these laws, in 1918 Eugene Debs, four-time candidate for president, was arrested and convicted of "hindering enlistment" and was hit with a 10-year prison sentence—just for expressing an opinion.

The pendulum swung again: in his first year in office (1933), Franklin D. Roosevelt pardoned all those still in jail under Espionage or Sedition Act violations. Partly in response to and in revulsion over the new Sedition Acts, the American Civil Liberties Bureau (now known as the America Civil Liberties Union, or ACLU) was founded in 1920. And the pendulum continued in the Jeffersonian direction with the 1971 U.S. Supreme Court ruling upholding the publication of the Pentagon Papers (which revealed the corruption of the Nixon administration).

The U.S.A. PATRIOT Acts, I and II

Democratic processes are often curtailed (and rights removed) as a result of some attack, real or imagined. As with the Espionage and Sedition Acts after World War I, citizens must (and can) be vigilant to restore democracy as soon as possible.

After 9/11, Attorney General John Ashcroft gave testimony to Congress in which he said those who question government policy are "aiding the enemy." He subsequently proposed Operation TIPS, in which ordinary neighborhood workers such as UPS drivers, letter carriers, and utility workers would be asked to peer into our houses and call an 800 number if they saw anything suspicious. This program was successfully shouted down by loud public outcry.

2003: Force all dissent out of sight.

In the first years of the twenty-first century, the First Amendment is again under attack. Increasingly, at political events and protests, police are ordered by the U.S. Secret Service to segregate spectators into two groups. Those who support the administration are allowed to be in the area of the presentation or event. Those who oppose the administration are assigned to cages made of chain-link fencing, often as much as a mile away from the event.

For example, on October 24, 2002, Brett Bursey of South Carolina showed up for a speech by George W. Bush and stood with thousands of Republicans at the Columbia, South Carolina, airport. Bursey was carrying a sign that said "No More War For Oil."

After a few minutes, police approached Bursey and told him he'd have to move a half mile away and out of the sight and hearing of the president or the press. "It's the content of your sign," an officer informed Bursey.

When Bursey failed to move, he was arrested and charged with trespassing. But the local police, simply following instructions from the Secret Service, didn't know that it's not possible to arrest someone for trespassing on public property, so South Carolina subsequently dropped the charges against him. He was then rearrested and charged (by Federal prosecutor Strom Thurmond Jr.) with a federal crime, under Title 18, U.S. Code, sec. 1752:

> [i]t shall be unlawful for any person or group of persons—
> (1) willfully and knowingly to enter or remain in . . . (ii) any posted, cordoned off, or otherwise restricted area of a building or grounds where the President or other person protected by the Secret Service is or will be temporarily visiting . . .

But Bush supporters in the same area at the same time were not arrested. Can there be any doubt that the actual agenda was to use the law to suppress dissent?

With Bursey facing hard prison time and substantial fines, Congressman Barney Frank weighed in, writing a letter coauthored by 10 other members of Congress to Attorney General Ashcroft. "As we read the First Amendment to the Constitution," the members wrote, "the United States is a 'free speech zone.' We ask that you make it clear that we have no interest as a government in 'zoning' Constitutional freedoms, and that being politically annoying to the President of the United States is not a criminal offense. This prosecution smacks of the use of the Sedition Acts two hundred years ago to protect the President from political discomfort. It was wrong then and it is wrong now."

Ashcroft never replied to the letter, and on January 6, 2004, Bursey was found guilty and told me a few days later that he intends to appeal his conviction.

At the moment, the mentality of John Adams is prevailing. The next few years will probably tell if what de Tocqueville called "the grand experiment" of truly free speech and genuine freedom of assembly will again flower or forever die in the nation of its modern birth.

Theocrats attack democracy.

The first settlers of this colony were Englishmen, loyal subjects to their king and church, and the grant to Sir Walter Raleigh contained an express proviso that their laws "should not be against the true Christian faith, now professed in the church of England.". . .

But the first republican legislature, which met in '76, was crowded with petitions to abolish this spiritual tyranny. These brought on the severest contests in which I have ever been engaged. . . . Among these, however, were some reasonable and liberal men, who enabled us, on some points, to obtain feeble majorities.

—THOMAS JEFFERSON, *Autobiography*, 1821

I am approached with the most opposite opinions and advice, and by men who are equally certain that they represent the divine will. . . . I hope it will not be irreverent of me to say that if it is probable that God would reveal his will to others on a point so connected with my duty, it might be supposed he would reveal it directly to me.

—PRESIDENT ABRAHAM LINCOLN (1861–1865)

Religious fundamentalism—those who claim a special right to political power because they say their god gave it to them—represents one of the greatest threats to modern-day democracy worldwide. America is currently under a double attack: Christian theocrats have infiltrated our government and are siphoning off hundreds of millions of our tax dollars, while Moslem theocrats have put us into a state of constant terror alert.

"America is a Christian nation": No; it's a nation where a lot of Christians live.

Alabama Supreme Court Chief Justice Roy Moore, the "Ten Commandments Judge" who lost his seat in 2003 for refusing to remove a two-ton graven monument of the Ten Commandments from the court's rotunda, said the controversy he and Fox News stirred up was about religion. "It's about the acknowledgment of almighty God," he said, "and I will never, never deny the God upon whom our laws in our country depend."[95]

In fact, the First Amendment prohibits "establishment of religion." But aside from the judge's misinformed assertion that our laws are based on religion, the court's battle with its chief justice was not really about religion: it was about power. A power that seeks, ultimately, to replace democracy (the will of the people). And Judge Moore's case—the media sensation in late 2003—is a good example of hundreds of similar arguments being made by lawyers, judges, churches, and religious power advocates across America and in other democracies around the world.

The judge's main arguments for keeping an image of the Ten Commandments in the Alabama Supreme Court rotunda were, he said, that America is a Judeo-Christian nation founded by Christians, and that the foundation of American law is the Bible and the Ten Commandments.

The most well known of the Founders and Framers of this nation would strongly disagree on both counts.

It was fine, in their minds, for people to exercise religious freedom. A good thing, in fact: Jefferson wrote at length, for example, about how Jesus provided an example for all of us about how to conduct one's own personal life. Although Washington, Jefferson, and Franklin rarely participated in church services or other religious ceremonies beyond those necessary for state or political purposes, they all nonetheless had great respect for "the Mystery."

But while religion must be safe and free from control by government, so, too, must government be free from control by religion.

The record tells us that they believed that secular democracy is a more powerful unifying force for a decent and peaceful civil society than any religion ever was or could be. Although most were spiritual in their own ways, and many were also openly religious, the Founders and Framers understood the damage that organized religion could do when it gained access to the reigns of political power.

And, with the memory of the Salem witch trials and other religious atrocities still fresh in their minds, the Founders knew that those among the organized religions who sought to add political power to their own religious power would be unrelenting and could be deadly to democracy.

The Founders who rejected that day's Christians

Our Founders were both well schooled in the history of the Crusades and knew from firsthand experience with Puritanism how oppressive religious men could be with even small amounts of political power. Ben Franklin fled Boston when he was a teenager in part to escape the oppressive environment created by politically powerful preachers, and for the rest of his life he was openly hostile to the idea of secular power being wielded by those who also hold religious power. Although he was fascinated by the spiritual experience, Franklin had little use for the organized religions of the day. In his autobiographical *Toward the Mystery,* he wrote, "I have found Christian dogma unintelligible. Early in life I absented myself from Christian assemblies."

In his autobiography, Franklin talks about how he came to this way of thinking: "My parents had early given me religious impressions, and brought me through my childhood piously in the dissenting [Puritan] way. But I was scarce fifteen, when, after doubting by turns of several points, as I found them disputed in the different books I read, I began to doubt of Revelation itself.

Some books against Deism fell into my hands; they were said to be the substance of sermons preached at Boyle's lectures. It happened that they wrought an effect on me quite contrary to what was intended by them; for the arguments of the deists, which were quoted to be refuted, appeared to me much stronger than the refutations; in short, I soon became a thorough deist."

Franklin—like most of the more well-known Founders—was a Deist, subscribing to a philosophy made popular by early Unitarians who held that the Creator made the universe long ago and has since chosen not to interfere in any way, that neither Jesus nor anybody else was divine (or, alternatively, that we are all divine), and that there is only one God and not three.

Another founding Deist who resisted giving political power to those with religious power was George Washington.

Jefferson's diary entry for February 1, 1799, reads, "when the clergy addressed General Washington on his departure from the Government, it was observed in their consultation, that he had never, on any occasion, said a word to the public which showed a belief in the Christian religion, and they thought they should so pen their address, as to force him at length to declare publicly whether he was a Christian or not. They did so.

"However," Jefferson noted, "the old fox was too cunning for them. He answered every article of their address particularly except that, which he passed over without notice." Jefferson concluded that Washington "never did say a word on the subject in any of his public papers" and "that Gouverneur Morris," a close friend of Washington's, "has often told me that General Washington believed no more of that [Christian] system than he himself did."

In fact, President George Washington supervised the language of a treaty with African Muslims that explicitly stated that the United States was a secular nation.

The Treaty with Tripoli, worked out under Washington's guidance and then signed into law the next year by John Adams in 1797, reads: "As the government of the United States of America is not in any sense founded on the Christian Religion,—as it has in itself no character of enmity against the laws, religion or tranquility of Musselmen,—and as the said States never have entered into any war or act of hostility against any Mehomitan nation, it is declared by the parties that no pretext arising from religious opinions shall ever produce an interruption of the harmony existing between the two countries."

But for the Founders this wasn't just an issue of being Christians or not: they didn't want *any* organized religion mixing its functions with government.

For example, on February 21, 1811, President James Madison vetoed a bill passed by Congress that authorized government payments to a church in Washington, D.C., to help the poor. Faith-based initiatives were a clear violation, in Madison's mind, of the First Amendment doctrine of separation of church and state and could lead to a dangerous transfer of political power to religious leaders.

Caring for the poor was a public and civic duty—a function of government—and should not be allowed to become a hole through which churches could reach and seize political power or the taxpayer's purse. Funding a church to provide for the poor would establish a "legal agency"—a legal precedent—that would break down the wall of separation the Founders had put between church and states to protect Americans from religious zealots gaining political power.

Thus, Madison said in his veto message to Congress, he was striking down the proposed law because it helped a church to "provide for the support of the poor, and the education of poor children of the same," which, Madison warned, "would be a precedent for giving to religious societies."[96]

What Thomas Jefferson really said

Jefferson was perhaps the most outspoken of the Founders who saw religious leaders seizing political power as a naked threat to American democracy. One of his most well-known quotes is carved into the stone of the awe-inspiring Jefferson Memorial in Washington, D.C.: "I have sworn upon the altar of God eternal hostility against every form of tyranny imposed upon the mind of man." Modern religious leaders who aspire to political power often cite it as proof that Jefferson was a Bible-thumping Christian.

What's missing from the Jefferson Memorial (and almost all who cite the quote), however, is the context of that statement, the letter and circumstance from which it came.

When Jefferson was vice president, he wrote to his good friend, the physician Benjamin Rush, who started out as a Christian and ended up, later in his life, a Deist and Unitarian. Here, in a most surprising context, we find the true basis of one of Jefferson's most famous quotes:

"DEAR SIR, . . . I promised you a letter on Christianity, which I have not forgotten," Jefferson wrote, noting that he knew to discuss the topic would add fuel to the fires of electoral politics swirling all around him. "I do not know that it would reconcile the *genus irritabile vatum* [the angry poet/prophets/preachers (the same root word as "Vatican")] who are all in arms against me. Their hostility is on too interesting ground to be softened.

"The delusion . . . on the clause of the Constitution, which, while it secured the freedom of the press, covered also the freedom of religion, had given to the clergy a very favorite hope of obtaining an establishment of a particular form of Christianity through the United States; and as every sect believes its own form the true one, every one perhaps hoped for his own, but especially the Episcopalians and Congregationalists.

"The returning good sense of our country threatens abortion to their hopes, and they [the preachers] believe that any portion of power confided to me [such as being elected president], will be exerted in opposition to their schemes. And they believe rightly: for I have sworn upon the altar of God, eternal hostility against every form of tyranny over the mind of man. But this is all they have to fear from me: and enough too in their opinion."

Jefferson's famous quote about "hostility against every form of tyranny" was presented in the context of *not* supporting religions that try to control the mind of man! He says, explicitly, that he opposes their "schemes" to have their religion adopted throughout the United States. And the implication is that he would consider any such religious move to be "tyranny over the mind of man."

Thus began a long and thoughtful correspondence—mostly about religion. In later years, Jefferson would put together what is now called *The Jefferson Bible,* in which he deleted all the miracles from the New Testament and presented Jesus to readers as an inspired philosopher. *The Jefferson Bible* is still in print, and well received, if online sales and readers' comments are any indication.

In his autobiography, Jefferson wrote an interesting historical footnote about the religious leaders seeking political power he confronted head-on when he authored the Statute of Virginia for Religious Freedom, and who the other Framers confronted when they submitted the First Amendment, which specified, "Congress shall make no law respecting an establishment of religion, or prohibiting the free exercise thereof."

Speaking of the Virginia law, the inspiration for the First Amendment, he noted, "Where the preamble declares that coercion is a departure from the plan of the holy author of our religion, an amendment was proposed, by inserting the word 'Jesus Christ,' so that it should read, 'a departure from the plan of Jesus Christ, the holy author of our religion.' The insertion was rejected by a great majority, in proof that they meant to comprehend, within the mantle of its protection, the Jew and the Gentile, the Christian and Mahometan, the Hindoo, and Infidel of every denomination."

But it wasn't just religious tolerance that was the issue for Jefferson—it was preventing any one religion from claiming it was uniquely the American religion, and then using that claim to grasp at political power. Thus, secular government must allow even pagans and pantheists to coexist, while at the same time rigorously preventing any of them from gaining power over it. In his *Notes on Virginia,* Jefferson laid it out clearly: "The legitimate powers of government extend to such acts only as are injurious to others. But it does me no injury for my neighbor to say there are twenty gods, or no God. It neither picks my pocket nor breaks my leg."

Religious leaders grasp for political power.

Yet in the days of the Founders, as today, many religious leaders claimed that their right to influence government was legitimate because government itself was founded on their territory—the Ten Commandments. This assertion—that British common law as well as American law derived from the Ten Commandments—was particularly infuriating to many of the Founders.

First, there's the simple fact that there isn't that much overlap between the Ten Commandments and American legislation. Our laws don't specify a single god who must be worshipped, ban graven images, require us to take a day off work every week, mandate that we "honor" our parents, make it illegal for men to "covet" other men's wives or sleep with unmarried women, or make it illegal to lie (in fact, corporations have recently asserted the explicit "right to lie" under the First Amendment). The only things in common are prohibitions on killing and stealing.

Of greater concern to the Founders, though, was the power grab religious leaders were trying to pull off. In a February 10, 1814, letter to Dr. Thomas Cooper, Jefferson addressed the question directly: "Finally, in answer to Fortescue Aland's question why the Ten Commandments should not now be a part of the common law of England we may say they are not because they never were." Anybody who asserted that the Ten Commandments were the basis of American or British law was, Jefferson said, mistakenly believing a document that was "a manifest forgery."

The reason was simple: British common law, on which much American law was based, existed before Christianity had arrived in England.

"Sir Matthew Hale lays it down in these words," wrote Jefferson to Cooper, "'Christianity is parcel of the laws of England.'"

But, Jefferson says in rebuttal of Hale, it couldn't be. Just looking at the timeline of English history demonstrated that this was impossible: "Christianity was not introduced till the seventh century; the conversion of the first Christian king of the Heptarchy having taken place about the year 598, and that of the last about 686. Here, then, was a space of two hundred years, during which the common law was in existence, and Christianity no part of it. . . . In truth, the alliance between Church and State in England has ever made their judges accomplices in the frauds of the clergy; and even bolder than they are."

In a January 24, 1814, letter to John Adams, Jefferson went through a detailed lawyer's brief to show that the idea that the laws of both England and the United States came from Judaism, Christianity, or the Ten Commandments rests on a single man's mistranslation in 1658, often repeated, and totally false.[97]

"It is not only the sacred volumes they [the churches] have thus interpolated, gutted, and falsified, but the works of others relating to them, and even the laws of the land," he wrote. "Our judges, too, have lent a ready hand to further these frauds, and have been willing to lay the yoke of their own opinions on the necks of others; to extend the coercions of municipal law to the dogmas of their religion, by declaring that these make a part of the law of the land."

It was a long-running topic of agreement between Jefferson and John Adams, who, on September 24, 1821, wrote to Jefferson noting their mutual hope that America would embrace a purely secular, rational view of what human society could become:

"Hope springs eternal. Eight millions of Jews hope for a Messiah more powerful and glorious than Moses, David, or Solomon; who is to make them as powerful as he pleases. Some hundreds of millions of Mussulmans expect another prophet more powerful than Mahomet, who is to spread Islamism over the whole earth. Hundreds of millions of Christians expect and hope for a millennium in which Jesus is to reign for a thousand years over the whole world before it is burnt up. The Hindoos expect another and final incarnation of Vishnu, who is to do great and wonderful things, I know not what." But, Adams noted, the hope for a positive future for America was—in his mind and Jefferson's—grounded in rationality and government, not in religion. "You and I hope for splendid improvements in human society, and vast amelioration in the condition of mankind," he wrote. "Our faith may be supposed by more rational arguments than any of the former."

Democracy is a moral system, too.

In a modern revival of religious leaders seeking political power, e-mails fly around the Internet saying that Founders like Madison claimed the United States was based either on Christianity or the Ten Commandments. Many originate in the writings of a right-wing group whose president helped prepare the history and social studies standards for Texas and California schoolchildren and are so taken out of context that they can only be called deliberate attempts to fool people. Others are simple fabrications, like so many fraudulent e-mails—"urban legend" quotes created from nothing.

Moral precepts against killing or stealing are found not only in the Bible but exist among every tribe on earth, some of whose cultures and languages date back over 60,000 years. They're part of the social code of animals ranging from prairie dogs to gorillas. They're rooted in the biological imperative of survival.

Jefferson wrote in a June 5, 1824, letter to Major John Cartwright, "Our Revolution commenced on more favorable ground [than the foundation of English or Biblical law]. It presented us an album on which we were free to write what we pleased. We had no occasion to search into musty records, to hunt up royal parchments, or to investigate the laws and institutions of a semi-barbarous ancestry. We appealed to those of nature, and found them engraved on our hearts."

Jefferson then thanks and congratulates Cartwright for writing that the American Constitution as well as both American and British common law are entirely secular in their origin: "I was glad to find in your book a formal contradiction, at length, ... that Christianity is a part of the common law. The proof of the contrary, which you have adduced, is incontrovertible; to wit, that the common law existed while the Anglo-Saxons were yet pagans, at a time when they had never yet heard the name of Christ pronounced, or knew that such a character had ever existed."

Jefferson concluded his letter by denouncing the efforts of churchmen to seize the fledgling United States of America, and paraphrased *The Lottery*, a 1732 play by Henry Fielding, which lamented that in the lottery of life foolish brutes all too often seize power and destroy the good and the wise. At the end of the play, a character says that when "we all are undone," the opportunists will "Sing Tantarara, Fools all, Fools all."

"What a conspiracy this," Jefferson closed his 1824 letter to Cartwright, "between Church and State! Sing Tantarara, rogues all, rogues all, Sing Tantarara, rogues all!"

The new aristocracy:
corporatism and monopolies

There is an evil which ought to be guarded against in the indefinite accumulation of property from the capacity of holding it in perpetuity by ... corporations. The power of all corporations ought to be limited in this respect. The growing wealth acquired by them never fails to be a source of abuses.

—PRESIDENT JAMES MADISON (1809–1817)

"Corporatism" returns—in "human" clothing.

While much of the world is striving to emulate the American experiment, contemporary America is moving in the direction of the corporate-state partnership.

▸   Executives from regulated industries are heading up the agencies that regulate them. Agencies like the FDA, FAA, and USDA have had their missions corrupted by corporate influence on the political process from ones of regulating industries to protect the safety of consumers to promoting the interests of the industries themselves (leading to lax protections for Mad Cow Disease, among other things).

▸   Widespread privatization has become a euphemism for shifting control of a commons resource (like water supplies) from government agencies to corporations.

▸   And corporations and their agents have become the largest contributors to politicians, political parties, and so-called think tanks that both write and influence legislation.

In America today we've become numb to this issue—we take it for granted that big companies have the right to do what they want. But this flies in the face of history. As President Andrew Jackson (1829–1837) said: "In this point of the case the question is distinctly presented whether the people of the United States are to govern through representatives chosen by their unbiased suffrages or whether the money and power of a great corporation are to be secretly exerted to influence their judgment and control their decisions."[98]

Even within our grandparents' lifetime, the priority was strictly on living, breathing humans, and companies were expected to respect humans and stay out of human politics. If a company made a political contribution, the responsible people could be jailed, and the company could even be put out of business.

Consider the following 1905 Wisconsin law, which resembles

other laws across America dating back to the founding of this nation.

> **Political contributions by corporations.**[99] No corporation do-
> ing business in this state shall pay or contribute, or offer consent
> or agree to pay or contribute, directly or indirectly, any money,
> property, free service of its officers or employees or thing of
> value to any political party, organization, committee or individ-
> ual for any political purpose whatsoever, or for the purpose of
> influencing legislation of any kind, or to promote or defeat the
> candidacy of any person for nomination, appointment or elec-
> tion to any political office.
>
> **Penalty.**[100] Any *officer, employee, agent or attorney or other represen-
> tative of* any corporation, acting for and in behalf of such cor-
> poration, who shall violate this act, shall be punished upon
> conviction by a fine of not less than one hundred nor more than
> five thousand dollars, or by *imprisonment in the state prison* for a
> period of not less than one nor more than five years, or by both
> such fine and imprisonment in the discretion of the court or
> judge before whom such conviction is had and if the corporation
> shall be subject to a penalty then by forfeiture in double the
> amount of any fine and *if a domestic corporation it may be dissolved,* if
> after a proper proceeding upon quo warranto, in either the cir-
> cuit or supreme court of the state to be prosecuted by the attor-
> ney general of the state, the court shall find and give judgment
> that section 1 of this act has been violated as charged, and if
> a foreign or non-resident corporation *its right to do business in this
> state may be declared forfeited.* (Italics added.)

Why don't we have such laws today? Corporations paid politicians to get them struck down.

The distinction between corporate control and human control is absolutely pivotal: governments that derive their just powers from the consent of the governed are responsible to citizens
and voters, and their agencies are created exclusively to administer and protect the resources of the commons used by citizens
and voters. Corporations are responsible only to stockholders
and are created exclusively to produce a profit for those stock-

holders, even if it involves harm to humans. When aggressive corporations are in seats of power, the results are predictable.

We have recently seen, all too often, the strange fruits borne by placing a corporate sentry where a public guardian should stand: for instance, we now know that the California energy crisis of 2001 was largely manipulated into existence by Enron and a few other Texas energy companies who had gained influential positions in government policymaking. The cost to humans of this corporate plunder was horrific; but who was accountable, and who will go on trial? And more to the point, how did it come about that corporations had the ability to do such things while the public protested?

Corporations got "human rights" due to a court recorder's error.

It turns out, says the Supreme Court, that corporations have human rights. In several different decisions, all grounded in an 1886 case, the Court has ruled that corporations are entitled to a voice in Washington, just like you and me.

But that is a peculiar thought. Our nation is built on equal protection of people (regardless of differences of race, creed, gender, or religion), and corporations are much bigger than people, much more able to influence the government, and don't have the biological needs and weakness of people. And therein lies the rub—a subtle shift that happened 136 years ago, which put us on this road.

The path from government of, by, and for the people to government of, by, and for corporations was paved largely by an invented legal premise that corporations are, in fact, people—a premise called "corporate personhood." This states not just that people make up a corporation, but that each corporation, when created by the act of incorporation, is a full-grown "person"— separate from the humans who work for it or own stock in it— with all the rights granted to persons by the Bill of Rights.

This idea would be shocking to the Founders of the United

States. James Madison, often referred to as "the father of the Constitution," wrote: "There is an evil which ought to be guarded against in the indefinite accumulation of property from the capacity of holding it in perpetuity by . . . corporations. The power of all corporations ought to be limited in this respect. The growing wealth acquired by them never fails to be a source of abuses."[101]

And in a letter to James K. Paulding, March 10, 1817, Madison made absolutely explicit a lifetime of thought on the matter. "Incorporated Companies," he wrote, "with proper limitations and guards, may in particular cases, be useful, but they are at best a necessary evil only. Monopolies and perpetuities are objects of just abhorrence. The former [i.e., monopolies] are unjust to the existing [generations], the latter [are] usurpations on the rights of future generations."

Yet the concept of "corporate personhood" hasn't been around forever; it arrived long after the death of James Madison. It happened in 1886, when the U.S. Supreme Court's reporter inserted a personal commentary called a "headnote" into the decision in the case of *Santa Clara County v. Union Pacific Railroad.*

For decades the Court had repeatedly ruled against the doctrine of corporate personhood, and it avoided the issue altogether in the *Santa Clara* case, but Court reporter J. C. Bancroft Davis (a former railroad president) added a note to the case saying that the Chief Justice Morrison R. Waite had said that "corporations are persons" and should be granted human rights under the free-the-slaves Fourteenth Amendment.

The comment wasn't a ruling.

In fact, Davis had recorded a remark made in a side conversation that was never part of a ruling by the Court; he phrased it in a way that implied it was part of the decision, but it wasn't. To the contrary: in the Library of Congress archives, there is a note in Waite's handwriting, specifically saying to Davis, "We avoided meeting the constitutional question in the decision."

Nonetheless, the headnote for that decision was published in 1887 (a year Waite was so ill he rarely showed up in court; he died the next year). Since then corporations have claimed that they are persons—pointing to that decision and its headnote—and, amazingly enough, in most cases the courts have agreed. Many legal scholars think it's because the courts didn't bother to read the case, but instead just read the headnote. But at this point, after a century of acceptance, the misreading has essentially become law, like a common law marriage.

The impact has been almost incalculable. As "persons," corporations have claimed the First Amendment right of free speech and—even though they can't vote—they now spend hundreds of millions of dollars to influence elections, prevent regulation of their own industries, and write or block legislation. Tobacco companies and horrible polluters have used it to claim protection against searches, using the Bill of Rights, which was intended to protect the small and weak. Before 1886 in most states this was all explicitly against the law. Since 1886 they sued to have these "unequal" restrictions removed.

As "persons," corporations can (and do) claim the Fourth Amendment right of privacy and prevent government regulators from performing surprise inspections of factories, accounting practices, and workplaces, leading to uncontrolled polluters and hidden accounting crimes. Before 1886 this was also, in most states, explicitly against the law. (Corporations have also successfully claimed that when people come to work on "corporate private property," those people are agreeing to give up their own constitutional rights to privacy, free speech, etc.)

As a "person," a corporation can claim that when a community's voters pass laws to ban it, those voters are engaging in illegal discrimination and violating the corporation's "human rights" guaranteed in the Fourteenth Amendment—even if the corporation has been convicted of felonies. The laws the corporations overturn are often referred to as "bad boy laws" because they reference past crimes committed by the corporations (which cannot be jailed, so they pay fines instead). The result has been an *Alice in Wonderland* situation where a corporation convicted of felonies can and does own television stations (General Electric, for example, has been convicted of felonies but owns many television stations), but when a man in the Midwest was recently convicted of a felony, the FCC moved to strip him of his TV station.

The irony is that corporations insist on the protections granted to humans, but not the responsibilities and consequences they bear. Corporations don't have human weaknesses—don't need fresh water to drink, clean air to breathe, uncontaminated food to eat, and don't fear imprisonment, cancer, or death. While asserting their own right to privacy protections from government regulators, they want workers to relinquish nearly all their human rights of free speech, privacy, and freedom from self-incrimination when they enter the "private property" of the workplace.

This is an absolute perversion of the principle cited in the Declaration of Independence, which explicitly states that the government of the United States was created by people and for people and operates only by consent of the people whom it governs.

The result of corporate personhood has been relentless erosion of government's role as a defender of human rights and of its duty to respond to the needs of its human citizens. Instead, we're now seeing a steady insinuation of corporate representatives and those beholden to corporations into legislatures, the judiciary, and even the highest offices in the land.

We stand before a historic opportunity.

We have reached the point in the United States where corporatism has almost triumphed over democracy. If events continue on their current trajectory, the ability of our government to respond to our needs and desires as humans—things like fresh water, clean air, uncontaminated food, independent information sources, secure retirement, and accessible medical care—may vanish forever, effectively ending the world's second experiment with democracy. We will have gone too far down Mussolini's road and will most likely encounter similar consequences: a militarized police state, a government unresponsive to its citizens and obsessed with secrecy, a ruling elite drawn from the senior ranks of the nation's largest corporations, and war.

Alternatively, if we awaken soon and reverse the 1886 mistake that created corporate personhood, we can still return to the democratic republican principles that animated Jefferson and brought this nation into being. Our government can shake off the past 30 years of exploding corporatism and throw the corporate agents and buyers of influence out of the hallowed halls of Congress. We can restore our stolen human rights to humans and keep corporate activity constrained within the boundaries of that which will help and heal and repair our earth rather than plunder it.

The path to doing this is straightforward and is now being taken across America. Ten communities in Pennsylvania have passed ordinances denying corporate-owned factory farms the status of persons. The city of Point Arena, California, passed a resolution denying corporate personhood, and other communities are considering following their example. Citizens across the nation are looking into the possibility of passing local laws denying corporate personhood, in the hope that one will eventually be brought before the Supreme Court so the court can explicitly correct its reporter's 1886 error. Taking another tack, some are suggesting that the Fourteenth Amendment should be re-amended to insert the word "natural" before the word "person," an important legal distinction that will sweep away a century of legalized corporate excesses and reassert the primacy of humans.

The concern is not corporations per se; the bludgeon of corporate personhood is rarely used by small or medium-sized companies but only by a handful of the world's largest, to force their will on governments and communities. This means that a very few parties (the biggest corporations) are all that stand in the way of reform. The corporate personhood doctrine is the weakest link in the chain of corporate power.

Once again, we must do what Jefferson always hoped: "The people, being the only safe depository of power, should exercise in person every function which their qualifications enable them to exercise, consistently with the order and security of society."[102] We must seize the moment to take back the power, for our children and our children's children.

MODERN DEMOCRACY:
ITS HISTORY AND WHY IT WORKS

*The farther backward you can look, the farther forward you are
likely to see.*
—SIR WINSTON CHURCHILL, British prime minister
(1940–1945 and 1951–1955)

The oldest democratic cultures

Although we touched on the influence of Native Americans on the Founders in an earlier chapter, it's important to revisit and look more deeply into the structure of indigenous people in the context of the history of democracy itself. Tribal democracies were a model for ancient Athens and still survive around the world, in many cases after tens of thousands of years of stability.

A democratic indigenous culture is sometimes described as being similar to a Garden of Eden. It's a stable culture, living in peace and relative abundance. People have figured out their relationship to all other living and natural things, and to one another. They live within their means, not taking more from their environment than it can naturally regenerate within their lifetimes. They live in peace.

Peter Farb noted that the Native American Shoshone tribe had no word for war in their vocabulary.[103] The Shoshone considered conflict—between families, tribes, individuals, or between humans and the natural world—as an obscenity, a great embarrassment. The Shoshone were a democratic indigenous culture. (In *The Last Hours of Ancient Sunlight* and other writings, I referred to democratic indigenous cultures as "Older Cultures." And, as a form of metaphorical shorthand, I referred to warlike cultures as Younger Cultures.)

When robert wolff,* author of *Original Wisdom,* lived in Malaysia in the early 1960s, studying Malay village life, he found a democratic culture within a seemingly hierarchical society.[104] There was a Western-style government, where a district commissioner appoints a village chief but when in a village he visited twice a week, the village chief died, it took a year and a half of seemingly random talk among the village people, and an occasional visit of a friend of the commissioner, to have a new head appointed that everyone was comfortable with. When robert asked what the duties of the village head were, he was told, "He is the face of the village." In Malay culture, robert says, nobody can tell another what to do. That would be rude and un-Malay. The village chief (called *kepala,* which means "head") cannot order anyone to do anything; parents cannot "order" their children to do anything.

The Malays of Malaysia are modern in many ways, but in village life there is no hierarchy. No one is higher or more important than anyone else.

These ideas are deeply rooted in the cultures of Southeast Asia. In village life people know not to stand out in any way. Someone may own a car but will park it far outside the village. Someone may be a Western-educated nurse, but her house is

---

*robert writes his name in lowercase.

like all the other houses in the village. Things get done through discussions that seem at first little more than casual remarks bandied back and forth under a tree, but in time a consensus is formed. It is we in the West, robert said, who impose our standards and expectations on indigenous people; they learned long ago that that does not work.

In democratic indigenous cultures, people have a rich community life. Individuals draw their sense of identity more from their community (tribe, family, clan) than from their own personal accomplishments. Many democratic indigenous cultures don't even have a word for "I" or "me" in their language; they have discovered that egocentrism (the culturally toxic idea that "Greed is good!") can trigger the beginning of the end of democracy.

They understand the concept of "the empty spirit," which Meister Eckhart wrote was the most important work and the most powerful prayer we could live. As Maxim Gorki said: "This vile life, unworthy of human reason, began on that day when the first individual tore himself away from the miraculous strength of the people . . . [and] called itself 'I.' It is this same 'I' which is the worst enemy of man."[105]

Democratic indigenous cultures are lazy by our standards. They rarely "work" more than two to three hours a day, that being what is necessary to gather food and keep their shelter together. They pass much of their lives raising children, talking, singing, dancing, telling stories, creating art, and interacting with the natural world.

When the Sng'oi were offered a chance to make money working on the rubber plantations the government of Malaysia was planting on the edge of their forests in the 1960s, for example, they simply said, "No, thank you." Why work to get money to buy things they didn't need? Life was already good.

So good, in fact, that to this day robert mourns the loss of their culture. Many "modern, civilized" people have found appeal in the "stone age" or "primitive" or "savage" lifestyle of aboriginal people.

Over a hundred years after the "discovery" of America by Columbus, so many Europeans had defected to join various Indian tribes that in the early 1600s Sir Francis Bacon (one of the founders of empiricism) wrote: "It hath often been seen that a Christian gentleman, well-born and bred, and gently nurtured will, of his own free will, quit his high station and luxurious world, to dwell with savages and live their lives, taking part in all their savagery. But never yet hath it been seen that a savage will, of his own free will give up his savagery, and live the life of a civilized man."

The "white Indians" discover tribal democracy.

Over the next hundred years, as more and more whites encountered Native Americans, the incidence of whites joining Indian tribes dramatically increased. Derisively termed "white Indians" by the colonists, thousands of European immigrants to the Americas simply walked away from the emerging American society to join various Indian tribes. Ethnohistorian James Axtell wrote that these early settlers joined the Indians because "they found Indian life to possess a strong sense of community, abundant love, and uncommon integrity." Axtell quoted two white Indians who wrote to the people they'd left behind that they'd found "the most perfect freedom, the ease of living, the absence of those cares and corroding solicitudes which so often prevail with us."[106]

In 1747, Reverend Cadwallader Colden wrote of the growing exodus of whites for Indian life: "No Arguments, no Intreaties, nor Tears of their Friends and relations, could persuade many of them to leave their new Indian Friends and Acquaintance; several of them that were by the Caressings of their Relations persuaded to come Home, in a little Time grew tired of our Manner of living, and ran away again to the Indians, and ended their Days with them."[107]

While most people in the modern world think of contemporary tribal people as hungry to join our civilized world, wolff found the Sng'oi just as happy with their own democratic culture as Colden found Native Americans in the 1700s.

Similarly, Colden wrote: "... Indian Children have been carefully educated among the English, cloathed and taught, yet, I think, there is not one Instance, that any of these, after they had Liberty to go among their own People, and were come to Age, would remain with the English, but returned to their own Nations, and became as fond of the Indian Manner as those that knew nothing of a civilized Manner of living."

Not being fettered to eight or more hours of work a day to enrich some person or corporation at the top of an economic food chain, people in democratic indigenous cultures spend much of their time interacting with their children. James Bricknell, who was captured by the Delaware in the early 1800s and lived among them for several years before returning to his family, wrote in 1842: "The Delawares are the best people to train up children I ever was with.... Their leisure hours are, in a great measure, spent in training up their children to observe what they believe to be right.... They certainly follow what they are taught to believe right more closely, and I might say more honestly, in general, than we Christians.... I know I am influenced to good, even at this day, more from what I learned among them, than what I learned among people of my own color."[108]

The religious practices of democratic indigenous cultures are ecological; they always involve interaction with, rather than separation from, the rest of the physical (and metaphysical) creation. They maintain harmony with nature, and problems like disease or the failure to find adequate food are seen as imbalances that must be corrected rather than as the actions of angry gods or punishments.

Similarly, democratic indigenous cultures have no police or prisons. The closest they may come are places of refuge, to which totally incorrigible people are exiled (the oldest written record of them is in the Bible).

In democratic indigenous cultures human nature is considered to be basically good and generous, and when people misbehave it's assumed there is an imbalance in them or in their immediate circle of acquaintances. If harmony can't be restored, most tribes simply tolerate the unusual behavior as eccentricities. robert wolff tells of visiting one Malay village where a man was darting from tree to tree, as if he were trying to hide or remain invisible. When he asked who the man was, they replied, "Oh, he's our thief." The hapless thief would steal things from people, acting out some incurable inner compulsion, but somehow the objects always got returned. It would be silly to lock the man up: he was a member of their tribe.

Democratic indigenous cultures rarely have armies. Like Costa Rica, which had no army for several decades, they put their resources into the well-being of their people. They may have very competent hunters, but the job of these armed individuals is to find food, not to conquer or kill other humans.

Democracy is built into our genetic code, which is why indigenous people throughout history have always—given enough time—worked it out by trial and error. It also explains why so many early colonists—living under seventeenth-century New England theocracies or fleeing the feudal poverty of big cities—instantly recognized democracy and never turned back.

These "Indian" lessons in democracy were vital to the Founders and Framers, and continue to teach us the highest values of both democracy and human society.

Roots in Rome and Greece

If liberty and equality are chiefly to be found in democracy, they will be best attained when all persons alike share in the government to the utmost.

—ARISTOTLE (384–322 B.C.), *Politics*

While it's clear that the Founders and the Framers were familiar with the histories of tribal and Saxon England as well as the details of the many Native American democracies that existed during their time, one of their greatest influences was the example of Athens, Greece. Among the Greek historians, Jefferson's favorite was Herodotus.[109]

The Greek problems with democracy

Being educated men, Jefferson, Hamilton, Madison, Adams, Franklin, Jay, Mason, and the others who helped put together the United States of America had undoubtedly all read the *Histories of Herodotus.*

If anything, the debates between Otanes, Megabyzus, and Darius—in which they discuss how putting "the mob" in charge of political power would ultimately lead to tyranny by the mob itself—were the ghosts in the corner of the room in Philadelphia where Jefferson penned the Declaration of Independence, and downstairs in that same building where the Constitution was later worked out.

Probably the main barrier against the formation (or reformation) of Athenian-style democracy for two millennia was the antidemocratic position held by Plato and his student Aristotle. Both carried a grudge against the Athenians for having sentenced Plato's teacher Socrates to death, and Plato went so far as to bury the details of Socrates' crime so well that even today only a few Greek scholars know the "scoop" that journalist I. F. Stone discovered in the 1970s and published in his 1988 book *The Trial of Socrates*—that Socrates was sentenced to death because he was involved with, and maybe even behind, a revolt that briefly overthrew Athenian democracy.

Athenian democracy functioned largely on a simple premise: that the people should rule themselves. Even the *thetes*—the poorest of the Athenians—participated in the government and served as the majority of the sailors in Athens's navy. Many historians consider Athens's navy so powerful because its seamen were fully empowered citizens of their nation.

Socrates thought democracy was crass and inherently riddled with weaknesses. The mob would listen to public orators who would stir them up in various ways that might not be best for the nation. These orators were called "demagogues," a word that literally means "leaders of the people," although it was a term of derision when used by Socrates and his students.

Socrates suggested that leadership was as specialized a field as medicine, and that governance was too important a function to be left to the average person. The rabble would always, he thought, be more concerned with their own shortsighted immediate gratification than with the larger and loftier ideals of governance and the survival of a nation.

Socrates was proved wrong and ultimately convicted by his own people. His antidemocratic teachings led, in part, to two of his closest students, Critias (Plato's cousin) and Alcibiades overthrowing the democratic government of Athens in two coups known as the oligarchies of the 400 and of the 30. Critias was a brutal leader during his brief reign as one of the 30. Many people died, and, contrary to Socrates' teachings, Critias and his other "professional politicians" stole from the public purse and used their power to enrich themselves and their cronies. During Critias' reign, his old teacher Socrates was well taken care of, not having to flee or hide as did so many of those who had previously advocated democracy or forms similar to it.

Thus, when democracy was restored to Athens following the collapse of the coups of the 400 and of the 30, Socrates was put on trial and, by a jury of 501 of his peers, sentenced to death for "corrupting the youth" like his student Critias.

Plato and Xenophon, both students of Socrates, were furious. Brilliant writers and orators, they and their students (such as Aristotle) proceeded to paint democracy with such a black brush that it didn't resurface for two thousand years.

Socrates didn't know what modern scientists do about democracy.

The Greeks struggled with their core belief that democracy wasn't the natural state of humankind and would always be vulnerable to overthrow by an oligarchy or a despot. Socrates taught Plato, Plato taught Aristotle, and Socrates, from his grave, would have felt vindicated when his student's student Aristotle undertook to tutor the young Alexander the Great, who would ultimately rule Athens with an iron fist. It's even possible that Aristotle's subtle embrace of Socrates' skepticism about democracy infected Alexander with the idea that one could conquer and rule Greece the way Aristotle's own students had done more than once.

Building American democracy from scratch

It was against this two-thousand-year history of the antidemocratic writings of Plato, Aristotle, Xenophon, and other students (or students of students) of Socrates that the Framers—the men who would write the constitution for a new nation—met in Philadelphia to debate the future structure of its government.

They were well aware of Socrates' objections to democracy, and some—particularly Hamilton and Adams—felt some form of modified oligarchy was necessary, with a president appointed for life and at least half the legislature being drawn from the upper classes and not subject to election or the will of the rabble.

On the other hand, Franklin, Jefferson, Madison, and other "small-d" democrats knew that democracy had worked well in ancient Athens. It had provided both a resilient form of government, and more than two centuries of prosperity and high quality of life for its citizens.

There were, however, a few challenges.

First, like the Roman republic that ultimately failed in part because people outside of Rome couldn't vote, the Athenian form of democracy wasn't suited to a large and sprawling land like North America. Athens covered a relatively small area and peer pressure was strong. A person couldn't easily commit a crime or corrupt the government and then leave town with his ill-gotten gains.

Second, there was still a strong sense of family and tribe in ancient Athens, particularly among those who originally formed the ruling class (the nation-state became progressively more and more democratic over time; until just before its conquest by Alexander the Great, even the poorest were represented).

Third, at one point the Athenians used a very direct democracy, with as many as six thousand citizens being necessary to form a quorum on important issues. For other issues and the courts, the Athenians used a lottery system to bring to power their representatives every year, figuring that the gods would direct the draw. Being a legislator or juror was like yearlong jury duty, and those who didn't or couldn't serve were known as the *idiotes*.

And, fourth, Athens didn't aspire to be anything more than a city. There was never a plan to unite all the Greek cities into one larger democracy as the Founders envisioned for uniting the states of America.

In the only democracy that had survived any length of time in a modern civilized context, Athens had a number of features and problems that made it impossible to simply clone or even graft onto the Articles of Confederation to invent American democracy in its final form. Something more was necessary, and the biggest debate was whether the danger facing the new republic was too much, or too little, democracy.

How much democracy is too much?

Reading James Madison's narratives of the Constitutional Convention of 1787, it's apparent that one of the biggest issues before the delegates was how much democracy was possible. The man who had spent the most time among the Indians—Benjamin Franklin—was an open advocate for as much as possible. Others were worried that democracy might end up as mob rule, and all their work in separating from England would dissolve into chaos.

The entire world was watching, and the consensus among most nations was that the "American experiment" was doomed to fail. Oligarchy and aristocracy were known quantities—they had survived rather well in Europe, at least for the past few centuries (although France was in ferment). And everybody knew that the Greek experiments with democracy had ultimately been over-thrown, albeit not exactly in the ways Socrates implied were inevitable.

As Jefferson later wrote in an August 26, 1816, letter to Isaac H. Tiffany, the Greek democracies (of which Athens was the most developed) were only a starting point for the thinking of the Founders: "They had just ideas of the value of personal liberty, but none at all of the structure of government best calculated to preserve it. They knew no medium between a democracy (the only pure republic, but impracticable beyond the limits of a town) and an abandonment of themselves to an aristocracy, or a tyranny independent of the people."

One of the biggest failings of the Greeks, Jefferson noted, was that their citizens simply showed up to participate in govern-ment, rather than electing representatives as the Romans did in a rather undemocratic fashion. "The full experiment of a govern-ment democratical, but representative, was and is still reserved for us."

Thus, Jefferson wrote, we were embarking into entirely new territory. "My most earnest wish is to see the republican element of popular control pushed to the maximum of its practicable exercise. I shall then believe that our government may be pure and perpetual."

Jefferson's opponents doubt democracy.

But back in 1787, one of Jefferson's most steadfast foes to the idea of a truly republican democracy was Alexander Hamilton, who was also one of the first speakers at the Constitutional Conven-tion. He called the British form of government "the best in the world," pleaded for a president to be appointed for life, and argued that "real liberty neither is found in despotism or the extremes of democracy, but in moderate governments—if we incline too much to democracy, we shall soon shoot into a monarchy."

Worried about what fellow Federalist John Adams called "the rabble," Hamilton warned John Jay that "the same state of the passions which fits the multitude . . . for opposition to tyranny and oppression naturally leads them to a contempt and disregard of all authority."

Nonetheless, Hamilton lost out on many important points to Madison (who spoke on behalf of Jefferson, who was in France at the time of the Convention) and other advocates of democracy over modified oligarchy or monarchy. As William Samuel Johnson of Connecticut said of Hamilton, "The gentleman from New York [is] praised by everybody . . . [but] supported by none."

Democracy as a guiding principle—with all being able to participate by choosing their representatives in free, fair, and honest elections—was an idea that wasn't just fermenting in North America: it was sweeping around the world.

Back in 1712, Abbé de Saint Pierre published a small book titled *Paix perpetuelle (Perpetual Peace)* in which he proposed that the best way to stop the European nations from feuding and warring with each other was for them to form a loose—and somewhat democratic—federation.

Jean-Jacques Rousseau wrote extensively about Saint Pierre's ideas in his own *Confessions,* another book that was widely read in North America and heavily influenced the thinking of America's Founders.

By 1770, both America and Europe were ablaze with discussion of democracy. That year saw the publication in Germany and England of *L'An 2240,* the bestselling futurist novel about a democratic state, by Sebastien Mercier, and in France Abbé Morellet wrote about the concept, mostly citing Saint Pierre. In 1772, another book—*On Public Felicity*—spread like wildfire. It was written by Chevalier de Chastellux, who, within the year, would serve in the American Continental Army and later fight in the Revolutionary War.

In *On Public Felicity,* Chastellux wrote that if the Americans could actually pull off the goal of creating a democratic government, it would lead humanity out of the hellish conditions of sweatshop England, Reign of Terror France, and post-Inquisition Spain, allowing its citizens to live "in external and domestic peace, abundance and liberty, the liberty of tranquil enjoyment of one's own."

Writers espousing democracy were not just well published in America (the demand was so much greater than their supply that such books were often bought by reading groups), but they also emigrated here to avoid persecution at home.

The keys to understanding liberal democracy

The Founders and Framers were well schooled in the history of politics in Europe, from ancient Sumeria and Greece to the reign of "Mad" King George III of England. They'd read the first texts of democracy, often in the original Greek and Latin, and were immersed in the philosophers of the Age of Enlightenment, in which they lived.

Leon P. Baradat, in his landmark book (often used as a college text) *Political Ideologies: Their Origins and Impact,*[110] points out that the core liberal philosophy of democracies is grounded in the following:

> Human rights
> Rationalism (natural law)
> Equalitarianism (all people are created equal)
> Personal liberty (possible when you assume human
>   nature is inherently good)
> Internationalism (possible when you assume others
>   will work together with you for mutual self-
>   interest)

The keys to understanding the philosophy of modern democracy are twofold. First, if people are inherently good and democracy is "normal," then we don't need an elite class to control us. Second, liberals believe that any sort of concentrated power is inherently a force that will corrupt democracy—be it governmental force, individual force, or corporate force.

Feudalism, Protestants, and democracy

Prior to the thirteenth century, when conservative kings and theocrats ruled the "civilized" world, liberal democracies were found only among indigenous people (with the exception of a few short-lived experiments like Athens). But the rise of feudalism represented the first emergence of liberal thinking in Europe since the European detribalization by the Celts, Romans, and popes, in that the feudal lords of the United Kingdom were the first to challenge the idea of the so-called divine right of kings.

The Hanseatic League emerged in the late twelfth century, a semidemocratic trading alliance that started between the cities of Hamburg and Lübeck to protect their mutual access to each other's salt and fish. Cologne joined the League in 1201, and the shadow government—which had its own form of a democratic parliament with representatives from each city member—grew over the next century. Kings still dominated Europe, however, and the League initially collapsed under the attack of Waldemar Atterdag, King of Denmark, in 1361, and by a century later had vanished.

In 1215, the feudal lords of England organized together and forced King John to sign the Magna Carta and cede to them some power over their own lives, property, and destiny. The Magna Carta was the first modern European written social contract between a government and those people it governed.

Even though it granted rights only to feudal lords and not to average people, the Magna Carta created the climate of reform and challenged hierarchical authority. Three hundred years later in Germany, Martin Luther similarly defied the divine right of the pope when he nailed his "95 Theses" to the door of the castle/church in Wittenberg in 1517 and kicked off the Protestant Reformation.

Defiance of the divine right of popes paralleled that of the divine right of kings. Democracy gathered momentum in the seventeenth century with the anonymous British publication in 1660 of *Vindiciae Contra Tyrannos (A Defense of Liberty Against Tyrants)*.[111] Although it was ordered burned by Oxford University in 1683, *Vindiciae* survived (and is still available) and had such a powerful impact on European thinking that it is sometimes credited as heralding the dawning of the Age of Enlightenment.

Consider, for example, this rejection from *Vindiciae* of that era's conservative belief that political power (laws) comes from those who govern, instead of the liberal democratic idea that power must be granted by the consent of the governed: "And absolutely rejecting that detestable opinion . . . that princes give laws to others but received none from any; we will say, that in all kingdoms well established, the king receives the laws from the people which he ought carefully to consider and maintain. And whatsoever he does against them, either by force or fraud, must always be reputed unjust."

The book ends with this straightforward, declarative statement of liberal democratic values: "Justice requires that tyrants and destroyers of the commonwealth be compelled to reason. Charity challenges the right of relieving and restoring the oppressed. Those who make no account of these things, do as much as in them lies to drive piety, justice, and charity out of this world, that they may never more be heard of."

The era of classical liberalism

British philosopher John Locke (1632–1704) is usually considered the father of modern liberal democracy, and with good reason. He directly challenged the notion that human nature is essentially evil. Instead, Locke said, human beings are inherently moral, competent, and intelligent: so much so, in fact, that they can rule themselves without help from a king, a pope, or a feudal lord supervising the process.

During Locke's lifetime King Charles I was executed in 1649, and for a short time Oliver Cromwell, and then his son—neither part of the royal lineage—led the kingdom as lord protectors. Cromwell's disastrous rule collapsed in large part because of an alliance he made with religious leaders of the time, bringing them into government and giving them political power, thus leading to a religious dictatorship. The people of England had been willing to accept a kingdom, but a theocracy was just too much.

When the monarchy was restored, it was greatly weakened, and in 1689 Parliament demanded and passed a "Bill of Rights" that guaranteed free elections, the right of Parliament to meet frequently and legislate, and the right to petition the king. The Bill of Rights also forbade the king from suspending acts of Parliament, increasing taxes, or keeping a standing army except with the approval of Parliament. It was a move toward democracy, but the king still held dictatorial powers that wouldn't be repealed for another two centuries.

Locke wrote about the philosophical base of the 1688 Glorious Revolution (whereas the conservative Thomas Hobbes supported restoring the Stuart dynasty) and emphatically rejected the notion of divine rights in favor of natural rights.

Although Locke was an advocate of personal liberty and the rights of property—these two were among his key points—he also strongly believed that it was possible for an individual to accumulate so much personal property that it would prevent others from enjoying liberty and rights to property. This, he felt, was the area where government should step in, because if somebody was accumulating property in a way that was destructive to society, then that person was actually violating other people's rights to liberty and property. (In this, Locke was echoing traditional tribal wisdom. In almost every tribal society on earth, including—according to de Thoyras—the tribal British culture before the Norman invasion, excessive accumulation of "things" was considered mentally ill behavior.)

Adam Smith on competition, monopolies, and war

Adam Smith weighed in on some of these issues in 1776 in *The Wealth of Nations*. While the phrase "invisible hand" of the marketplace occurs only once in Smith's book, conservatives have seized on it to suggest that Smith said there is a mechanism in the marketplace that is much like the mechanism of nature, in that it can and will regulate and fix all imbalances. In fact, his suggestion of allowing markets to self-regulate was an argument in favor of competition exclusive of large monopolies, because in his time kings set up monopolies for themselves and their friends, thus preventing most healthy competition. Competition can exist only in the absence of monopolies, Smith's theories argued.

There is also an important distinction between competition and war. In competition, which is useful in the marketplace, you improve yourself in order to prevail over your competitor. In economic war, which leads to monopolies in the marketplace, you destroy your competitor.

Smith also argued in favor of a high inheritance tax, enough to prevent family dynasties from arising and creating new anticompetitive aristocracies, which he saw as destructive elements in society. He believed that each generation must gain its own wealth from its own abilities, rather than through inheritance. (Jefferson echoed Smith's thinking when he wrote: "If the overgrown wealth of an individual be deemed dangerous to the State, the best corrective is the law of equal inheritance to all in equal degree.")

Who owns the means of production?

During the time of both Locke and Smith, the main way people could be productive was to own the means of their production. A carpenter, weaver, or silversmith owned his own tools, a farmer his own farm, a merchant his store. Both Locke and Smith agreed that when government owned the means of production—and in their day the only governments in the world were kingdoms or theocracies—then both liberty and the economy would suffer. This was, after all, the essence of feudalism—the feudal lords owned the croplands (the means of the production of crops) of their serfs and exercised economic power over their serfs through controlling access to that means of production. Serfdom and feudalism, in the minds of both Locke and Smith, were evils.

But the Industrial Revolution brought a new factor into the equation. With the development of huge machines and factories, most workers no longer owned the means of their own production. Corporations and wealthy families owned the factories, and the Industrial Revolution is legendary as an era when workers were treated like serfs. People by the millions abandoned their farms and small shops to travel to areas where there were mills and factories, transforming the land- and cityscape of Europe and America. Feudalism had returned to the scene, and social unrest rumbled across much of the world as a result.

One response to this came from Karl Marx, who suggested that the people—collectively, through the state—should own the means of production. His suggestion, which largely defines socialism, led to a worldwide workers' revolt against the feudal lords of factories and the kings who supported them.

It's fascinating to note that all of the countries that embraced communism were dictatorships at the time: none were democracies. In many places, like Tsarist Russia, the revolutionaries executed the kings and their families.

Yet the Bolsheviks, and later the communists, overthrew none of the democracies of the world, because democracies have a built-in stabilizing system that prevents them from being overthrown from within and immunizes them from the seeming lure of Marxism.

That mechanism was twofold.

The first part is democracy itself. When people believe that they rule themselves, they're unlikely to revolt. (In fact, the only way that Hitler was able to seal his overthrow of Germany's newborn democracy was by convincing the people—through his book

Mein Kampf, his speeches, and his and his party's many newspaper commentaries—that they were simultaneously under attack and also secretly ruled by a cabal of Jews instead of a democratically elected parliament.*

The other response to the neofeudalism of the Industrial Revolution was the trade union movement. While Marx spoke well of unions—a reference often commented on by conservatives who seek to portray the trade union movement as Marxist—the actual roots of the union movement are found in feudal-era Europe and Japan when guilds arose to protect the interests of their member-workers from exploitation by kings and feudal lords. One of the earliest was the guild of people who worked in stone and built great buildings—the Masons—and most of the Founders of America were members of the later, more philosophical remnant of that ancient guild.

In more modern times, the rise of unions tracked the rise of industry. If capital and businesses could organize into corporations and trade associations, the logic went, then workers should organize into trade unions to provide balance.

It was a sentiment that caught on as industrialization was happening across America in the middle of the nineteenth century. Carl Sandburg, in his brilliant biography of Lincoln, notes that the word "strike" was so new during Lincoln's era that newspapers put it in quotation marks when it appeared in their headlines. And, Sandburg notes, Lincoln was the first U.S. president to explicitly defend the rights of strikers, intervening in several situations where local governments were planning to use police or militia to break strikes, and preventing local governments from cooperating with the local corporate powers against workers.

The trade union movement went international in the late nineteenth century, growing out of the November 1888 meeting

---

*A fascinating exercise for today is to take *Mein Kampf* and replace the word "Jew" with the word "Liberal." It reads eerily like many of today's conservative screeds.

in London of unions from all around the world. Out of that first International Trade Union Congress came a number of international trade secretariats representing, according to *The International Transportworkers Federation, 1914–1945: The Edo Fimmen Era,* "cigar makers, hatters and shoemakers (1889), miners (1890), glass workers and typographers (1892), tailors, metal workers and railwaymen (1893), furriers and textile workers (1894), lithographers, brewery workers, seafarers and dickers [pawnbrokers] (1896) and foundry workers (1898)."[112] By 1900 there were more than 30 international unions, as the ancient guild response to feudal lords was being replaced by the trade union response to the new feudalism of giant corporations.

Modern liberalism and democracy

Ancient and tribal democracies inspired the writings of the early founders of liberalism, who inspired the first tries at liberal democracy (exclusively among the princes and merchants) in European city-states like Florence, Siena, and Venice, and the semidemocratic (it was mostly a trading bloc, and the underclass still had no rights) Republiek der Zeven Verenigde Nederlanden or Provinciën, or Republic of the Seven United Netherlands or Provinces, which lasted (contentiously) from 1588 until the French invasion in 1795.[113]

Probably the high point of modern liberalism in the United States came with the administration of Franklin Delano Roosevelt, who argued that the first and foremost function of a government of the people was to serve the people. Thus, government became the employer of last resort during the Great Depression, Social Security was put into place, and labor unions were empowered to balance the power of industry.

In the following years, Harry Truman made passage of a national single-payer health-care system one of his top priorities (although he was thwarted in that effort by the insurance industry), John Kennedy began tearing down apartheid in America, and Lyndon Johnson made a good (although flawed) try at providing a social safety net.

Although America is well behind other modern democracies in important indicators like infant and child mortality, public health, and education, and embarrassingly ahead of other modern democracies in the number of people we have in prison and the power corporate special interests have over government, we made a great start in 1776 and have been more or less steadily improving on it ever since (at least until the administration of America's first CEO president, George W. Bush).

And it's not just America that has benefited from the efforts of Jefferson, Madison, and Franklin (among others). Modern democracy has spread across the world with startling speed in the past century, particularly during the years after World War II. Today full or partial/emerging democracies represent more than three-quarters of the nations in the world. Even more startling, according to information compiled by Ambassador Mark Palmer in *Breaking the Real Axis of Evil,* the gross domestic product (GDP) of the fully free democracies of the world (46 percent of the world's nations) represents 89 percent of total world activity. By contrast, the planet's remaining dictatorships and communist nations—about a quarter of the world's nations—produce, in total (and even including China), only 6 percent of world economic activity.[114]

Modern democracies provide peace, prosperity, and a high quality of life for their citizens. They hold the greatest hope for the future of the world, because they're grounded in the most ancient and stable of social systems.

The State of Democracy in the World Today

I am more than ever convinced of the dangers to which the free and unbiased exercise of political opinion—the only sure foundation and safeguard of republican government—would be exposed by any further increase of the already overgrown influence of corporate authorities.

—President Martin Van Buren (1837–1841)

Democracy spreads across the world in a single century, 1920–2000.

There were no national democracies for over six millennia, and in 1800 only three democratic nations. By 1900 there were 13, and there's been a steady explosion in the number of liberal democracies in the world since the 1950s, as documented earlier.

The vigorous trend of nations turning to democracy in the last half of the twentieth century took most professional politicians and pundits by surprise.

Henry Kissinger's worldview was typical of those cynics who assumed that dictatorship was the natural state of humankind.

On February 3, 1976, then Secretary of State Kissinger introduced the concept of "détente," telling California's famous Commonwealth Club that "the USSR has achieved a broad equality with the United States," and such political/military equality "was inevitable for a large nation whose rulers were prepared to impose great sacrifices on their people and to give military strength the absolute top priority in allocation of resources."[115]

Kissinger—like nearly all policy analysts who started with the assumption that people are inherently evil and are born to rule or be ruled—flatly stated, "This condition [of communist dictatorship] will not go away, and it will perhaps never be conclusively 'solved.' It will have to be faced by every Administration for the foreseeable future." He was wrong; within three administrations, the Berlin Wall fell, then the Soviet Union. Instead of idealistically working to promote democracy in the Soviet Union, Kissinger said we must "promote the habits of mutual restraint, coexistence and ultimately, cooperation."

Time has proved Kissinger wrong: dictatorships, even under the guise of socialism, don't fare well in a world where all easily see the benefits of democracy.

The explosion of democracy

No matter how you define democracy, there's been an explosion of it in the twentieth century. And in order to measure when a country becomes democratic (or loses its democracy, as Germany did), it's useful to have a working definition.

One of the best definitions for modern purposes comes from Samuel P. Huntingdon's 1991 book *The Third Wave: Democratization in the Late Twentieth Century.*[116] Huntingdon says a nation is "democratic to the extent that its most powerful collective decision makers are selected through fair, honest, and periodic elections in which candidates freely compete for votes and in which virtually all the adult population is eligible to vote." He adds that the Bill of Rights freedoms such as the "freedoms to speak, publish, assemble, and organize" must be intact as well.

By such a definition, the United States didn't become a true democracy until 1920 and England until 1928, when all women over 21 were allowed to vote nationwide. In fact, by that standard New Zealand was the only democracy prior to 1900 (including ancient Greece), according to chroniclers of democracy like Freedom House, largely because women were disenfranchised worldwide until the twentieth century. Using their statistics, there were no democracies worldwide in 1900, 22 in 1950, and 119 in the year 2000.

Using a somewhat broader definition of democracy that would have included the United States since its founding, Francis Fukuyama notes in *The End of History and the Last Man* that in 1790 there were already 3 democracies in the world (the United States, France, and Switzerland), 5 in 1848 just before our Civil War (Belgium, The Netherlands, and Great Britain were added, while France lost its short-lived democracy until 1870), 13 in 1900, and the rest arrived in a steady progression interrupted only by Germany's conquest of so many European democracies during World War II.[117]

Huntingdon, on the other hand, lays out three "waves" of democracy, punctuated by three reversals when countries slipped back into dictatorship. The first wave ran from 1828 to 1926 and saw 33 of the 71 countries he tracked become democratic. During the first reversal, 1922–1942, 22 nations lost their democratic status. The second wave began toward the end of World War II, and from 1942 to 1962 Huntingdon counts 40 nations moving up to democratic status. This was followed by the second reversal (1958–1962), when 22 nations dropped democracy. The third and final wave Huntingdon documents began in 1974, leading to the addition of 33 more nations up to the 1991 publication date of his book.

The final triumph—or reversal—of democracy

Looking at statistics cited by Democracy House and the United Nations Development Programme, it appears that as of now

Huntingdon's third reversal has not yet begun. Nations continue to make the transition from dictatorship to democracy, with the most recent, as of this writing, being Afghanistan.

The feudal corporate lords take over the world?

But what if a new governmental form has emerged and not yet been recognized or identified by the pundits? A state led not by a dictator or theocrat, nor by its citizen/voters, but by corporations? A state in which corporations write laws, passed by legislators beholden to corporations, and always incrementally benefiting corporations?

This wouldn't be the "strong state" that Mussolini envisioned with his "fascism," where the corporations serve the state, but would represent a new type of state of, by, and for the corporations.

The state would merely supply a façade of governance. The real decisions would be made by corporate chiefs on issues ranging from how much mercury is in the air, to what candidates would run for elective office, to how the nation conducts its energy and foreign policies.

Corporate CEOs holding wealth and power that would have made Henry VIII jealous, living in private-jet and penthouse luxury beyond the imagining of most citizens, would decide what news people would see, what music they would hear, and what kind of medical care they could get.

There is not, to the best of my knowledge, a word to describe this sort of nation-state, although corporatist and corporatism seem to work. It's not a purely fascistic state because it doesn't include the "belligerent nationalism" part of the definition (if anything, nationalism is often celebrated in slogan but suppressed in policy), nor is it democratic because it's not run by or for its entire populace. It's not a dictatorship, yet neither is it a republic. It's not a theocracy—although it has its own belief system in the almost-supernatural powers of the "free market"—but it is no longer a constitutionally limited government.

Its parallel can be found in the thirteenth-century era of feudalism, when the lords had enough power to force the king to
grant them rights under the Magna Carta. This time, the government isn't hereditary, but its individual members come from (and
nearly all aspire to go to) the elite world of corporate wealth and
power. The closest I can come to describing it is as a corporate-
controlled semifeudal pseudodemocracy.

And the trend to transform democracies (and even dictatorships, like Russia) into corporate-controlled semifeudal pseudo-
democracies is already well under way.

The United States has succumbed and has laid plans to take
Iraq with it. Canada is on the brink, as is Germany, and Putin's
Russia is just beginning to fight back against corporate powers,
albeit using the weapons of dictatorship. Perhaps a third of the
smaller democracies of the world—particularly those rich in natural resources or cheap labor with strongman leaders or elite
ruling families or corporations (like Botswana, Colombia, and
Singapore)—are already democracies in name only.

The World Trade Organization (WTO) has replaced the
United Nations as the most powerful intergovernmental organization in the world, and in the WTO, corporations are equal part-
ners with nations. Soon corporations will be the masters of
nations; some suggest they already are.

This is the dark side of corporate globalization promoted in
works like Thomas L. Friedman's *The Lexus and the Olive Tree*. It
could displace democracy entirely from Greece and America, the
ancestral lands of its birth.

And so we are left with the question: will people who have
tasted freedom once again rise up and throw this century's version of tea into the harbor? Or will the people of previously
democratic nations find themselves powerless against the new
corporate feudal lords?

Where we are now

Which brings us back to Emmanuel Kant, the man who first proposed that worldwide democracy could bring about worldwide peace.

I first visited his hometown, Kaliningrad, in December 1994, just after the fall of the Soviet Union and the very week that Russia was holding its first democratic election in its thousand-year history. The city was gray and dismal, the people dispirited, the infrastructure crumbling.

In just ten years, the city has become vital and vibrant, as democracy and free enterprise have crept into Russia. At the same time, however, the claws of unregulated capitalism have caught the Russians unawares, and the streets of the city are filling with beggars, teenage prostitutes, petty criminals, gangsters, and the other symptoms of a nation that has embraced the individual liberty aspects of democracy without fully understanding the need for governmental care for the commons and legislative restraint of predatory corporate behavior. As this book is being written, Russian president Vladimir Putin has taken steps to stifle critics, an often-fatal first mistake for the survival of a democracy.

As Thomas Jefferson poignantly informed John Adams when Adams signed the Alien and Sedition Acts, a government that will not tolerate dissent—even offensive dissent—is a government that cannot survive as a democratic republic. And while the world murmurs concern about Putin's actions, similar alarm bells are being raised at the loss of speech and assembly in the United States.

Yet while democracy may be challenged in Russia and the United States, it seems that our Founders planted a seed that is thriving (although not without challenges) elsewhere in the world. In 2002, the United Nations Development Programme's *Human Development Report* points out that among the world's wealthy nations, Sweden has the lowest human poverty index (6.8 percent) and the United States has the highest (15.8 percent).[118]

"There have been great improvements in human political and civil rights," the UNDP notes. "Since 1980, 81 countries have taken significant steps in democratization, with 33 military regimes replaced by civilian governments. . . . but only 47 of these are considered full democracies today." On the other hand, "106 governments still restrict many civil and political freedoms."

Democracies are the most efficient at producing wealth, the UNDP data suggest: "With just two exceptions, all the richest countries of the world—countries with per capita income above $20,000 (in 2000 purchasing power parity US$)—have democratic regimes, and 42 of the 48 high human development countries are democracies."[119]

And democratic nations are more stable: "Dictatorships are more prone to violent upheavals than democracies, experiencing a war every 12 years, on average, compared with every 21 years in democracies."[120]

Nonetheless, even democracies are facing challenges, from a new type of antidemocratic aristocracy. Fully 80 percent of the world's people lived in nations where the rich got richer while the middle class and poor became poorer in the past 50 years, whereas only 4 percent of the world's people lived in nations where inequalities were reduced. Differences in equality are normal and healthy in democracies, but when the imbalance between rich and poor becomes too great, it often means an antidemocratic aristocracy has seized or is trying to seize control of the nation, and democracy itself is at risk in that country.

Democracy is inevitable.

If democracy is the natural state of all mammals, including humans, it must be something purely temporary that has prevented it for during so much of the "civilized" period of the past few millennia (even though it has continued to exist throughout this time among tribal people). The force that slowed its inevitable emergence was a dysfunctional story in our culture, which led to thousands of years of the sanctioning of slavery, the oppression of women and minorities, and the deaths of hundreds of millions. It was the story that our essential nature is sinful.

The fundamental issue of sin and punishment

Hobbes and others have assumed that we'd need a time machine to know how bad life really was 20,000 or 50,000 years ago. But there are still humans living essentially the same way your ancestors and mine did, and if we look at their lives we find, by and large, that Hobbes was mistaken.

I remember vividly the first time I experienced this. I was sitting around a campfire with half a dozen or so men who were members of a southwestern Native American tribe. We'd just done a sweat, and after some of the heavy talk and ritual associated with that sacred ceremony, the conversation gradually turned to "guy talk": telling stories, making each other laugh, and poking fun.

They were making jokes mostly about another tribe, which lived about six hundred miles away. Not cutting or hurting comments, but jokes that pointed out—with a humor born of respect—the historic and cultural differences between the two tribes. Because I'd never interacted with the other tribe, I made a comment typical of modern American culture: a put-down joke, with the man sitting opposite me around the fire as its butt. It was the kind of remark you'll hear within five minutes of turning on any sitcom on American television.

The group fell silent, and everybody looked down or into the fire. I realized I'd had breached some protocol. And I didn't know how to make it right or how they'd punish me for my sin.

After a long and, for me, uncomfortable silence, the oldest

man in the circle roused himself, as if he knew his age gave him the obligation to speak first.

"I remember a time when I was young," he said, "and, well, I won't say, 'stupid,' but let's say, 'not so wise.' Not that I'm all that wise now," he added with a small laugh, "but I've learned a few things over the years. Anyhow, I remember when I was young and I was sitting with some friends, and I said something hurtful about one of the men who was there with us. I remember how badly I felt, immediately knowing that I had put a pain on his heart. I remember how confused I felt, not sure what I should do to restore balance to the circle. And I remember one of the men telling a story of a time when he'd hurt somebody's feelings, and how he'd made it right by acknowledging that, and retracting the comment, and asking the rest of the group to help him bring back balance and harmony."

The man spoke for several minutes, and my version of it is from memory so probably not exact, but it captures the essence of his comments. He was teaching me—without ever once mentioning my name—how to remedy what I had done.

Then the man next to him cleared his throat and said, "I, too, remember a time I said something impulsive that hurt my friend." And he went on to tell the story of what he did to make it right. His story was followed by one from the man I'd made the joke about, and this continued all the way around the circle until it got to me.

By then, I knew how each person felt and had learned how I could make it right with each individual or rebalance the situation in the group. It took a few minutes, but I did it, and the oldest man gently interrupted me by hand-rolling tobacco into a corn shuck, lighting it, and passing it around the circle. It was as if something heavy had been lifted from the group. We were soon again laughing and telling tall tales.

What's important in this story is that nobody had called me a sinner. Nobody implied that I was doing what was normal or natural. Everybody accepted that I'd made a mistake, I hadn't known better, and each man had done his best to politely tell me how I could restore harmony.

This is one aspect of how a society can live without police and prisons.

This is how humans, for the most part, lived for the past 40,000 years and longer.

This is beyond the imagining of Thomas Hobbes and the people of his day who were struggling in a largely antidemocratic kingdom with the issue of whether those who rule over others—restraining sinful impulses and punishing those who err—should be appointed by gods or men (but never women).

When society agrees with the story that people are fundamentally flawed and evil, it creates repositories for those evil people or puts them to death. It assigns to some of its members the job of human trash collector who performs therapy, provides drugs, or restrains them. If they acted badly enough, they're put into a prison where it's assumed that others of equal evil and lacking restraint of their human nature will bully, beat, and even rape the newcomer.

On the other hand, when a society agrees with the democracy-grounded story that people are fundamentally good, born in balance with the world and each other, then something quite different happens when a person acts badly. It becomes the responsibility of the entire community to bring that person back into balance. The bad behavior is seen either as an indication that the person has not yet learned something or matured, or that the person is suffering from a form of spiritual sickness. The solemn responsibility and work of every person in the community becomes that of teaching or healing the individual. Usually, once harmony is restored, a small ceremony is performed to acknowledge the return of the person and the community to its natural state.

Some would argue that this way of life may work well for

small tribes where everybody knows everybody else but isn't viable in a city-state society where it's possible for predators and sociopaths to prey on innocent people if unrestrained by the force of law and threat or reality of imprisonment. There's considerable truth to this argument: Hobbes was writing from the midst of the British Empire in the seventeenth century, the belly of the beast of one of history's mightiest and most bloodthirsty antidemocratic cultures to rule the earth.

And yet we do have this simple metric today: generally, the more democratic a nation is, the fewer people it will have in prison.

Democracy is resilient, always rising from the human spirit.
Most scientists who have examined the relationship between democracy and biology have concluded that democracy is so resilient an idea, so biologically ingrained an imperative that it will continue to grow and prosper around the world even if the Texas oil barons and New York corporations do succeed in turning America back into a Dickensian world consistent with the vision of dictators, pseudoconservatives, and those who don't understand democracy.

Professor Rudolph Rummel, mentioned earlier, made the following points in an e-mail discussion we had in November 2003:

▸   Freedom is a basic human right recognized by the United Nations and international treaties and is the heart of social justice.

▸   Freedom—free speech and the economic and social free market—is an engine of economic and human development, and scientific and technological advancement.

▸   Freedom ameliorates the problem of mass poverty.

▸   Free people do not suffer from and never have had famines and, by theory, should not. Freedom is therefore a solution to hunger and famine.

▸ Free people have the least internal violence, turmoil, and political instability.

▸ Free people have virtually no government genocide and mass murder, and for good theoretical reasons. Freedom is therefore a solution to genocide and mass murder; the only practical means of making sure that "Never again!"

▸ Free people do not make war on each other, and the greater the freedom within two nations, the less violence between them. While they may declare war on autocratic regimes that threaten them, people in a democracy never vote to attack other democracies.

▸ Freedom is a method of nonviolence—the most peaceful nations are those whose people are free.

As Per Ahlmark, former deputy prime minister of Sweden, said in his remarks to the European Parliament on April 8, 1999: "In a democracy it is impossible, or at least extremely difficult, to get enough support from the people to initiate a military confrontation with another democracy. Such people know each other too well. They trust each other too much. For democratic governments it is usually too easy and natural to talk and negotiate with one another—it would look and feel ridiculous or totally irresponsible to start shooting at a nation which is governed in the same way as your own country."[121]

On his website, Dr. Randolph J. Rummel has a "Peace Clock" that shows that in 1900, only 8 percent of the world's people lived in nations that were democratic.[122] By 1950, the number had increased to 31 percent, and, Dr. Rummel says, "Now is the dawning of a new world," as by the year 2000 fully 58.2 percent of the world's people lived in democratic nations.

Rummel also coined the word "democide" (mentioned earlier by Per Ahlmark of Sweden) in his book *Death by Government* to describe the deliberate murder (or allowing the deaths) of a state's own citizens.[123] Rummel points out that the world was shocked when the Chinese Communists slaughtered people in Tiananmen Square but should not have been shocked: the Chinese state had killed over 35 million of its own citizens prior to that time and continues to kill them to this day.

As awful as that number is, the Soviets hold the world record, having killed an estimated 54–61 million human beings, according to Rummel. Although we all know about the wars incited by Nazi Germany and Imperial Japan, what most people miss is that in the twentieth century, up to four times as many people died at the hands of their own governments as in all the wars combined. The cause? According to Rummel and many other experts on the topic, it's a lack of democracy.

In his book *Breaking the Real Axis of Evil: How to Oust the World's Last Dictators by 2025,* former U.S. ambassador to Hungary Mark Palmer says that there are only 45 dictators left in the world, and that with thoughtful and nonviolent effort, we may be able to end all of their reigns before the year 2025.[124] The worldwide trend is, Palmer says, solidly toward peace. In a November 2003 interview, he told me, "If you could foresee a world which was 100 percent democratic, there would be no war." There would be competition, Palmer notes, but not war, and the result would be an increased standard of living among people all across the planet.

And the trend is good. Palmer is vice chairman of the board of directors of Freedom House, which produces an annual report on democracy around the world.[125] "In 2002, the last year that we covered," he told me, "we saw roughly 26 countries moving in the right direction [toward democracy] and only about 11 doing some reversal."

We may be standing on the edge of a new era of peace, because democracies have a built-in mechanism (the will of the people) to prevent aggressive wars. So long as our democratic institutions can resist being taken over by a new version of war-lords, aristocrats, and kings in the form of multinational corporations (particularly those in the defense industry), we could see the prospect of the biblical "thousand years of peace"—following the brutality of the last century—in our or our children's lifetime.

Reinventing democracy

Democracy doesn't just appear, fully formed. In every part of the world, over and over, it has to be refigured out, developed, put together piece by piece. This is why it can appear so different in different parts of the world, yet always share the same set of basic values.

Democratic indigenous cultures almost always have their own laws, appropriate to their time and place, to ensure stability and peace. The Australian Aborigines, for example, have carried for as long as 80,000 years the belief that if they engage in intensive (single crop, tilled soil) agriculture, the gods will punish them with terrible famines.

So how do people find their way from a violent warlord, theocrat, or feudal culture into a peaceful and stable democratic culture?

1. The people have learned they must live in a sustainable fashion, in balance and harmony with their environment.
2. They've agreed that they're no longer willing to live in a violent society characterized by extremes of wealth and power.
3. They've agreed that power must be locally held and locally exercised.

Eventually, enough people re-remember the basic tenets of democratic life and figure out how to apply them to their own particular time and place. When enough people "wake up" to the possibility of living in a democracy, the nondemocratic culture dissolves and a newly formed and unique democracy emerges, as we see in examples from New Caledonia to the Iroquois to the American Revolution, to the dramatic shift around the world toward democracy in the past century. Today, all across the world, people are creating fledgling democracies with the hope they can successfully transit them into multigenerational, long-term democratic nations.

A Vision for the Future of America and the World

I speak the pass-word primeval, I give the sign of democracy,
By God! I will accept nothing which all cannot have their
counterpart of on the same terms.

—WALT WHITMAN, "Song of Myself," 1855

Jefferson was an extraordinary visionary. He saw that democracy could be a long-lasting, healthy, robust form of government; in this, he saw the future far more accurately than did John Adams. In his last days, Jefferson foresaw the Civil War, 30 years into the future. How many visionaries do we have today whose forecasts are so accurate? And what would Jefferson do, if he were alive today?

We've strayed far away from the Founders' vision of American democracy, which was grounded in the Enlightenment and John Locke's belief that no institution—governmental, ecclesiastical, or corporate—should ever have the rights and powers reserved exclusively for We the People.

Corporations have reached out and grasped rights and powers that Samuel Adams and George Hewes directly challenged at the Boston Tea Party when they lit the fuse of the American Revolution.

Churches have created unholy (literally) alliances with politicians and governmental institutions to provide "faith-based" services ranging from prisons in Florida to schools in Washington, D.C., all as ways of insinuating themselves into the arterial flow of governmental tax dollars and to gain power over politicians.

And our government itself has been so infiltrated by agents of special interests—from a CEO president and vice president to corporate-funded "conservative" think tanks writing public policy—that many of our constitutional rights have already been usurped.

Add to this the war-intoxicated executive branch of the government granting draconian police powers to our law-enforcement agencies and disabling the 227-year-old wall of separation that forbade the U.S. military from operating within the United States against U.S. citizens and you have a prescription for the transformation of democracy into a modern feudal state.

But there are ways we can revive Jefferson's dream of a constitutionally limited democratic republic, and they're getting increasing interest in the media and among the public.

What follows are only intended as proposals, to start a discussion. That, of course, is how Jefferson himself would have wanted it—his dream of people creating a future by putting their heads together to derive a vision they can all share.

Register and vote.

The Founders dedicated their lives to our ability to participate in democracy. Do it. And encourage others to do the same.

Return war powers to Congress and end nonwars.

In the novel *1984* by George Orwell, a seemingly democratic president kept his nation in a continual state of repression by having a continuous war. Cynics suggest the lesson wasn't lost on Lyndon Johnson or Richard Nixon, who both, they say, extended the Vietnam War so it coincidentally ran over election cycles, knowing that a wartime president's party is more likely to be reelected and has more power than a president in peacetime.

On April 20, 1795, James Madison, who had just helped shepherd through the Constitution and Bill of Rights, and would become president of the United States in the following decade, wrote: "Of all the enemies to public liberty war is, perhaps, the most to be dreaded because it comprises and develops the germ of every other. War is the parent of armies; from these proceed debts and taxes. And armies, and debts, and taxes are the known instruments for bringing the many under the domination of the few."[126]

Reflecting on war's impact on the executive branch of government, Madison continued his letter about the dangerous and intoxicating power of war for a president.

"In war, too, the discretionary power of the Executive is extended," he wrote. "Its influence in dealing out offices, honors, and emoluments is multiplied; and all the means of seducing the minds, are added to those of subduing the force of the people. The same malignant aspect in republicanism may be traced in the inequality of fortunes, and the opportunities of fraud, growing out of a state of war . . . and in the degeneracy of manners and morals, engendered by both.

"No nation," he concluded, "could preserve its freedom in the midst of continual warfare."

The last war that Congress declared was World War II. Since then we've seen both the dilution of the meaning of the word "war" and a simultaneous abdication by Congress of its constitutional responsibility to be the sole body capable of declaring war. We have a "war on poverty," a "war on drugs," and a "war on illiteracy," among many others. We should strip the word "war" from all of these efforts.

Similarly, we must acknowledge that the "war on terrorism," which George W. Bush says could last indefinitely, is not a war. Wars are declared between nations, have specific beginning and ending points, and specific leaders who can initiate and sue to end hostilities.

While Osama bin Laden and al Qaeda have embraced the tactic of terrorism, they do not constitute a sovereign state, and to declare "war" on them only elevates them in the eyes of Muslims all over the world. It also confers on the president—for the duration of a war that Bush has said may last for generations—powers that the Founders meant a president to have only for very short and clearly defined periods of national emergency while in a declared state of war.

The appropriate response to the attacks of 9/11 would have been to identify the perpetrators (as of this writing in early 2004, this has still not been done officially), label them as criminals, and enlist the help of Interpol and police agencies all around the world to bring them to justice.

Immediately after 9/11, we had the sympathy and empathy of the world. France's largest newspaper, Le Monde, ran a front-page headline in two-inch-tall letters that said, in French, "We Are All Americans Now." People marched in solidarity with us in nearly every capital city in the world. When Bush tentatively identified the son of his father's business partner—Osama bin Laden—as the perpetrator, the government of Afghanistan offered to arrest bin Laden and put him on trial, Bush refused and instead attacked Afghanistan, killing more than ten thousand innocent civilians and leaving bin Laden at large.[127]

If bin Laden and al Qaeda are responsible for 9/11—and it certainly appears that is the case—the best way to respond is the same way other democracies have dealt with terrorist threats:

identify the crime and the criminals, gain international support for dismantling their organizations and arresting them, and prosecute them. Germany did it with the Red Army Faction, Italy against the Red Brigades, and Greece in response to the 17 November terrorist group. All three of these terrorist groups had spread to multiple nations and required international efforts to bring them to justice. Even the United Kingdom never made the blunder of "declaring war" on the IRA—and therefore now Northern Ireland is far more peaceful than it was a few decades ago.

But George W. Bush—floundering without a clear voter mandate and seeing his economic policies failing—needed the bounce in the polls that his father got by declaring war on Saddam, and Iraq sits atop a sea of oil over which Bush's campaign contributors were salivating. Bush defied international opinion and international law to declare a preemptive war—the first in the 227-year history of the United States—on a nation that had not first attacked us and didn't represent a demonstrable threat to us.

At the same time, Bush used powers designed for a time of real war—when the United States was under attack by another nation—to cut into the civil rights and liberties held and cherished by Americans since the days of this nation's founding.

Terrorism is not a threat to democracy—it's only a tactic. The threat to democracy comes from leaders who cynically exploit acts of terror—as Hitler successfully did with the burning of the Reichstag building—to hypermilitarize a nation.

It's time to declare the wars over—both the "war against terrorism" and the "war against Iraq"—and return civil liberties to Americans. We should disband the Pentagon's disinformation department, rein in the Justice Department, reinstall the firewall the prevents our military from acting against our civilians, and return America to a sense of normalcy. Even in the face of another (probable) al Qaeda attack on American soil, it's crucial for the survival of our democracy—as James Madison pointed out—to bring the police agencies of the world together to arrest and prosecute terrorists who attack us while not going over the edge into the abyss of perpetual war.

Repeal the PATRIOT Act and other antiliberty laws.

Like John Adams's Alien and Sedition Acts, the U.S.A. PATRIOT Act steps over the line from enhancing national security to damaging the very fabric of democracy itself. It's bad for America and a terrible example for the rest of the world.

The PATRIOT Act owes much of its passage to the arrival of anthrax-laden letters in the offices of the two Democrats in the U.S. Senate who were in a position to stop it: then Senate leader Tom Daschle and Senate Judiciary chairman Patrick Leahy. Not only did both have to evacuate their offices for the duration of the deliberations, but the reluctance the then-Democratically controlled Senate initially felt about the law evaporated when Congress found itself under attack.

It's time now for Congress to look back on those hysterical times and recognize—and repeal—the error of their hasty actions.

Provide free high-quality public education for all—through college.

Free public education is one of the greatest forces for producing mobility between economic classes. In those nations (and there are many) where any child can attend school all the way up to the Ph.D. or M.D. position with no cost to him or his family, you find the smallest differences between rich and poor, and the least rigidity of the remnants of caste and class systems.

This, of course, is not what conservatives want. When Ronald Reagan was elected governor of California, one of the first things he did was to eliminate public funding for attendance at the University of California system.

Any claim that eliminating this funding was an economic necessity is baseless; necessity is subjective and ultimately must be subject to the will of the people. And just as we saw in the discussion of child labor laws, the inevitable result is a less-educated populace.

Prior to Reagan's reign, any resident of California could get a *free* education through the UC system. The originator of this idea was Jefferson. In a letter to Colonel Charles Yancy on January 6, 1816, he argued for publicly funded free education for all as the main foundation of freedom.

"If the legislature would add to that a perpetual tax of a cent a head on the population of the State," Jefferson wrote, "it would set agoing at once, and forever maintain, a system of primary or ward schools, and an university where might be taught, in its highest degree, every branch of science useful in our time and country; and it would rescue us from the tax of Toryism, fanaticism, and indifferentism to their own State."

He added bluntly, "If a nation expects to be ignorant and free, in a state of civilization, it expects what never was and never will be."

And, Jefferson noted, a well-educated citizenry was ultimately the only defense against an overreaching government. "The functionaries of every government have propensities to command at will the liberty and property of their constituents. There is no safe deposit for these but with the people themselves; nor can they be safe with them without information. Where the press is free, and every man able to read, all is safe."

It was a core concept for Jefferson, as it was for many of the Founders (which is why they went along with most of his proposals). In a letter to Joseph C. Cabell, January 31, 1814, he made it clear that free public education and grass-roots politics were the key to the survival of America, saying that "public education" was so critical to democracy that "I shall claim a right to further [it] as long as I breathe."

Jefferson repeatedly wrote and spoke about how there must be free college available to any student able to demonstrate the ability to perform at the university level. In a letter to J. Correa de Serra dated November 25, 1817, he wrote:

"My bill proposes:

"1. Elementary schools in every county, which shall place every householder within three miles of a school.

"2. District colleges, which shall place every father within a day's ride of a college where he may dispose of his son.

"3. An university in a healthy and central situation, with the offer of the lands, buildings, and funds of the Central College, if they will accept that place for their establishment."

In both the colleges and universities, Jefferson expected to find "a selection from the elementary schools of subjects [students] of the most promising genius, whose parents are too poor to give them further education, to be carried at the public expense through the colleges and university.

"The object," Jefferson summarized, "is to bring into action that mass of talents which lies buried in poverty in every country, for want of the means of development, and thus give activity to a mass of mind, which, in proportion to our population, shall be the double or treble of what it is in most countries."

The result of his efforts was that on March 7, 1825, the University of Virginia finally opened. As a nineteenth-century biographer of Jefferson noted, "It must have been a day of unspeakable satisfaction for him."[128] After all, on his tombstone he asked that his accomplishments as president of the United States be not mentioned because that was not the most important work of his life. His epitaph reads simply: "Author of the Declaration of American Independence, and of the Virginia Statute for Religious Freedom, and Father of the University of Virginia."

Just as Jefferson argued for "a system of general instruction which shall reach every description of our citizens, from the highest to the poorest," we must now work to reverse Reagan's legacy and put a full education back into the reach of all of our citizens.

Require that any benefits Congress gives itself, it gives to all citizens.

Being in Congress should not be a way of enriching oneself; that would be using one's role in government for personal gain. Plain and simply, Congress should not be allowed to vote itself any benefit that doesn't apply to all citizens.

The biggest single example at the moment is health care. There is no reason on earth why our representatives should guarantee themselves something that's not job related if they're not willing to guarantee it to all of us.

Obviously, exceptions would be made for expenditures that are directly job-related, such as their office expenses. But even then, the rules for what's a legitimate business expense should be no different for their offices than for ours.

Provide health care for all.

Insurance companies take between 8 percent and 60 percent (with an average of 15 percent) of the money that flows through them to cover their overhead, administration, and profits. Medicare operates on an average overhead of 1 percent. Medicare, of course, doesn't pay million-dollar salaries to its executives, or pay for corporate jets, fancy headquarters, buildings, advertising, marketing, or lobbying and political contributions. Nor does it have to pay between 3 and 10 percent of its revenues as dividends to stockholders to prevent stockholder revolts.

It turns out, according to a study published in the *New England Journal of Medicine* that if all of America's health insurance companies, HMOs, and other middlemen were eliminated, and the government simply paid your medical costs directly to whomever you chose to provide you with health care, the savings would be so great that without increasing the health-care budget we could provide cradle-to-grave health-care cost to every American.[129]

This is the "single payer" system adopted in Canada and most other democracies. The health-care system itself is still private, and you can choose any doctor, hospital, or pharmacy. Government pays the bills, and the only losers are the insurance companies that have fastened themselves onto our backs like giant leeches.

This being the case—and it is in every other industrialized democracy in the world—why doesn't the average American know it? Why do they persist in believing that Canadians are crossing the border looking for health care in the United States, when the reverse is true and Americans are traveling to Canada? The reason is simple: the health insurance and HMO industry spends hundreds of millions of (our) dollars on advertising and lobbying to keep our legislators under their thumbs and us in the dark.

In the meantime, we rank 20th to 25th in the world in life expectancy, infant mortality, and immunization rates, 54th in the world in "fairness" of access to health care, and drive more than a half-million families a year into the desperation of bankruptcy with medical expenses. We can do better.

Require a living wage.

One of the core liberal ideas—which helped build the American middle class when other nations were floundering—was the notion that workers should earn enough to participate fully in society.

James Couzens was one of the first to advance in a big way the idea advocated by the progressive movement so active in America from the 1880s to the early 1920s. When Couzens invested $2,500 to help Henry Ford start the Ford Motor Company in 1903 and became one of Ford's business partners and his business manager, Ford was paying its laborers $1.50 per day. Couzens convinced Ford's wife, Clara, that it was both immoral and bad business to pay people the minimum they were willing (or desperate enough) to work for, and proposed that Henry pay his employees what the corporation could afford—$5 a day (more than double what his competitors were paying)—with a working week reduced from six days to five. Henry at first fought both Clara and Couzens, but finally relented in order to maintain business and domestic harmony.

The result was the start of a solid middle class in Michigan, an increase in the loyalty and productivity of Ford's workforce, and an improvement in the quality of the cars he produced. The cost of a new Ford car dropped from over $800 to under $400, and sales boomed.

Taking credit for Couzens's suggestion, Henry Ford said, "If you cut wages, you just cut the number of your customers," explaining how with "his" $5 a day wage, Ford employees could now buy the product they were producing. Instead of increasing profits by extracting concessions from labor, Ford began to echo Couzens's progressive idea that profits could be increased by smarter manufacturing methods, and well-paid labor would then become a market for the product they produced. "I can find methods of manufacturing that will make high wages," said Ford in 1914, essentially reversing the most commonly held notion of business as being dependent on low wages for success.[130]

Couzens split with Henry Ford in 1915, sold his stock (representing his original $2,500 investment) in the Ford Motor Company for $29.3 million, and became first the mayor of Detroit, then a Republican senator from Michigan. Although the Republicans embraced him as a wealthy industrialist, he continued to promote his own progressive/liberal agenda. For example, the top income tax rate was 73 percent when Couzens came to the Senate in 1922. Over his loud objections, the Republican Harding and Hoover administrations passed six successive tax cuts, ultimately slashing the top rate from 73 down to 24 percent in 1929, creating tottering towers of upper-tax-bracket wealth that crashed and brought on the Great Depression. Couzens's support of progressive positions so enraged Republicans that they refused to renominate him to a third term in 1936.

The conservative rebuttal to a living wage is that if corporations can get their labor cheaper, it will mean cheaper goods for you and me. But few people noticed a drop in prices of Nike's shoes when they moved to offshore (and very cheap) labor through the late 1980s and 1990s. Instead, we mostly saw Nike's president, Phil Knight, become one of the richest men in the world. Even the much-vaunted low prices of Wal-Mart, often attributed to cheap Chinese labor, are nothing new. Your grandparents remember the dime stores that crisscrossed America, selling at a low price products made in the United States by workers earning a living wage. The main result of Wal-Mart's acquisition of cheap overseas labor has been the transformation of the Walton family into one of the world's wealthiest dynasties; it's had only a minimal impact on the cost of products sold. Labor is only a small part of the cost of most products, and history shows that when "conservative" business owners can drive down the cost of labor, they usually keep the difference for themselves.

Support organized labor or organize your workplace.

"Cheap labor" is the core mantra of the conservatives, and ultimately destroys communities, eviscerates the middle class, and harms democracy.

If capital can organize in the form of a corporation, and corporations can organize as conglomerates, chambers of commerce, and trade and lobbying associations, then labor must have an equal and guaranteed-by-law right to organize. Strong unions are the only thing standing between you and serfdom at the hands of corporate masters, and without the unions of the past there would be no American middle class today.

For more information about the union movement, visit the website of the AFL-CIO at www.aflcio.org. You'll find a wealth of news and facts, as well as information about how to unionize your current workplace.

Use tariffs and trade policy to balance labor's playing field.

Tenche Coxe was a friend of many of the Founders of America. A small businessman who never achieved the prominence of a John Hancock, he was nonetheless constantly active in the politics of the day. He'd originally opposed separation from England because he feared it would hurt business; after the Revolution he embraced democracy with fervor.

One of Coxe's biggest concerns was that the newly emerging American industries would be wiped out by foreign competition. The British were using slave-wage labor (and often actual slave labor) in India, Asia, and Africa to manufacture products for export to America, and Coxe saw the loss of jobs and destruction of domestic industries as both an economic and a national security issue. He agitated for a national commercial system, starting with a system of tariffs to protect American products and workers.

Coxe's logic was simple. If a product had an hour of labor in it and was imported from a country where labor cost one-tenth of what it did in America, it should have a tariff or tax added to it upon import equal to the missing nine-tenths of the labor cost. To put it in today's terms, if it cost two dollars in labor to make a pair of shoes in the United States, but only 25 cents in China, then there should be a $1.75 tariff on the shoes upon import to level the playing field between laborers.

Coxe created the first chamber of commerce in America (in Pennsylvania) and then, according to his biographer, Jacob E. Cooke, got "enacted in September 1786 at the behest of artisans and mechanics and over the opposition of many merchants, not only [what was to become] representative tariff legislation in New York and Massachusetts, but also served as the prototype for the first federal tariff in 1789."

Coxe's law was titled in a straightforward manner: "An Act to Encourage and Protect the Manufacturers of This State." While it exempted products from the tax that "it is not in our interest to manufacture," it would "lead us to encourage" the growth of domestic industry. This, Coxe felt, was the heart of true patriotism. America's "own interests must be our principal rule," Cooke notes that Coxe wrote in April 1786.

From 1786 until 1996 when Bill Clinton signed NAFTA and GATT/WTO, the United States (and every other signatory nation) had protected its domestic industries and workers by leveling the playing fields of labor and manufacturing costs. With the stroke of a pen, Clinton put the interests of the world's largest multinational corporations (and campaign donors) above those of America's small and medium-sized businesses and America's middle class and created the "giant sucking sound" Ross Perot predicted in 1992.

George W. Bush taught us that we can simply walk away from treaties. NAFTA and GATT/WTO should be among the first we dispose of.

Strengthen the social safety net.

"Welfare has failed," proclaimed the conservative talk-show host. "There are still poor people." This, he suggested, was why we should scrap welfare programs and tolerate the explosion of homeless people, suicides, and crime that would ensue.

Extending this logic, we should do away with our fire departments. After all, there are still fires. And get rid of our police because there are still criminals.

The Founders thought long and hard about this issue, as poverty isn't just something that came along with the modern era. In the winter of 1766, Benjamin Franklin submitted a pseudonymous letter to the editor of *The London Chronicle,* which they published on November 29.[131] Franklin, representing himself as a farmer, "one of that class of people that feeds you all, and at present is abus'd by you all," wrote a lengthy and sarcastic screed about the regulated price policies of London. "Bring your corn to market if you dare," Franklin claimed the city fathers were saying to farmers, and "we'll sell it for you, for less money, or take it for nothing."

Franklin then points out that the rationale offered by the city officials for regulation of the prices of agricultural goods was so that the poor could afford to buy foodstuffs. "But, it seems," he wrote, "we Farmers must take so much less, that the poor may have it so much cheaper. This operates then as a tax for the maintenance of the poor."

Working himself up into full lather—he was writing under the pen name "Arator"—Franklin then railed about the British welfare system. "I am for doing good to the poor, but I differ in opinion of the means.—I think the best way of doing good to the poor, is not making them easy in poverty, but leading or driving them out of it."

In this, Franklin made the observation—bluntly stated—that when incentives for people to work are gone, some people will choose not to work at all. "In my youth I travelled much," he wrote, "and I observed in different countries, that the more public provisions were made for the poor, the less they provided for themselves, and of course became poorer. And, on the contrary, the less was done for them, the more they did for themselves, and became richer."

With this, Franklin identified a critical problem for those who want a viable social safety net but don't want to create a dependent class of people, living on the dole from generation to generation. His suggestion of leading the poor out of poverty is a key point: the world's best antipoverty program, we have seen again and again, is a program that ensures there is a strong middle class with an abundance of well-paying jobs and high levels of worker security. Without governments stepping in to tell businesses how to operate, this is achieved by the simple step of having the law authorize the existence of corporations and providing for their security and similarly authorizing the existence of labor unions and guaranteeing their security.

When organized capital and organized labor have relatively equal levels of power, society stabilizes, as we saw throughout the period from the 1940s to the 1970s, the golden age of the American middle class. When government—which defines the rules by which the game of business is played in all cases—tilts its policies in favor of corporations and against labor, as Reagan began and has been happening state by state ever since, then job security vanishes, wages drop, corporate profits soar, CEOs start taking multimillion-dollar paychecks, and corporate corruption runs rampant.

For people capable of working, Franklin was right when he noted that welfare systems that simply hand out cash to the poor will take "away from before their eyes the greatest of all inducements to industry, frugality, and sobriety, by giving them a dependence on somewhat else."

But Ronald Reagan appointing Alan Greenspan as chairman of the Federal Reserve Board in 1987 has complicated the issue of employment. Greenspan, a former devotee and friend of Libertarian cult leader Ayn Rand, believes a main job of the Fed's interest-setting mechanism is to maintain a constant pool of a few million unemployed people so that employers won't find themselves bidding against each other for employees, thus driving up the cost of labor to corporations. Thus, when times are good for workers, Greenspan turns up interest rates to cool down the economy and throw people out of work. When times are bad and more are unemployed than he feels necessary, he reduces interest rates to heat up the economy.

As the *Wall Street Journal* noted in a front-page article about him on January 27, 1997:

> Workers' fear of losing their jobs restrains them from seeking the pay raises that usually crop up when employers have trouble finding people to hire.
>
> Even if the economy didn't slow down as he expected, he [Alan Greenspan] told Fed colleagues last summer, he saw little danger of a sudden upturn in wages and prices.
>
> "Because workers are more worried about their own job security and their marketability if forced to change jobs, they are apparently accepting smaller increases in their compensation at any given level of labor-market tightness," Mr. Greenspan told Congress at the time.

The *Wall Street Journal* added, a few months later, "Mr. Greenspan, for one, scrutinizes worker insecurity. He has said in recent remarks that he believes a pervasive fear of unemployment has kept wage demands modest, but he is worried that the robust labor market would soon embolden workers to demand more."[132]

So we see a swing, from London in Franklin's day regulating business and causing pain to farmers, to Greenspan today regulating unemployment and causing pain to workers. The middle ground, of course, is to do neither, but to give labor the same authorities and limitations that business has to organize, negotiate, and fully participate in the marketplace.

That takes care of those capable of working and shows how LBJ's Great Society was just as flawed as Clinton's "end of welfare as we know it," which simply tossed people off the dole and into

the hands of employers who don't allow unionization or pay living wages. Restoring balance to the workplace would resolve both
issues to a large extent.

And during times of such economic distress that there aren't
enough jobs to go around—as was created by both Herbert Hoover
and George W. Bush's nearly identical economic policies—it's
important for government to step in as the employer of last resort as FDR did with the WPA to help America recover from
Hoover's Great Depression.

But there are also people who simply cannot work: the old,
the sick, the infirm, the handicapped, and single mothers during
their first year of motherhood. If this group doesn't have the
means to support itself, the resulting pain is felt by all of society.

For this reason, the Founders put into place the first welfare
plans at the same time they were putting together the United
States. As Thomas Jefferson noted in his 1787 *Notes on Virginia,*
"The poor who have neither property, friends, nor strength to
labour, are boarded in the houses of good farmers, to whom a
stipulated sum is annually paid. To those who are able to help
themselves a little, or have friends from whom they derive some
succours, inadequate however to their full maintenance, supple-
mentary aids are given, which enable them to live comfortably in
their own houses, or in the houses of their friends. Vagabonds,
without visible property or vocation, are placed in workhouses,
where they are well cloathed, fed, lodged, and made to labour.
Nearly the same method of providing for the poor prevails
through all our states; and from Savannah to Portsmouth you will
seldom meet a beggar."

This was "without comparison better," he added, than the
sort of system where the only medical care or assistance available
to the poor would be "in a general hospital, where the sick, the
dying, and the dead are crammed together, in the same rooms,
and often in the same beds."

To fill these holes in the modern-day social safety net, we
must pass universal single-payer health insurance and strengthen

the Social Security system, while keeping its trust fund away from the grasping fingers of Wall Street's brokers.

Bring back the middle class by restoring the tax laws that created it.

As Thomas Jefferson pointed out, people living on the edge of existence shouldn't pay taxes on the necessities of life. On the other hand, those who have accumulated so much wealth that it may be "dangerous to democracy" should be subject to substantial taxation, particularly upon their death. America was created in part in response against hereditary aristocracy, and eliminating the inheritance tax—the traditional bulwark against dynastic behavior—is a terrible mistake.

In Sweden, one of the most democratic nations on Earth with one of the most vital middle classes and highest qualities of life, CEOs typically earn about 13 times as much as their average blue-collar workers. In Germany it's 15 times. Both nations have tax laws that discourage CEOs from moving into a royalty class with private jets and solid-gold bathroom fixtures. In the United States, however, the average CEO makes more than 411 times as much as the average worker.

The simple reality is that they are not working as hard as 411 people all at the same time. It's impossible. Nor are our CEOs 411 times smarter than their fellow workers.

Abusive pay for senior executives in American business not only harms companies by depriving them of operating revenue (every CEO means 411 workers who can't be hired, for example, or requires poverty-level pay from many workers to support), but implicitly sends the message that's explicit in royal societies— some people are simply much, much, much better and more deserving than others.

While hard work should and must be rewarded in order for a free and open society to exist, returning to the more steeply progressive tax rates that led to the creation of the American middle class in the era of 1947–1980 will be good for America and, ultimately, for corporate America as well.

Keep Social Security out of corporate hands.

Regardless of the current scare tactics of the investment banking industry—usually echoed by conservatives in the media—the Social Security trust fund is fine. At current levels of funding, it'll be solvent for at least another 30 years, and with only a tiny increase in taxes it can remain solvent forever.

So why all the hysteria? Because Wall Street is salivating at the prospect of getting its hands on the billions of dollars we've put into Social Security. They can take fees, administrative costs, and transaction costs. They can churn accounts and make money with our money. They can make billions, and they are spending millions on advertising and to buy conservative politicians to get the message out.

But, some ask, if Wall Street can make money investing Social Security, why shouldn't the government? The reason is simple: Social Security isn't a speculative investment. Social Security is a trust fund. It covers many things beyond old age and must be continuously solvent and available.

Along with this, Social Security must be accounted for separately on the government's books (the "lockbox" that Al Gore talked about in 2000). The Bush Jr. administration, like the Reagan and Bush administrations before it, has been lowering the deficit numbers given to the public each year by counting the Social Security surplus as "income from taxes" and then spending it out of general revenues. This looting of our pensions—so much like Enron and others looted their employees pensions—must stop, and only an act of Congress can make it happen.

Institute universal conscription.

One of the interesting features about many of the mature democracies of the world is that they require every high-school graduate to serve a year of either military or nonprofit service. At first blush, this may seem like an oppression by government, but history shows it's actually one of the best ways to prevent a military from becoming its own insular and dangerous subculture, existing within and threatening to influence the democracy that funds it, and to prevent the lower ranks of the military from being overwhelmed by people trying to escape poverty.

The Founders of America had long considered this same issue. Many were strongly against there ever being a standing army in America during times of peace, although they favored a navy, and today would no doubt favor an air force. The theory was that an army had too much potential for mischief, to oppress people or even stage a military coup and take over an elected government, as recently happened in Pakistan and has happened in several other nations over the past century.

Jefferson first suggested that we not have a standing army and wrote a series of letters in 1787, as the Constitution was being debated, urging James Madison to write it into the Constitution. The idea was for every able-bodied man in the nation to be a member of a local militia, under local control, with a gun in his house. If the nation was invaded, word would come down to the local level and every man in the country would be the army.

Switzerland has such an army, and many have suggested it's one reason why Hitler never tried to invade this neighbor.

To facilitate this, it was suggested that three things were necessary: a ban on a standing army, a provision making every able-bodied male a member of a local militia that could come under national control if the nation was attacked, and a provision making sure every male had a weapon handy if that day ever came. The debates led to a clumsy compromise, and the first two items ended up chopped away, leaving only the third. This remnant of that discussion is today known as our Second Amendment to the Constitution.

As president, Jefferson again tried to revive his argument. He cut the size of the army from over 300,000 men to fewer than 10,000, closing forts and cutting costs, while enlarging the navy. But he could never kill off the army altogether, because the citizen's militia had never been formalized at a federal level.

After he left office, he came to the conclusion that if every man couldn't be a member of a militia, every man should be a member of the army. This would ensure diversity of opinions in the army and minimize the chances of a military coup or a military culture that could become so powerful it would influence the government or seduce the president into playing commander in chief too often. He was also offended by the idea of an army that people would join only because they were so poor there was no other way to get an education and a job (for such people, he wanted universal free public education).

He wrote his thoughts on the topic in a June 18, 1813, letter to his old friend and future president James Monroe.

"It is more a subject of joy that we have so few of the desperate characters which compose modern regular armies," he wrote, pleased that his army had taken on a different nature during his tenure as president, just completed five years earlier. "But it proves more forcibly the necessity of obliging every citizen to be a soldier; this was the case with the Greeks and Romans, and must be that of every free State. Where there is no oppression there will be no pauper hirelings."

As history shows, Jefferson was more often right than wrong. We should institute a universal draft in the United States, with a strong public service option for those young men and women who don't want to go into the military. The result will be a generation of citizens who feel more bonded with and committed to their nation, who have experienced the critical developmental stage of a "rite of passage" into adulthood, and who have experienced more of America and the world than just their own neighborhood.

It would also help calm Dwight D. Eisenhower's fears. The old general left us the following warning as he left office in 1960: "In the councils of government, we must guard against the acquisition of unwarranted influence, whether sought or unsought, by the military-industrial complex. The potential for the disastrous rise of misplaced power exists and will persist.

"We must never let the weight of this combination endanger our liberties or democratic processes. We should take nothing for granted."

As Jefferson wrote to Monroe: "We must train and classify the whole of our male citizens, and make military instruction a regular part of collegiate education. We can never be safe till this is done."

Clean up the environment and public lands.

In 1970 a Democratic Congress presented Richard Nixon with the Environmental Protection Agency, and, seeing the handwriting on the wall, he embraced it. The truth that Nixon realized is that we cannot afford to continue to poison our own nest. The average American has more than one hundred different detectable cancer-causing synthetic compounds in his or her bloodstream, and part of the reason for this is that we test and regulate only the smallest fraction of those produced.

As mentioned earlier, the EPA has been spectacularly unsuccessful in protecting the health of Americans—and we're seeing an explosion in rates of everything from autism to birth defects as a result. Today one in three Americans will contract cancer, a disease that was so rare at the time of this nation's founding that— even with all the different names it went by—it's hard to find records of it occurring.

The same is true of the USDA's responsibility for our food

products, including its unwillingness to require genetically modified organisms be labeled despite overwhelming consumer sentiment in favor of such labels.

Responsibility for these failings falls squarely at the feet of corporate lobbyists and the conservative politicians who not only allow themselves to be bought and controlled by dirty industries but proclaim that such "support for industry" is a positive political virtue.

Conservative proposals for "Clear Skies" and "Healthy Forests" are cynical shams, bills largely written by the regulated industries themselves in tacit exchange for fat campaign contributions. It's time for we humans to take back the commons of our air and water, and the first step is to reject corporate participation in politics.

Strengthen the Sherman Anti-Trust Act and break up monopolies.

Since its passage in 1890 the Sherman Anti-Trust Act—which decreed monopolies that restrained trade illegal—has been modified numerous times by subsequent legislation. The last time it was used in a serious way was by President Jimmy Carter, in forcing the breakup of AT&T. The Reagan administration not only effectively stopped enforcement of the Act, but signaled to industry that monopolies and mergers were just fine. The result was the "M&A (mergers and acquisitions) Mania" of the 1980s that created some of the largest and most monopolistic enterprises the world had ever seen.

President Martin Van Buren (1837–1841) told Congress: "I am more than ever convinced of the dangers to which the free and unbiased exercise of political opinion—the only sure foundation and safeguard of republican government—would be exposed by any further increase of the already overgrown influence of corporate authorities."[133] As Jefferson had predicted two generations earlier, and Jimmy Carter tried to stop in the 1970s, the influence of corporate authorities has done nothing but grow since then.

If America is ever again to be the land of entrepreneurial opportunity, we must break up the large monopolies that sit on our body politic and economic like giant cancers. The process will lead—as it did with the breakup of AT&T—to an increase in shareholder value, innovation, and competition.

Bust up the media conglomerates and restore a robust free press.

True freedom of the press isn't just a function of the press having freedom from government regulation, but, most important, having freedom from corporate power. Several very simple and straightforward laws, the media equivalents of the Sherman Anti-Trust act, can facilitate this.

First, pass a law that any media outlet (newspaper, radio station or network, television station or network) must have a single owner, be it human or corporate. That owner cannot be owned by, beholden to, or subject to the manipulation of any other person or corporation.

The Sherman Act states: "Every contract, combination in the form of trust or otherwise, or conspiracy, in restraint of trade or commerce among the several States, or with foreign nations, is declared to be illegal. Every person who shall make any contract or engage in any combination or conspiracy hereby declared to be illegal shall be deemed guilty of a felony."

Similarly, the Media Single Ownership Act could state something to the effect of: "Every contract, combination in the form of trust or otherwise, or conspiracy, in restraint of freedom of the press by individual ownership and management of each press outlet, is declared to be illegal. Every person or corporation who shall make any contract or engage in any combination or conspiracy hereby declared to be illegal shall be deemed guilty of a felony." Furthermore, to ensure that a free press both serves and responds to its local community, its owners should be required by law to reside within the listening, viewing, or daily delivery area of that media.

As of this writing, the FCC is fighting Congress over whether a single corporation should be able to own radio stations that reach a total of 35 percent or 45 percent of American citizens (among other things). This is absurd. Each individual station should be completely locally owned. And, for democracy to become uncontaminated, networks must be stand-alone corporations devoted to the single purpose of providing their programming, rather than parts of larger business empires with their fingers in defense contracting, industries that produce toxic waste, or other areas that produce conflicts of interest with news operations.

In *Democracy in America,* de Tocqueville envisioned a time when democracy itself would teeter on the brink. He was at an apparent loss to describe his vision of America's future. The term "megamedia" hadn't yet been invented, and so, he wrote, "I am trying myself to choose an expression which will accurately convey the whole of the idea I have formed of it, but in vain; the old words despotism and tyranny are inappropriate: the thing itself is new; and since I cannot name it, I must attempt to define it."

Describing a future with an "innumerable multitude of men, all equal and alike, incessantly endeavoring to procure the petty and paltry pleasures with which they glut their lives," de Tocqueville saw "an immense and tutelary [care-giving] power, which takes upon itself alone to secure their gratifications."

In a startling description of a television-addicted nation, he added, "The will of man is not shattered, but softened, bent, and guided: men are seldom forced by it to act, but they are constantly restrained from acting: such a power does not destroy, but it prevents existence; it does not tyrannize, but it compresses, enervates, extinguishes, and stupefies a people, till each nation is reduced to be nothing better than a flock of timid and industrious animals."

Timid and industrious animals is not the prescription for a vibrant democracy, and applying the philosophy of the Sherman Act to any media that purports to produce news is an important first step toward revitalizing our system of government.

Make the "revolving door" between industry and regulatory agencies illegal.

Today it's not uncommon for executives of regulated industries to go directly from industry into the halls of government, serve for a year or two while supervising the revision of laws affecting their industry, and then return to their industry with an ample increase in salaries and bonuses. Similarly, it's common for corporations that contract with the military to recruit senior military officials—at large salaries—to their companies in the years immediately following those officials having negotiated or authorized major military purchases from the same companies.

To restore integrity to government, the revolving door must close. All government employees—including retired elected officials—should be barred for at least three years from working in any industry or any position that principally involves or derives its revenues from, or is regulated by, the government agencies with which they have dealt. Similarly, government employees in regulatory decision-making capacities should face the same prohibition against working in the private sector when it involves an industry in the area they regulated.

Use tax incentives and grants to jump-start alternative energy.

Jimmy Carter pioneered this during his time in the White House, and the alternative energy industry was birthed from his tax cuts, tax credits, and grants for solar, wind, water, and other power sources. When Ronald Reagan came into office heavily indebted to the oil industry, one of his first acts of office was to remove Jimmy Carter's solar collectors from the roof of the White House. He then proceeded to gut Carter's alternative energy programs, and they've lain dormant ever since.

But building a civilization on liquefied fossils and then thinking it will last forever makes no sense. According to figures on the British Petroleum website, world oil reserves divided by current rates of consumption imply we'll run critically low of oil in our children's lifetimes.[134] In the absence of viable and functioning alternatives, this will cause a world-devastating shock to the world's economies and threaten democracy worldwide.

To prevent finding ourselves in a dangerously resource-poor situation, we must immediately move to make the United States energy independent and to convert our centralized electric grids into more efficient and local (and locally owned) sources of power generation.

Reserve human rights for humans, not "aggregated capital."

In April 1993, Nike Corporation argued before the United States Supreme Court that, as a "person," it should have the constitutionally protected right to lie. It wasn't under oath, after all, when it engaged in a PR campaign to claim that its subcontractors had cleaned up their labor practices. If humans can say, "Honey, that looks great on you" and not mean it, then a corporation should be able to say any damn thing it wants to, too. After all, doesn't the First Amendment apply to corporations as well as to humans?

The Supreme Court chose not to rule in the case, kicking it back the California Supreme Court—which had already ruled that Nike didn't have the right to lie—and the case was settled out of court with a payment by Nike to Marc Kasky, the plaintiff. But it illustrates the growing trend among corporations to claim human rights such as privacy, rights against self-incrimination, and the right to cry "discrimination" when a community says no to a big-box retailer.

This trend is incredibly dangerous to democracy. The solution is to pass legislation defining "person" as "a human being" so corporations can no longer claim the Bill of Rights. Communities in several states have already done this, but for the campaign to be successful overall it'll have to be national. Let your legislators know.

And regarding the principle of equal access to government process, ask yourself this: would *you* have been able to afford to take such a ridiculous request all the way to the Supreme Court, just in case you might win?

We need to fully understand that the way the system works today, the deck is extremely stacked in favor of the monstrously large players. Usually, that's the biggest corporations.

Keep church and state separate.

In the second year of his presidency, Thomas Jefferson decided that he would not follow the example of John Adams and declare a national day of fasting and prayer. He was so firmly committed to the idea that the church should be separated from the state that, having already outlawed federal subsidies to churches (even for charitable work), he wouldn't allow himself, as president, even to mention prayer.

As he noted in a January 21, 1802, note to Attorney General Levi Lincoln, "I do not proclaim fastings and thanksgivings, as my predecessors did. . . . I know it will give great offence to the New England clergy; but the advocate of religious freedom is to expect neither peace nor forgiveness from them."

Just as the wall between feudal corporate forces and state has been weakened since Jefferson's time, so, too, has the wall between church and state. Churches should be absolutely free to go about their business, and even have their houses of worship exempt from taxation (although nothing else). But the multimillion-dollar funding of church charities affiliated with Jerry Falwell, Pat Robertson, Reverend Moon, and other religious leaders who have traded their influence with their parishioners for the state's bag of silver must come to an end. The state should no more subsidize churches—regardless of the good they may do—than should churches tell the state how to govern. Both are matters between people and their churches, and people and their government.

Make the United States more democratic in its elections.

Set limits on campaign spending; consider public funding.

Almost every other mature democracy has dealt with the problem of corporations corrupting politicians through one of two simple measures. Either they have public funding of campaigns, or they put spending caps on political campaigns and ban lobbying (which, in America, was called "bribery and influencing" until relatively recently). If every American taxpayer contributed $5 each per year, it would generate over a billion dollars every two years to pay for election campaigns across the nation. Combine that with shortening the campaign cycle to a few months and a requirement that radio, TV, and newspapers devote a certain small amount of time or space to political debate, and you have kicked the corporate special interests out of government and restored decency to politics.

This is not a new idea. President Theodore Roosevelt, for example, was one of its most ardent proponents, saying, "I again recommend a law prohibiting all corporations from contributing to the campaign expenses of any party.... Let individuals contribute as they desire; but let us prohibit in effective fashion all corporations from making contributions for any political purpose, directly or indirectly."[135]

Institute "instant runoff" voting, to make minority parties viable.

Most democracies in the world today have healthy multiparty systems, but older ones (such as America and the UK) don't. The reason is simple: the idea of *proportional representation* hadn't been conceived when the older democracies were formed.

It wasn't until the 1840s that John Stuart Mill first wrote about it, which is why most democracies formed after 1850 have healthy multiparty systems that represent a broad range of political opinions. Older democracies are usually two-party states.

Knowing that there was a deficiency in the American system, James Madison wrote long letters and articles begging America's politicians not to form political parties, but it was all for naught. By the late 1790s, the Democratic Republicans had split off from the Federalists and we've had a two-party system in the United States ever since.

The problem is that we have winner-take-all elections. If more than two candidates run, it's possible for a candidate to take the seat with fewer than a majority of the votes—and, as Madison noted, then the people are represented by a candidate whose opinions reflect only a minority of Americans. (A good example was the presidential election of 2000, in which Bush got three million fewer votes than his opposition, Gore and Nader.)

There are two solutions to this problem. The first is proportional representation, as they have in Israel, Germany, and many other nations. If there are 100 seats in parliament, and party "A" gets 22 percent of the vote, they get 22 seats. Party "B" that got 19 percent of the vote gets 19 seats, whereas Party "C" that got 31 percent of the vote gets 31 seats, and so on, to 100 percent. The result is that politicians have to form alliances and coalitions, and learn to work together, and it guarantees that pretty much all the opinions of We the People are represented by *somebody* in parliament.

Given that it's unlikely we'll amend our Constitution to allow for proportional representation any day soon, a quick solution is Instant Runoff Voting (IRV), as proposed by legislators in over 30 states and already instituted in some cities such as San Francisco.[136] If an IRV system had been in place during the 2000 presidential election, for example, everybody would have been presented with a two-tiered ballot. For each office, you could have selected your first choice and a second choice if you want.

Let's say that your first choice was Ralph Nader, but you'd tolerate Al Gore. You could have picked Nader as number one and Gore as number two.

Then, if no candidate got more than 50 percent of the vote (as none of them did), all ballots that didn't go for one of the top two candidates would be counted again, using the second-choice votes. Most of Nader's votes would have become Gore votes, and Gore would have been declared the winner. No candidate could win without being selected (first or second) on a majority of ballots.

IRV encourages multiparty participation in elections without creating the odd situation we have today in which, when you vote for a third (or fourth) party candidate, you actually hurt the mainstream candidate with whom he or she is most closely aligned. IRV works well, and Australia has adopted a form of it nationwide. Many communities across America have adopted it for their local elections, and a few states are considering it. Not surprisingly, the Green Party is working hard to get it passed everywhere in the United States.

And it should be passed. Because—regardless of your political beliefs—it enhances the vitality of democracy and increases participation, because nobody need feel that their vote would be pointless.

Given Jefferson's belief in the value of giving people a voice, it seems certain that he would have approved.

Abolish the Electoral College.

The Electoral College separates We the People from the process of electing the president and was put into place as the result of a series of uneasy compromises during the Constitutional Convention and then went through several subsequent modifications. Its modern consequences are well known today: although George W. Bush "won" in the Electoral College, Al Gore received more than a half-million more votes than Bush.

On December 31, 1800, Thomas Jefferson, locked in his own electoral battle, wrote a letter to his old friend Tenche Coxe that was so private he noted he wouldn't trust it "to the fidelity of the post-office" (he suspected Adams of having his agents open and read his opponents' mail), in which he complained to Coxe that the Electoral College was a mistake. "The contrivance in the Constitution for marking the votes works badly, because it does not enounce precisely the true expression of the public will," he said bluntly.

It was true in 1800 and it's true today. The Electoral College is an anachronism and should be ended, finally allowing the people of America to directly elect their president.

Get corporations out of the voting process.

The beating heart of democracy is the vote. In Germany, as in many European nations, ballots are cast by paper and counted by government employees, with observers from the various parties looking on. News organizations conduct exit polls, and although it takes a few days to count the votes, the results are known within hours of the polls closing because the exit polls are never more than 1 percent off. With this system there is no doubt as to the accuracy of the vote; it is entirely in the hands of people who have no interest in controlling or manipulating it, and it is totally auditable.

In America, when we introduced electronic voting machines, suddenly our exit polls became so inaccurate that the polling companies shut down their operations in the 2002 elections. Stories of voting machine failures are legion, and the fact that conservative activists run several of the voting machine companies has raised eyebrows around the world. That those companies have also claimed that citizens have no right to know how their machines work (open source code) is a mockery of the open democratic process.

We must ban corporations from involvement in our vote. If we decide to use voting machines, they must be manufactured for government but owned by government, run by government in an open and transparent manner, and not be connected to insecure phone lines or the Internet, where they can be hacked. For-profit corporations, whose primary motivation is profit and not democracy, have no business in handling the heartbeat of democracy.

Make the UN more democratic.

Having cleaned up our own house, let's do the same with the United Nations.

Conservatives regularly dismiss the UN when its actions don't serve their desires, and the institution has suffered greatly over the years, particularly at the hands of Republican presidents. But the flaw in the UN isn't the one they point to—that we lose some power by agreeing to participate in an international democracy. The flaw in the UN is that it purports to be a democratic institution, with its members representing their people back home, but this is not true for the more than 40 member nations that are dictatorships.

If we want to ensure peace and our safety by bringing about worldwide democracy, and transforming the UN into a more democratic institution, let's begin by saying that only real democracies can participate fully, and strip voting and veto rights from any nation that the UN itself doesn't certify as being run by a democratic government elected in free and fair elections.

(This may put the United States at a slight disadvantage if the UN were to investigate the massive vote fraud perpetrated in Florida just before the 2000 election when Kathleen Harris and Jeb Bush conspired to purge the voter rolls and deny as many as seventy thousand law-abiding citizens of their right to vote— mostly from African American [and, thus, Democratic-voting] districts. Nonetheless, the risk is worth it. The UN could start certifying the United States with the next election cycle, as it'll take a while for them to get up to speed in certifying the democracies of many other nations as well.)

Take action.

This list is by no means complete as a template for restoring democracy to America, but it's a beginning. Some of its items are easily done in a single congressional session or by voter ballot initiative, whereas others may be the work of a generation. Hopefully it will stimulate discussion and debate—the lifeblood of democracy—about these and other issues, and lead us to take American democracy back from the corporate feudal lords who are working so hard to smother it.

What Would Jefferson Do?

Long before I was struck with cancer, I felt something stirring in American society. It was a sense among the people of the country—Republicans and Democrats alike—that something was missing from their lives, something crucial. I was trying to position the Republican Party to take advantage of it. But I wasn't exactly sure what "it" was.

My illness helped me to see that what was missing in society is what was missing in me: a little heart, a lot of brotherhood. . . . Love each other a little more, care about each other, and get away from that [dirty, negative] kind of politics.

—Lee Atwater (1951–1991),
Republican strategist and creator of G. H. W. Bush's
devastating "Willie Horton" attack ad; while dying of
brain cancer at age 40[137]

All of us—no matter what our current political persuasion— can participate in returning democracy to our nation. Let us not, like Atwater, wait until we're near death to take action.

Let us also not fall prey to the pervasive cynicism that has gripped much of the world today, which would encourage us to think there's no point in trying. People rarely show up for local democratic forums such as town council and school board meetings; even fewer people volunteer or run for such offices; and the number of "nonvoters" has exploded. This cynicism has led to an epidemic of nonparticipation in democratic processes, and we must end it.

Such resignation among voters certainly benefits those in power, because the less likely someone is to vote, the less chance there is that peaceable "regime change" will happen when voters throw them out. Thus, the mighty—in this case, the largest corporations and individuals with dynastic wealth—have a big stake in perpetuating the myth that democracy always fails. They want us to believe that there's no hope, no point in fighting, because they will win control of our nation, and therefore we should simply give up in our attempts at reform.

Should we just give up? Is despair an appropriate response to the overwhelming power of what President Cleveland called "aggregated capital"?

"We do not have the luxury of despair," answered Vermont's Independent congressman Bernie Sanders when I asked him that question on my radio program in December of 2003. "In fact," Sanders added, "despair is precisely what the people who own this country and have the power want you to feel. They don't want you to fight back."

Sanders said, "Progressive viewpoints are, in fact, held by the vast majority of the people. People want health care for all; they don't want the disgrace of having the highest rate of childhood poverty in the industrialized world."

And, he pointed out, "If we become burdened with despair and give up, Tom DeLay and George Bush will laugh all the way to the bank."

The reality is that every time Americans have confronted a serious social problem of political origin, it seemed at first impossible to overcome. But people of goodwill, vision, and perseverance fought for years to bring an end to slavery, the oppression of women, and the subjugation of Native Americans.

Although none of these battles is over, all are well past or near the turning point, showing that dramatic cultural and governmental change is possible—and, in fact, is inevitable when enough people wake up and speak out. True, systemic change never happens from the top down: it's always from the bottom up. In virtually every case of positive change in the history of democracy, there was each time a groundswell of popular support and a chorus of "average persons'" voices that preceded a nation's leaders taking action.

We can speak out.

One of the lessons that Congressman Sanders taught me is that members of Congress do listen to their constituents. Most read the "Letters to the Editor" section of their hometown newspapers regularly, and even if they don't listen to every call or read every e-mail or letter from their constituents, they have staffers who summarize these for them. And—as conservative activists have discovered over the past 20 years—politicians take citizens' opinions seriously: they realize their political survival may be at stake.

The phone number for the United States Capitol is 202-224-3121. You can ask for any congressperson or senator and speak with a member of his or her staff. Be sure to keep your calls to a single subject, and try to present your opinion in a single sentence or two: brevity increases the probability your concern will be understood and communicated to your representative.

More effective than calling, e-mailing, mailing, or faxing is to organize a small group (five to fifty is usually sufficient) of people who share your perspective and ask your representative for a personal meeting at his or her local office the next time he or she is in the district or state. Elected representatives rarely avoid such displays of people power, and if your group is articulate, brief, and to the point, you may well influence your representative's thinking.

Other ways to get on your elected representative's radar screen are to write op-ed articles for your local paper, create or join a local advocacy group and meet with the local media, and write personal letters to your elected officials.

And don't forget the option of running for elective office yourself.

Transforming democracy for the better

As Jefferson pointed out, times change and democracies must change to meet them. The disparities in wealth in America today would be mind-boggling to the Founders, as would the costs of health care and old age.

It's entirely appropriate for each generation to ask the simple question "What sort of nation do we want to live in?" and then look for ways, consistent with the Constitution and its processes, to create just that sort of nation. If Germany has learned some good lessons regarding single-payer health care, we should feel free to borrow them and incorporate them into our democracy. If Sweden has learned how to make retirement work, it's something we should consider. And so on.

Now we are confronted with the problem of a relative minority of people in our culture who hold massive wealth and power. They use this to mold our opinions in their media, to control our legislators by making obscene campaign contributions just to protect their wealth and power, and to control our lives by owning the great majority of jobs. They believe that the aristocracy and feudal power of giant corporations and enormous personal wealth entitles them to decide and dictate how all Americans should live—completely removing American freedoms from our hands.

They are wrong, and the vast majority of Americans know it.

We have not just a duty but an obligation to confront and

defy this sort of power. Our first obligation is to the generations that came before us and fought for democracy: they didn't fight, die, or work so hard to bring about a new corporate aristocracy.

Our second obligation is to the generations that will follow us: we hold this world in trust, having borrowed it from them, and they will not easily forgive us if we bequeath it to them in worse shape than we inherited it.

And our third obligation is to the present: to return democracy to America so that our foreign adventures will be restrained by democratic processes, our domestic taxing and spending priorities will reflect our true needs, and our courts, legislatures, and governors and president will answer to us, rather than corporate special interests.

The Founders endured enormous hardship and loss to break free of an oppressive government that was then the most powerful force in the world. The effort and sacrifice this required was extraordinary, and following that horrific war they established a liberal democracy whose purpose is to serve and protect the people, so that control should never again reside in a small set of powerful hands.

Conservative historians have, for centuries, asserted that selfish men founded the country, with only rhetorical concern for privacy, liberty, and human rights. John Adams said democracy couldn't last, and the grandfather of conservative thought, Edmund Burke, said some kinds of people just aren't good enough to be involved in government.

But democracy has lasted, and people from all walks of life have become good and effective leaders both locally and in Washington. The greatness of the Constitution has been proven, Jefferson's belief in We the People has been validated, and the American vision of democracy has infected and energized the world.

Yet today there are forces at work who again want to return us to a feudal world in which only a very few have power, and the masses are terrified to lose their jobs for lack of other prospects.

Thus, we must never forget the words the Founders set down in pen and ink when they began our country:

> We hold these truths to be self-evident . . .
>
> That Governments are instituted among Men, deriving their just powers from the consent of the governed,
>
> That whenever any Form of Government becomes destructive of these ends, it is the Right of the People to alter or to abolish it, and to institute new Government, laying its foundation on such principles and organizing its powers in such form, as to them shall seem most likely to effect their Safety and Happiness.
>
> When a long train of abuses and usurpations . . . [provides evidence of] a design to reduce them under absolute Despotism, it is their right, it is their duty, to throw off such Government, and to provide new Guards for their future security.

Despair is not an option, action is necessary, and both biology and history tell us that democracy is the right path to take. By exposing the conservative frauds and presenting the realistic and practical possibilities of a democratic republic uncontaminated by corporate special interests, we can bring about a healthier, happier, and more peaceful America and world. But to do so will require that we each become activists, we each become passionate, and we each speak our truth, promote our vision, and vote our conscience.

The Founders ended the Declaration of Independence with these words:

> For the support of this Declaration, with a firm reliance on the protection of divine Providence, we mutually pledge to each other our Lives, our Fortunes and our sacred Honor.

Can we do anything less?

AFTERWORD BY ROBERT WOLFF

When Thom and Louise came to visit me here in Hawai'i, a few years ago, we must have "talked story," as we say here, for many hours. I know we talked about indigenous and aboriginal peoples and how different their way of life is. I have lived among non-Western people most of my life and still find it difficult to live in our Western world. Yes, indigenous people are often poor, compared with us, but they live within the limits of their environment. They may not have all the gadgets and gimmicks we have, although almost everyone in the world now has heard radio and seen television, but native people, even now, have a different way of being with each other. People are more equal than we are in the West. Men do not dominate; in many countries of Southeast Asia, women are the entrepreneurs, not men. Children are wanted, cherished everywhere, and never "owned" as we think of ours. Children are not only seriously listened to, but heard. People accept and respect one another for who they are. Disagreements are worked out verbally, without courts and almost always without violence.

How else could we have survived for a hundred thousand years and more?

I grew up in Indonesia with people whose culture stressed the importance of never telling another what to do. In that culture a mother will ask a child of three if she wants to take this medicine. If the child says no, that's it. Parents do not have ambitions for their children other than to help them become who they are born to be.

We have lost that feeling of equality; we are forced to think hierarchically. Someone has to be the boss. Someone must own. Ursula K. Le Guin in one of her books says, "Owning is owing; having is hoarding." True, but we have forgotten. We have forgotten so much! Lost under layers of shoulds and mustn'ts. Lost because we have become used to being entertained instead of living our lives. Huge industries producing entertainment including advertising and propaganda have created a world that is not human any more.

In 1960 I was a research associate professor at the University of California, San Francisco Medical Center. They sent me and my family out to Malaysia to do research in "dietary behavior"— as a wit said, why people eat what they do and not what they should. I am a social psychologist and I speak Malay, the language spoken in Malaysia and Indonesia. I worked in a few villages that I visited regularly, finding again the world I had known as a child. Proud and kind people, patient, unambitious in our eyes perhaps, but knowing themselves rich in their culture. Never arguing, but discussing important matters in what must seem to a Westerner almost a dreamlike way: a word here, a short sentence, long pauses. People saying what is in their heart; people really listening to what is in other people's hearts. And always: respect.

In the West, discussions are often monologues; while someone else is talking we are formulating what we want to say when we can interrupt.

My daughter-in-law is from an island in the South Pacific. Their language has no word for "thank you" because, as she explained, "Of course we help when it is needed, why should we thank? We help each other!"

In Malaysia, quite by accident I meet the Sng'oi (also written Senoi), one of the tribes of the aboriginal peoples of Malaysia. It is still hard to express what I felt when I first met these simple, almost naked people. Their smiles . . . their wide open faces. A sense of recognition, something deep down . . .

Later I discovered that all travelers and writers who met other aboriginal people in Africa, in Australia, in other parts of Asia, and in South America, had very similar experiences. My favorite account is Peter Matthiessen's in his book *The Tree Where Man Was Born*. He and a companion meet a small band of Hadza, an aboriginal group of East Africa:

> Shy, they await in a half-circle, much less tall than their bows. *"Tsifiaqua!"* they murmur, and our people say, *"Tsifiaqua mtana,"* and then the hunters say, *"M-taa-na."* (*Tsifiaqua* is "afternoon" as in "good afternoon," and *mtana* is "nice" as in "nice day," and *"tsifiaqua m-taa-na,"* as the hunters say it, may mean "Oh beautiful day!") I am smiling wholeheartedly too, and so is Enderlein; my smile seems to travel right around my head. The encounter in the sunny wood is much too simple, too beautiful to be real, yet it is more real than anything I have known in a long time. I feel a warm flood of relief, as if I had been away all my life and had come home again—I want to embrace them all.

That was what I felt. I had come home, these people were the essence of humanness, this is how we have always been. This is what it was to be human.

In this book Thom has gathered information from scientists and philosophers through the ages who have come to the same conclusion. We, our species, survived for a hundred thousand years by living in close harmony with each other and the earth. As Native Americans say: "All my relations—all the people and animals and rocks and trees I have a relationship with."

Reading this book brought back experiences I had not seen in this light.

I was in Rotterdam when the Germans invaded Holland and Belgium on their way to France. May 1940. The Dutch government fled to England. For days, weeks, we were without any government. And the most amazing thing happened: *Nothing very much changed!*

Nobody went crazy. Of course we were concerned. We were scared. We did not know what would happen, or even what was happening a few miles away. Phones did not work, electricity went out, there was no water. Some stores opened and then closed, others opened for an hour. Few cars on the road. But life went on. Neighbors helped neighbors. We made do; we helped each other.

During an occupation that became a nightmare, this sense of community intensified. I discovered that when I needed support I could always find it among the poorest. Relying on each other was strong at the end of the occupation, a time of utter chaos. When Germany capitulated, there were no Allied troops to come to western Holland where I was. We, the Resistance, were given armbands and told to keep order. We had been trained in cellars, barely knew how to handle the guns we had, and many of us refused to carry them.

The Allies did not disarm the Germans, so they were told to stay in their barracks with their guns.

Even then, life went on. Everyone helped organize the distribution of food that was dropped from planes for a starving population. There was no electricity, usually no water, no gas, no fuel, no telephones. And no money. But again nobody went crazy. Neighbors helped neighbors. As far as I know, no hospital was working, but an old woman nursed an older woman, a man rode his injured son in a wheelbarrow to someone who was a nurse. I still remember how, starved as we were after what is now known as the Hunger Winter, we shared what food we had.

Under all the layers of what we call civilization, that basic quality of democracy was there. That is how we have always survived.

In the 1950s, when I was a student at the University of Michigan, the U.S. government did research on how people react in disasters (at the time we expected atomic war). A large federal grant made it possible to interview people in towns that had experienced a sudden and disastrous disruption of "the system." The results of this Disaster Project? Ordinary people picked up the pieces, instantaneously. Nobody panicked. When a city was burning and police and ambulances could not reach a large part of the city, a schoolboy directed traffic, a housewife took care of lost children. A teacher organized distribution of water. Life went on because our basic democracy, our basic instincts to cooperate, to help each other, immediately took over.

Yes, I like the idea that democracy is not a political system, but it is our basic humanity, it means we are in this together. "We the people," not as a bunch of individuals, each striving for power and wealth at the expense of others; "survival of the fittest" not interpreted to mean that only the most ruthless survive. No, "We the people" are a coherent group of humans who know and accept that we are dependent on each other for survival as a species.

"Democracy," as Thom uses the term in this book, is the most basic pattern of who we humans really are. We survived by living in close-knit groups as equals, learning how to live together by communicating with respect, not force.

It seems so obvious: how could we have survived any other way?

And I know that this basic pattern is still in us because I have experienced that when what we think of as the infrastructure of civilization suddenly disappears, we pick up that way of being without hesitation, we help each other, without distinction of gender or race or age.

Thank you, Thom, for reminding us who we are.

---

robert wolff is the author of *Original Wisdom: Stories of an Ancient Way of Knowing* (Inner Traditions, 2001).

Notes

1. UN Development Programme, "Deepening Democracy in a Fragmented World," www.undp.org/hdr2002/overview.pdf.

2. Holly Sklar, "Raw Deal for Workers on Minimum Wage Anniversary," Knight-Ridder/Tribune News Service, June 24, 2003 (www.commondreams.org/views03/0625=09.htm).

3. www.usatoday.com/money/perfi/general/2003-09-14-middle-cover_x.htm.

4. Consumer Bankruptcy Project at Harvard University, cited by *USA Today*, www.usatoday.com/money/perfi/general/2003-09-14-middle-cover_x.htm.

5. "2004: USA PATRIOT Act Update," news release from the American Civil Liberties Union (ACLU), January 9, 2004.

6. www.fair.org/activism/fcc-factsheet.html and ibid.

7. President Grover Cleveland's 4th Annual Message (what today we call a "State of the Union Address") (1st term) presented in written form to Congress, December 3, 1888.

8. From the Federal Election Commission's website, www.fec.gov/pages/tonote.htm: 2000, 51.3%; 1996, 49.6%; 1992, 55%; 1988, 50%; 1984, 53%; 1980, 53%; 1976, 54%; 1972, 55%; 1968, 60.4%; 1964, 62%; 1960, 63%.

9. UN Development Programme, *Human Development Report*, www.undp.org/hdr2002/facts.html.

10. Reprinted in 1972 in the journal *Industrial Research*.

11. J. David Singer and Melvin Small, *The Wages of War, 1816–1965: A Statistical Handbook* (New York: John Wiley, 1972), and *Resort to Arms: International and Civil Wars, 1816–1980* (Beverly Hills, CA: Sage, 1982).

12. Available free online at www.hawaii.edu/powerkills/note15.htm.

13. www.hawaii.edu/powerkills/personal.htm.

14. Jack S. Levy, "Domestic Politics and War," *Journal of Interdisciplinary History* 18 (1988): 653–673.

15. "How Democracy Prevents Civic Catastrophes" by Per Ahlmark, former deputy prime minister of Sweden, speech delivered to the European Liberal Democrats, European Parliament, Krakow, April 8, 1999; unwatch.org/speeches/demcat.html.

16. *Merriam-Webster's Dictionary* online, 2003, at www.merriam-webster.com.

17. Various sources, including www.quotedb.com/quotes/1274.

18. *American Heritage Dictionary* (Boston: Houghton Mifflin, 1983).

19. Alfons J. Beitzinger, *Edward G. Ryan: Lion of the Law,* State Historical Society of Wisconsin, May 1997.

20. UN Development Programme, "Deepening Democracy in a Fragmented World."

21. "Benjamin Franklin's Marginalia, 1770," in Leonard Labaree, ed., *Papers of Benjamin Franklin* (New Haven: Yale University Press, 1965), vol. 17, p. 381.

22. *Journals of the Continental Congress* (Washington, DC: Government Printing Office, 1904–1905), 3:433.

23. Richard Henry Lee letter to General Charles Lee, Philadelphia, May 27, 1776, Collections of the New-York Historical Society.

24. *Pennsylvania Gazette,* May 29, 1776.

25. Cara Richards, *The Oneida People* (Phoenix: Indian Tribal Series, 1974).

26. John Adams, *Defence of the Constitutions of Government of the United States of America* (Hall and Sellers), March 1787.

27. Thomas Jefferson letter to John Adams, June 11, 1812.

28. Horatio Hale, *The Iroquois Book of Rites* (D.G. Brinton, 1883), p. 21.

29. For example, if a person committed the ultimate crime of murder, Lafitan wrote that the killer's punishment was particularly fitting to his crime: "The dead man's body was stretched on poles in the air and the murderer was forced to stand under it and let fall on him the pus which flowed from the corpse. A plate, put beside him for his food, was soon filled with the filth which fell from above. To have this plate moved aside a little, cost him a present of seven-hundred beads of wampum [paid to the dead man's family]. Finally, he remained in this wretched position as long as the dead man's relatives wished and had to give them a new present after he had won their consent." Joseph Lafitan, *Customs of the American Indians Compared with Customs of Primitive Times* (Toronto: Champlain Society, 1974; originally published in 1724), vol. 1.

30. The British chieftain's name is often published as Galbacus, but Aikin notes: "The scene of this celebrated engagement is by Gordon (Itin. Septent.) supposed to be in Strathern, near a place now called the *Kirk of Comerie,* where are the remains of two Roman Camps. Mr. Pennant, however, in his *Tour in 1772,* Part II, P. 96, gives reasons which appear well founded for dissenting from Gordon's opinion. His account is as follows. 'Near this place (Comerie) on a plain of some extent, is the famous camp which Mr. Gordon contends to have been occupied by Agricola, immediately before the battle of Mons Grampius; and to which, in order to support his argument, he gives the name of Galgachan, as if derived from Galgacus, leader of the Caledonians, at that fatal engagement.' "

31. "*Peace given to the world* is the very frequent inscription on the Roman medals," notes Aikin in this book's footnote to this passage.

32. "We must, therefore, acquiesce in the necessity, which denounces our separation, and hold them [the English], as we hold the rest of mankind, enemies in war, in peace friends" (from Tacitus, noted earlier).

33. The first sentence of the U.S. Constitution says: "We the People of the United States, in Order to form a more perfect Union, establish Justice, insure domestic Tranquility, provide for the common defence, promote the general Welfare, and secure the Blessings of Liberty to ourselves and our Posterity, do ordain and establish this Constitution for the United States of America."

34. By the Electoral College.

35. Here's the act: ". . . it shall be felony for any Person, which now doth, or within four Years last past heretofore hath or here after shall Inhabit or belong to this Island, to serve in America in an hostile manner, under any Foreign Prince, state or Potentate in Amity with his Majesty of Great Britain, without special License for so doing, under the hand and seal of the Governour or Commander in chief of this Island for the time being, and that all and every such offender or offenders contrary to the true intent of this Act being thereof duly convicted in his Majesties supreme Court of Judicature within this Island to which court authority is hereby given to hear and to determine the same as other cases of Felony, shall suffer pains of Death without the benefit of Clergy.

"Be it further Enacted by the Authority aforesaid, that all and every Person or Persons that shall any way knowingly Entertain, Harbour, Conceal, *Trade or hold any correspondence by Letter or otherwise with any Person or Persons, that shall be deemed or adjudged to be Privateers,* Pirats or other offenders within the construction of this Act, and that shall not readily endeavour to the best of his or their Power to apprehend or cause to be apprehended, such Offender or Offenders, shall be liable to be prosecuted as accessories and Confederates, and to suffer such pains and penalties as in such case by law is Provided."

36. www.britannica.com.

37. Esther Forbes, *Paul Revere and the World He Lived In* (Boston: Houghton Mifflin, 1942).

38. Ibid.

39. Ibid.

40. George R. T. Hewes, *Retrospect of the Boston Tea Party with a Memoir of George R. T. Hewes, a Survivor of the Little Band of Patriots Who Drowned the Tea in Boston Harbor in 1773* (New York: S. S. Bliss, 1834).

41. A slang term of the time for *peasant,* based on the 1577 *Rusticus in Gallia* portrait of a French peasant by Hans Weigel.

42. Dennis Brindell Fradin, *The Signers: The 56 Stories Behind the Declaration of Independence* (New York: Walker & Company, 2002). Rush H. Limbaugh Jr. also wrote a marvelous summary of these men's lives, titled "The Americans Who Risked Everything," reprinted in his son's "Limbaugh Letter" in September 1997.

43. Ibid.

44. Ibid.

45. Ibid.

46. Adolf Hitler speech at Koenigsberg, March 25, 1938.

47. John Adams letter to John Taylor, April 15, 1814, in Charles Francis Adams, ed., *The Works of John Adams* (1851) 6:484.

48. Charles A. and Mary R. Beard, *The Rise of American Civilization* (London: The MacMillan Company, 1927). (All subsequent Beard quotes refer to this edition.)

49. Bernard Bailyn, *To Begin the World Anew: The Genius and Ambiguities of the American Founders* (New York: Knopf, 2003).

50. Kevin Phillips, *Wealth and Democracy: A Political History of the American Rich* (New York: Broadway Books, 2003).

51. Forrest McDonald, *We the People: The Economic Origins of the Constitution* (Chicago: University of Chicago Press, 1958).

52. George Washington turned this and the other records of the Convention over to the Department of State in 1796. Secretary of State John Q. Adams supervised their publication in 1819 and they now appear in numerous sources, including Farrand's *The Records of the Federal Convention of 1787*, published in 1911 by Farrand in New York.

53. Ibid.

54. Fawn M. Brodie, *Thomas Jefferson: An Intimate History* (New York: W. W. Norton & Company, 1974).

55. Thomas G. West, *Vindicating the Founders: Race, Sex, Class, and Justice in the Origins of America* (Lanham, MD: Rowman & Littlefield, 1997).

56. Ibid.

57. "The Forgotten Population: The Free Black Community in Washington County, 1800–1850," www.restoringthevoices.org/popwas4.html.

58. www.innercity.org/columbiaheights/newspaper/slavery. html.

59. The law read: "that each woman servant got with child by her master shall after her time by indenture or custome is expired be by the churchwardens of the parish where she lived when she was brought to bed of such bastard, sold for two years."

60. www.angelo.edu/events/university_symposium/1987/rhode. htm.

61. Susan B. Anthony letter to Gerrit Smith, Rochester, November 12, 1872 (www.lib.rochester.edu/rbk/women/women.htm).

62. Thomas W. Knox, *The Republican Party and Its Leaders* (New York: P. F. Collier, 1892).

63. Joseph Ellis, *American Sphinx: The Character of Thomas Jefferson* (New York: Vintage, 1998).

64. Ibid., p. 10.

65. Destutt Tracy, *A Treatise on Political Economy* (London, 1817).

66. Ibid.

67. Jefferson adds that although Adam Smith had some important things to say on the topic as well, *The Wealth of Nations,* which was published in 1776, is a bit difficult to read. "Adam Smith, first in England, published a rational and systematic work on Political Economy," Jefferson writes, "but his book, admitted to be able, and of the first degree of merit, has yet been considered as prolix and tedious." This book by Tracy, however, is, in Jefferson's opinion, brilliant, and so tightly written that it combines eight volumes of thinking into a single book. "It is certainly distinguished by important traits; a cogency of logic which has never been exceeded in any work, a rigorous

enchainment of ideas, and constant recurrence to it to keep it in the reader's view, a fearless pursuit of truth whithersoever it leads, and a diction so correct that not a word can be changed but for the worse; and, as happens in other cases, that the more a subject is understood, the more briefly it may be explained, he has reduced, not indeed all the details, but all the elements and the system of principles within the compass of 8 volumes, of about 400 pages."

68. Phillips, *Wealth and Democracy.*

69. www.ameristat.org/Content/NavigationMenu/Ameristat/Topics1/MarriageandFamily/More_U_S_Women_Outearning_Their_Husbands.htm.

70. news.bbc.co.uk/1/hi/health/3106451.stm.

71. news.bbc.co.uk/1/hi/health/234918.stm.

72. A. Page, S. Morrell, and R. Taylor, "Suicide and Political Regime in New South Wales and Australia During the 20th Century," *Journal of Epidemiology and Community Health* 56 (2002): 766–772, and M. Shaw, D. Dorling, and G. Davey Smith, "Mortality and Political Climate: How Suicide Rates Have Risen During Periods of Conservative Government, 1901–2000," *Journal of Epidemiology and Community Health* 56 (2002): 723–725.

73. Kendall Powell, "Suicide Rises Under Conservative Rule," *Nature,* www.nature.com/nsu/020916/020916–17.html.

74. news.bbc.co.uk/2/hi/health/2263690.stm.

75. "Unverified" quote from Alexander Fraser Tytler (1747–1813) listed as entry 424 in *Bartleby's Quotations,* online at www.bartleby.com/73/424/html.

76. *Merriam-Webster's Dictionary* online, 2003, at www.merriam-webster.com.

77. Speech by Theodore Roosevelt to the Ohio Constitutional Convention in Columbus, Ohio, 1912, reprinted nearly in its entirety in Thom Hartmann, *Unequal Protection: The Rise of Corporate Dominance and the Theft of Human Rights* (Emmaus, PA: Rodale, 2002).

78. Kurt Eichenwald, "Redesigning Nature: Hard Lessons Learned," *New York Times,* January 25, 2001.

79. Robert Monks and Nell Minow, *Power and Accountability* (New York: HarperCollins, 1991).

80. www.xmission.com/~mwalker/DQ/quayle/qq/One.Big.File.html.

81. Eichenwald, "Redesigning Nature."

82. Ibid.

83. Paul Hawken, *The Ecology of Commerce: A Declaration of Sustainability* (New York: HarperBusiness, 1994).

84. Anne Platt McGinn, "Detoxifying Terrorism," Worldwatch Institute, November 16, 2001.

85. Russell Kirk, *The Conservative Mind* (Washington, DC: Regnery, 2001).

86. L. Conradt and T. J. Roper, "Group Decision-Making in Animals," *Nature,* 421 (January 9, 2003): 155–158.

87. James Randerson, "Democracy Beats Despotism in the Animal World," *New Scientist,* January 8, 2003.

88. Albert Somit and Steven A. Peterson, *Darwinism, Dominance, and Democracy: The Biological Bases of Authoritarianism* (New York: Praeger, 1997).

89. Peter Farb, *Man's Rise to Civilization, As Shown by the Indians of North America from Primeval Times to the Coming of the Industrial State* (New York: Avon, 1976).

90. Charles Darwin, *The Descent of Man*, 1871.

91. Documented in John Ferling, *A Leap in the Dark: The Struggle to Create the American Republic* (New York: Oxford University Press, 2003).

92. Ibid.

93. www.digitalhistory.uh.edu/database/article_display.cfm?HHID=10.

94. Congressman George Thatcher in a letter now held at the Massachusetts Historical Society.

95. www.cnn.com/2003/US/South/08/25/moore.bio/.

96. From the Journal of the House of Representatives of the United States of America, letter from James Madison, February 21, 1811.

97. Here's the larger text, for those interested in the details of Jefferson's legal argument:

"TO JOHN ADAMS, MONTICELLO, January 24, 1814.

"DEAR SIR— . . . You ask me if I have ever seen the work of J.W. Goethe, *Schriften?* Never; nor did the question ever occur to me before, where get we the Ten Commandments? The book indeed gives them to us verbatim, but where did it get them? For itself tells us they were written by the finger of God on tables of stone, which were destroyed by Moses; it specifies those on the second set of tables in different form and substance, but still without saying how the others were recovered.

"But the whole history of these books is so defective and doubtful, that it seems vain to attempt minute inquiry into it; and such tricks have been played with their text, and with the texts of other books relating to them, that we have a right from that cause to entertain much doubt what parts of them are genuine: In the New Testament there is internal evidence that parts of it have proceeded from an extraordinary man; and that other parts are of the fabric of very inferior minds. It is as easy to separate those parts, as to pick out diamonds from dunghills. The matter of the first was such as would be preserved in the memory of the hearers, and handed on by tradition for a long time; the latter such stuff as might be gathered up, for imbedding it, anywhere, and at any time. . . .

Jefferson then carefully prepares a lawyer's brief to show that the entire idea that the laws of both England and the United States came from Christianity or the Ten Commandments rests on a single man's mistranslation in 1658, often repeated, and totally false.

"It is not only the sacred volumes they have thus interpolated, gutted, and falsified, but the works of others relating to them, and even the laws of the land. We have a curious instance of one of these pious frauds in the laws of Alfred. He composed, you know, from the laws of the Heptarchy, a digest for the government of the United Kingdom, and in his preface to that work he tells us expressly the sources from which he drew it, to wit, the laws of Ina, of Offa and Aethelbert (not naming the Pentateuch [the Old Testament]). But his pious interpolator, very awkwardly, premises to his work four chapters of Exodus (from the 20th to the 23d [where the Ten Commandments are found]) as a part of the laws of the land; so that Alfred's preface is made to stand in the body of the work.

"Our judges, too, have lent a ready hand to further these frauds, and have been willing to lay the yoke of their own opinions on the necks of others; to extend the coercions of municipal law to the dogmas of their religion, by declaring that these make a part of the law of the land. . . .

"Finch begins the business of falsification by mistranslating and misstating the words of [Chief Justice of the High Court] Prisot thus: 'to such laws of the church as have warrant in Holy Scripture our law giveth credence.' Citing the above case and the words of Prisot in the [margin] in [Finch's] law, B.I, c.3, here then we find 'ancient scripture,' 'ancient writing,' translated 'holy scripture.' This, Wingate, in 1658, erects into a maxim of law in the very words of Finch, but citing Prisot and not Finch. And Sheppard, titled *Religion*, in 1675 laying it down in the same words of Finch, quotes the *Year-Book*, Finch and Wingate.

"Then comes Sir Matthew Hale, in the case of the King v. Taylor, I Ventr. 293, 3 Keb. 607, and declares that 'Christianity is part and parcel of the laws of England.' Citing nobody, and resting it, with his judgment against the witches, on his own authority. . . .

"Thus strengthened, the court in 1728, in the King v. Woolston, would not suffer it to be questioned whether to write against Christianity was punishable at common law, saying it had been so settled by Hale in Taylor's case, 2 Stra. 834. Wood, therefore, 409, without scruple, lays down as a principle, that all blaspheming and profaneness are offences at the common law, and cites Strange.

"Blackstone, in 1763, repeats, in the words of Sir Matthew Hale, that 'Christianity is part of the laws of England', citing Ventris and Strange, ubi supra. And Lord Mansfield, in the case of the Chamberlain of London v. Evans, in 1767, qualifying somewhat the position, says that 'the essential principles of revealed religion are part of the common law.'

"Thus we find this string of authorities all hanging by one another on a single hook, a mistranslation by Finch of the words of Prisot, or on nothing. For all quote Prisot, or one another, or nobody."

98. President Andrew Jackson's 5th Annual Message (State of the Union) presented in written form to the United States Congress, December 3, 1833.

99. Section 4479a [Sec. 1, ch. 492, 1905].

100. Section 4479b [Sec. 2, ch. 492, 1905].

101. The Founders' Constitution, Volume 5, Amendment I (Religion), Document 64, press-pubs.uchicago.edu/founders/documents/amendI_religions64.html.

102. Thomas Jefferson letter to Dr. Walter Jones, written at Monticello, January 2, 1814.

103. Farb, *Man's Rise to Civilization.*

104. robert wolff, *Original Wisdom* (Rochester, VT: Inner Traditions, 2001).

105. Maxim Gorki quoted by René Dubos in *Beast or Angel* (New York: Scribner, 1971).

106. James Axtell, *The European and the Indian* (New York: Oxford University Press, 1981).

107. Cadwallader Colden, *The History of the Five Indian Nations of Canada* (London: 1747).

108. An article by James Bricknell about his capture and life among the Delaware Indians, *American Pioneer*, vol. 1, 1842.

109. In a 1785 letter to his 15-year-old nephew, Peter Carr, Jefferson made a comment of several to be found among his letters, placing Herodotus in the lead: "Then take up ancient history in the detail, reading the following books, in the following order: Herodotus, Thucydides, Xenophontis, Anabasis, Arrian, Quintus Curtius, Diodorus Siculus, Justin."

110. Leon P. Baradat, *Political Ideologies: Their Origins and Impact* (Prentice Hall, 2002).

111. Although published anonymously, *Vindiciae Contra Tyrannos* was generally thought to be written by Philippe Duplessis-Mornay (1549–1623) and Hubert Languet (1518–1581).

112. *The International Transportworkers Federation, 1914–1945: The Edo Fimmen Era*, edited by Bob Reinalda, 1997, is available from the ITF at www.itf.org.uk.

113. The elected representatives to the Dutch republic were, in theory, derived from among the people of each of the states. In reality, they were almost always princes of Orange-Nassau. Modern democratic Holland came into being in 1813 in concert with Belgium.

114. Mark Palmer, *Breaking the Real Axis of Evil: How to Oust the World's Last Dictator by 2025* (Lanham, MD: Rowman & Littlefield, 2003).

115. February 3, 1976, address to the Commonwealth Club, New York, by Henry A. Kissinger, then secretary of state.

116. Samuel P. Huntingdon, *The Third Wave: Democratization in the Late Twentieth Century* (Norman, OK: University of Oklahoma Press, 1991).

117. Francis Fukuyama, *The End of History and the Last Man* (New York: Avon, 1993).

118. UN Development Programme, *Human Development Report*, www.undp.org/hdr2002/facts.html.

119. Ibid.

120. Ibid.

121. Per Ahlmark, "How Democracy Prevents Civic Catastrophes," address to European Parliament, April 8, 1999.

122. www.hawaii.edu/powerkills/DP.CLOCK.HTM.

123. R. J. Rummel, *Death by Government* (Somerset, NJ: Transaction, 1997).

124. Palmer, *Breaking the Real Axis of Evil.*

125. www.freedomhouse.org.

126. Madison's quote has been widely circulated for over 200 years, usually in edited form, in hundreds of quote and political collections. The entire context is online at http://tiger.berkeley.edu/sohrab/politics/madison.html.

127. On Sunday, October 7, 2001, the Associated Press reported, in a story

titled "Taliban Offer to Detain bin Laden": "ISLAMABAD, Pakistan (AP)—In a desperate eleventh-hour appeal to halt U.S. attacks, Afghanistan's ruling Taliban offered Sunday to detain terrorist suspect Osama bin Laden and try him under Islamic law if the United States makes a formal request.

"The Bush administration, which has insisted that Afghanistan hand over bin Laden and his lieutenants, quickly rejected the Taliban proposal.

"'The president's demands are clear and nonnegotiable,' said White House spokesman Scott McClellan." (Archived at: dupagepeace.home.att.net/lastresort.html.)

Once the bombing started, Britain's *Guardian* newspaper reported, in an October 14, 2001, article titled, "Bush rejects Taliban offer to hand Bin Laden over," that "President George Bush rejected as 'non-negotiable' an offer by the Taliban to discuss turning over Osama bin Laden if the United States ended the bombing in Afghanistan" (www.guardian.co.uk/waronterror/story/0,1361,573975,00. html.)

128. From a 1905 speech by Albert Ellery Berch at the University of Virginia.

129. Steffie Woolhandler, Terry Campbell, and David U. Himmelstein, "Costs of Health Care Administration in the United States and Canada," *New England Journal of Medicine,* August 2003.

130. Archived at various sources, including the *Detroit News,* www.detnews.com/history/125th/page5a.htm.

131. Franklin's letter was published under the title "On the Price of Corn and Management of the Poor" by Arator.

132. *Wall Street Journal,* March 10, 1997, p. A2.

133. Martin Van Buren's 1st Annual Message (State of the Union) presented in written form to Congress, December 5, 1837.

134. www.bp.com.

135. Theodore Roosevelt's 6th Annual Message to Congress (State of the Union), December 3, 1906.

136. www.fairvote.org/irv/.

137. John Brady, "I'm Still Lee Atwater," *Washington Post,* December 1, 1996, as quoted in www.washingtonpost.com/wp-srv/style/longterm/books/bckgrnd/atwater.htm.

Index

A

Adams, John, 134, 258; and dissent, 157–58, 159–61, 164, 209, 224; and influences on Founders, 25, 27, 28, 29–30, 31, 35; Jefferson's relationship with, 158, 161, 172–73, 251; and modern democracy, 189, 191, 194; and myths about democracy, 65–66, 90, 96, 98; and religion, 167, 172–73, 247; and vision for future, 219, 224, 247

Agriculture Department, U.S. (USDA), 5, 125, 175, 241–42

Ahlmark, Per, 13, 215, 216

Albany Plan of Union, 26, 28

Alien and Sedition Acts, 157–60, 209, 224

"alpha" animals, 139, 142, 143, 144–45

American Civil Liberties Union (ACLU), 4, 162

American Revolution, 52, 53. See also Boston Tea Party

animal behavior, 139, 142, 143, 144–45, 146, 153

antidemocracies, 19–20, 189–92, 210

antitrust laws, 100, 115, 242–43, 245

apartheid, 13, 202–3

Aristotle, 188, 189, 190, 191

Articles of Confederation, 192

Ashcroft, John, 130, 134, 163, 164

Athens, Greece: democracy in, 17, 75, 96, 109, 189–92, 193, 196

Atwater, Lee, 138, 254

B

Bailyn, Bernard, 71–72

Beard, Charles, 67–69, 70–71, 72, 73, 74, 75

Beard, Mary, 68–69, 72

Bill of Rights, U.S., 3, 97, 155–56, 179, 205, 221, 247. See also specific amendment

biology of democracy, 142–44. See also animal behavior

Boston Tea Party, 41–52, 55, 112, 220

Burke, Edmund, 107–8, 132, 134, 258

Bursey, Brett, 162–64

Bush, George H.W., 16, 109, 112, 118–19, 125, 136, 137, 223, 238

Bush, George W., 106, 153, 203, 255; antidemocratic damage of, 136, 137, 138; and deficit spending, 136, 137, 238; and dissent, 162–64; and elections of 2000, 249, 251; and erosion of democracy, 3, 4, 5; and First Amendment, 3; and Fourth Amendment, 3; and regulation, 5; and social programs, 120, 234, 238; and taxation, 118–19; and terrorism, 223; and trade, 112, 232; and treaties, 232; and war powers, 222, 223 business: "big business" versus, 115–16. *See also* corporations/corporatism

C

campaign contributions. *See* political contributions
capitalism, 63, 115, 130–31
Carter, Jimmy, 118, 242, 243, 245–46, 250
change: working for, 254–59
Churchill, Winston, 56, 183
civil rights, 2, 3, 16, 20, 223. *See also* rights; *specific right*
classical liberalism, 197–98
Cleveland, Grover, 6–7, 255
Clinton, Bill, 6, 112, 118, 232, 234, 235–36
Clinton, Hillary, 104, 106, 107
common law, British, 171–72, 174
communism, 13, 56, 60, 62, 111, 200, 203, 205, 216
competition, 100, 113–14, 199, 216, 231
Congress, U.S., 11, 82, 160–61, 168, 221–24, 227, 241, 244, 245, 256–57. *See also* special interests
Conradt, L., 142, 143–44, 145
conservatives: antidemocratic damage by, 136–39; and deficits, 109–10; and education, 224–25; and employment, 105, 106; and environment, 242; and Founders as impractical dreamers, 95–96; and government as evil, 94–95; and labor, 107, 129, 201, 230; and modern democracy, 199, 201; meaning of term, 135; and media, 122–24; and privacy, 97; and regulation, 127; and shift to pseudo-conservative values, 135–36; and social programs, 119, 120, 232–33, 238; and socialism, 110, 111; and suicide rate, 105; and taxes, 102–3, 117, 118; and trade, 111, 112, 113, 114; and U.N., 252; what

became of real American, 132–39; and working for change, 256, 258, 259
Constitution, U.S., 3, 11, 29, 38, 174; "domestic tranquility" in, 38; economic interpretation of, 67–76; and elections, 250, 251; and gender, 87–89; and modern democracy, 189, 191; and military, 239; and power, 121; and privacy, 96–98; ratification of, 74–75, 76, 88; signers of, 67–68, 69–70; and slavery, 77–87, 88; Washington's views about, 76; and wealth of Founders, 67; as work in progress, 91–94; and working for change, 257, 258. *See also* Bill of Rights; *specific amendment*
Constitutional Convention, 39–40, 55, 69–70, 73–74, 75–76, 82, 134, 192, 193, 251
constitutions: of other nation states, 37, 58; state, 80, 103
consumer protection, 126, 175
Continental Congress, 28, 29
control: and what is democracy, 22–23
corporations/corporatism: as antidemocracy, 19–20, 136; and business versus "big business," 115–16; and deficit spending, 109; definition of, 3; and democracy in world today, 204, 207–8, 214, 217; dominance of, 4–7; and erosion of democracy, 2, 3, 4–9, 253; and failure of democracy, 60, 61, 62, 63, 64–65; and fascism, 23, 207; feudal lords in, 7–9; and globalization, 208; and government as evil, 95; and labor, 201, 230–31; and modern democracy, 196, 200, 201, 203; and means of production, 200, 201; media, 122–24, 243–45; multinational, 127–29, 217, 232; pay for senior executives in, 237, 238; political

contributions of, 8–9, 92, 175, 176, 179, 242, 248–49; and political parties, 89; and power, 64, 114–15, 121, 130, 219–20, 243; and regulation, 125–26; rights/personhood of, 16, 20, 94–95, 175–82, 219–20, 246–47; rise of, 174–82; and social programs, 234, 238; and taxation, 64, 100, 117, 119, 237, 238; and trade, 112–13, 114–15, 127–29, 232; and voting, 251–52; and what is democracy, 19, 22–23; and working for change, 257, 259; and working women, 104–7. *See also* monopolies; regulation; robber barons; special interests

Couzens, James, 228–30

Coxe, Tenche, 231–32, 251

D

Darwin, Charles, 111–16, 143, 144, 145, 147, 148, 149, 151, 153, 154

death penalty, 4

Declaration of Independence, 28, 34, 39, 52–53, 68, 79, 80, 112, 180, 189, 226, 259

deficit spending, 109–10, 135*n*, 136–37, 238, 258

Deism, 167, 169

democracy: basic tenets of, 217; characteristics of healthy, 20–21; as constant winner, 153–54; definitions of, 12, 14–18, 205–6; as enlightened self-interest, 146–47; erosion of, 1–9; as experiment, 153, 181, 192; failure of, 56–64; final triumph or reversal of, 206–7; how much, 192–93; inevitability of, 210–18; models of, 16–17; as moral system, 173–74; myths about, 65–131; as natural state, 210–11; and oldest democratic cultures, 183–88; pure, 17, 18, 66; reinventing, 217–18; resilience of, 214–17;

self-destruction of, 65–66; spread of, 7–8, 16, 17, 204–8, 215, 216, 258; stability of, 210; struggle for, 16; survivability of, 65–66; threats to, 9, 164–74; "waves" of, 206; as way of nature, 140–54; what is, 10–23; wolff's comments about, 261–65; in world today, 204–18. *See also* modern democracy; *specific topic*

Democratic Party, 89–91

disasters, 264–65

dissent, 62–63, 64, 66, 157–58, 159–60, 189–92, 209, 224. *See also* PATRIOT Acts; Sedition Act

divine right, 40, 133, 196–98

dominance, 139, 140–54, 261, 262

draft, military, 239–41

due process, 61, 88

E

East India Company, 41–48, 50–52, 92, 112

economics, 99–101, 129–30, 136

education, 9, 98, 224–27, 240

Eighth Amendment, 4

elections, U.S., 8, 20, 21, 221, 248–51, 252, 253. *See also* political contributions

employment/unemployment, 2, 4, 7, 104–7, 119, 130, 234–36. *See also* labor

energy, 177, 245–46

England, 105, 172, 206, 208; Constitution of, 37; de Rapin's views about history of, 34–40; as influence on Founders, 34–55; pre-Norman conquest in, 33–34, 36–38, 39, 40, 66, 188, 196, 198; representative government in, 40, 44; Tacitus' views of, 31–34; U.S. relationship with, 39. *See also* Boston Tea Party; East India Company; United Kingdom; *specific person*

Enlightenment, 22, 79, 95–96, 195, 197, 219
Enron, 8, 177
environment, 5, 6, 126, 136, 241–42. *See also* Environmental Protection Agency; *specific legislation*
Environmental Protection Agency (EPA), 95, 125, 127, 241
equal opportunity, 18, 20
equality, 195, 210, 261, 262, 265
Espionage Act (1917), 161, 162

F

faith-based initiatives, 168
Farb, Peter, 10, 149–51, 184
fascism, 19, 23, 56, 207
Federal Communications Commission (FCC), 95, 180, 244
Federal Drug Administration (FDA), 125, 126, 175
Federalist Party, 65–66. *See also specific person*
feudalism/feudal lords, 19, 110, 113, 200; and democracy in world today, 207–8; and liberal democracy, 196–97, 200; rise of corporate, 7–9; and vision for future, 220, 253; and working for change, 257, 258
Fifteenth Amendment, 88
Fifth Amendment, 4, 97
First Amendment, 3, 95, 161, 162, 163, 165, 168, 170, 171, 179
Founders, 134, 137, 173, 201, 209; and corporatism, 177–78; and economic interpretation of Constitution, 67–76; and education, 225; as idealistic dreamers, 95–96; influences on, 24–55, 66; intent of, 23, 67; and modern democracy, 188–89, 191, 193, 195, 201; and military, 239; and religion, 165, 166–68, 171; and slavery, 77–87; and social programs, 233, 236; and vision for future, 219, 222, 225, 233, 236, 239; wealth of,

67–76; and what is democracy, 14–15, 17–18, 22, 23; and working for change, 257, 258, 259. *See also specific person*
Fourteenth Amendment, 88, 178, 181
Fourth Amendment, 3, 95, 156, 179
Fox News, 123, 135, 165
France, 81, 157, 206, 222
Frank, Barney, 163
Franklin, Benjamin: and Constitutional Convention, 55; and Declaration of Independence, 52, 53; and influences on Founders, 26, 28; and liberal democracy, 189, 191, 192, 203; and religion, 165, 166–67; and social programs, 119, 233–34
free speech, 3, 58, 95, 156, 161, 162–64, 179, 180, 205, 209, 214. *See also* Alien and Sedition Acts
free trade/markets, 104–7, 111–16, 127–29, 207, 214
freedom, 9, 14, 134, 156, 214–15, 257. *See also type of freedom*
freedom of assembly, 162–64, 205, 209
freedom of the press, 122–23, 205, 243–45

G

Galgachan (British tribal leader), 33–34, 40
gender issues, 87–88. *See also* women
genocide, 215, 216
Germany, 196, 237, 251, 257; Constitution of, 58, 63; and democracy in world today, 206, 208; failure of democracy in, 55, 56–64, 205; Nazi, 13, 200–201, 216, 223; representative government in, 39, 63; U.S. compared with, 63–64; and what is democracy, 22–23. *See also* Hitler, Adolf
Gingrich, Newt, 17, 136, 138
"Goddess of Democracy" (statue), 22

Gore, Al, 238, 249, 250, 251
government: and education, 225; as
    evil, 94–95; functions of, 202;
    power of, 111, 112; revolving door
    for employees of, 245; and trade,
    111, 112; and tribal democracy,
    148; and vision for future, 220
Great Britain. *See* England; United
    Kingdom
Great Depression, 63–64, 202, 236
Greece, 22, 66, 206, 208, 223, 240.
    See also Athens, Greece
greed, 120–21
Greenspan, Alan, 234–35

H

habeas corpus, 58
Hamilton, Alexander, 133, 134, 189,
    191, 193–94
Hancock, John, 29, 53, 231
"happiness," 26, 38, 52
health care, 2, 5–6, 202, 227–28,
    236–37, 257
Hewes, George R. T., 44–51, 49*n*,
    219–20
hierarchy, 140–54, 261, 262
Hitler, Adolf, 12, 13, 23, 56–64,
    200–201, 201*n*, 223, 239
Hobbes, Thomas, 141, 141*n*, 148, 198,
    211, 213, 214
"the homeland," 59, 60–61, 63
Hoover, Herbert, 91, 230, 234, 236
House of Representatives, U.S., 88,
    160. *See also* Congress, U.S.
Hume, David, 34–35
Huntingdon, Samuel P., 205, 206,
    207

I

income taxes, 101, 117
Indians, American. *See* Native
    Americans; tribal societies
indigenous cultures, 96, 183–88, 196,
    217, 261–63. *See also* Native
    Americans; tribal societies

industry. *See* corporations/corpora-
    tism
inheritance taxes, 101, 103, 199, 237
intelligence services. *See* national
    security
Iraq, 207, 208, 223
Iroquois Indians, 22, 29, 30–31, 66

J

Jefferson, Thomas: Adams's rela-
    tionship with, 158, 161, 172–73,
    251; and antidemocratic conser-
    vative damage, 137–38; and Con-
    stitution, 38, 92–94, 121; and
    corporatism, 181, 182; and Decla-
    ration of Independence, 39, 79,
    80, 92, 189, 226; and deficit
    spending, 136; and democracy as
    moral system, 173–74; and dis-
    sent, 209; and education, 98,
    225–27, 240; and elections, 250,
    251; and erosion of democracy, 6;
    as founder of Democratic Party,
    89–91; and freedom of the press,
    122; as impractical dreamer, 96;
    and influences on Founders, 11,
    24–28, 29, 30, 31–32, 33, 34–35,
    36, 38, 39, 66; and labor, 107;
    and liberal democracy, 189, 191,
    193–95, 203; Lincoln's letter on
    birthday of, 89–91; and military,
    239, 240, 241; and monopolies,
    242–43; and power, 121; and
    presidential power, 158, 159,
    160–61; and privacy, 98; and
    protection from harm clause, 21;
    and religion, 21, 164, 165, 167,
    168–71, 172–73, 247; and slavery,
    77–81, 83, 84–86, 89, 90–91,
    138; and social programs, 234;
    and survivability of democracy,
    66; and taxation, 99–103, 199,
    237; as visionary, 219, 220; wealth
    of, 73; and what is democracy,
    21, 22; and working for change,
    257, 258

jobs. *See* employment/unemployment
Johnson, Lyndon B., 203, 221, 234

K

Kant, Immanuel, 10–11, 12, 209
Kirk, Russell, 133–35
Kissinger, Henry, 204–5

L

labor, 2, 5, 69, 104–8, 129–30, 136,
    201, 223–32, 234–35. *See also*
    employment/unemployment;
    unions
law of the jungle, 113–14
liberal democracy, 12, 21, 55, 67, 106,
    111, 112, 195, 197, 202, 258. *See also*
    modern/liberal democracy
liberals/liberalism: and bias of
    media, 123–24; classical, 197–98;
    and failure of democracy, 62;
    and government as evil, 94; high
    point of U.S., 202; and labor
    issues, 107–8; modern, 202–3;
    and social programs, 119–21; and
    taxation, 103. *See also* modern
    democracy
liberties, 52, 97, 200, 223, 258; and
    definition of democracy, 18; and
    influences on Founders, 37, 38;
    and modern democracy, 195, 198,
    200; and 9/11, 157; and privacy, 98
lies, 61–63, 95, 124, 171
Limbaugh, Rush, 1, 97, 104, 106–7,
    135
Lincoln, Abraham, 89–91, 164, 201
lobbying. *See* special interests
Locke, John, 35, 69, 96, 197–98,
    199–200, 219

M

Madison, James: and Constitutional
    Convention, 75, 192; and corpo-
    ratism, 174, 178; and democracy
    as moral system, 173; and elec-
    tions, 249; and Founders as

impractical idealists, 96; and
    influences on Founders, 38; and
    liberal democracy, 189, 191, 192,
    203; and military, 239; and presi-
    dential power, 156; and religion,
    168; and war, 221, 223; and wealth,
    69; and what is democracy, 18
Magna Carta, 196, 208
Marx, Karl, 200
McDonald, Forrest, 73–75
media, 95, 160, 165, 257; and anti-
    democratic conservative damage,
    136, 138; as conglomerates, 122–
    23, 243–45; corporations, 243–
    45; and erosion of democracy, 6,
    9; and failure of democracy, 58,
    60, 61, 62; liberal bias of, 123–24;
    and shift to pseudoconservative
    values, 135; and vision for future,
    220, 243–45; and what is democ-
    racy, 13, 21; wolff's comments
    about, 262. *See also* freedom of
    the press
Medicare/Medicaid, 120, 227
middle class, 128, 210, 234; and fail-
    ure of democracy, 63, 64; and
    labor, 104–8, 130, 228, 229, 230,
    231; and taxes, 102, 237–38; and
    trade, 128, 232; wealth/income
    of, 2, 3
military, 21, 111, 121, 223, 239–41,
    245
Mill, John Stuart, 155, 249
Milligan, Joseph, 99, 102–3
modern/liberal democracy, 7, 55,
    110–11; benefits of, 203; and
    definition of democracy, 17, 18;
    essential components of, 21;
    greatest threat to, 19–20; history
    of, 183–203; keys to understand-
    ing, 195–96; and Kirk's conser-
    vatism, 134; purpose of, 258;
    resilience of, 214; spread of, 203;
    and working for change, 251–58;
    workings of, 183–203

monopolies, 174–82, 199, 242–43
Mussolini, Benito, 3, 19, 23, 111, 181, 207

N

national security, 3, 21, 57, 60–61, 63, 156–64. *See also* terrorism
Native Americans: as influence on Founders, 24–31; and myths about democracy, 77; and oldest democratic cultures, 183–88; and sin and punishment, 211–13; and survivability of democracy, 66; tribal democracy among, 148–53; war among, 151–53; wolff's comments about, 263. *See also* tribal societies
natural law, 18, 114–15, 195
natural rights, 35, 40, 100
natural selection, 143, 145
Nineteenth Amendment, 69
9/11, 157, 222–23
Ninth Amendment, 97
Nixon, Richard M., 162, 221, 241

O

Ontasseté, 24–25, 26–27

P

Palmer, Mark, 203, 216
PATRIOT Acts, 3, 4, 162–64, 224
peace, 209, 215, 216–17
Pentagon Papers, 162
Plato, 189, 190, 191
police agencies, 58–59, 63, 163, 213, 220, 222, 223–24
political contributions, 20, 92, 95, 257; of corporations, 8–9, 92, 175, 176, 179, 242, 248–49; and erosion of democracy, 8–9; and vision for future, 242, 248–49
political participation, 7, 21, 193, 220, 242, 250. *See also* voting
political parties, 21, 89–91, 135, 159, 160, 249

poor/poverty, 102, 104–5, 130, 154, 168, 210, 214–15, 226, 232–37
power, 217, 258; absolute, 121; and corporations, 64, 114–15, 121, 130, 219–20, 243; corruption of, 121; and military, 241; of presidency, 156–64; and religion, 165, 170–73; where is, 112–13; wolff's comments about, 265
preemptive war, 61, 215, 223
presidency, 9, 156–64, 221. *See also specific president*
privacy, 4, 58, 95, 96–99, 179, 180, 247, 258
privatization, 175
privileges, 14–15, 37, 94
production: ownership of, 199–202
Progressives, 69, 89, 110, 228, 229, 230
property, 37, 71, 87–88, 101, 102–3, 134, 156, 198
punishment, 211–14
pure democracy, 17, 18, 66

R

Rapin Thoyras, Paul de, 34–40, 198
Reagan, Ronald, 112, 242; deficit spending of, 109, 135n, 136, 238; and definition of democracy, 16, 17; and education, 224–25, 227; and erosion of democracy, 2, 6; and social programs, 120, 234; and taxation, 118–19, 250
regulation, 5, 100, 104–7, 108, 124–27, 130–31, 175, 179, 199, 233, 235, 242, 245
religion, 9, 21, 121, 133, 141, 164–74, 196–97, 198, 220, 247–48
representative government, 39–40, 82–83, 193, 249–50
republic, 18, 55, 66
Republican Party, 89–91, 103, 135, 161, 229–30, 252

rights, 14, 15, 16, 59, 64, 90, 94, 155–64, 214, 246–47, 258. *See also type of rights*

robber barons, 70, 71, 103, 112, 136*n*, 214

Roman Empire, 22, 39, 66, 191, 193, 240

Roosevelt, Franklin D., 64, 91, 130, 162, 202, 234

Roosevelt, Theodore, 1, 115–16, 248–49

Roper, Tim, 142, 143–44, 145, 146

Rousseau, Jean-Jacques, 69, 194

Rove, Karl, 106, 138

rugged individualist ideal, 146–47

Rummel, J. Rudolph: 12, 214–16

Russia/Soviet Union, 13, 135–36*n*, 200, 205, 208, 209, 216

"Rusticus," 34, 47, 48

S

Sanders, Bernie, 255, 256

search and seizure, 3, 179

Second Amendment, 240

Secret Service, U.S., 3, 162, 163

Sedition Act (1918), 161–62, 163

Senate, U.S., 69, 224. *See also* Congress, U.S.

separation of powers, 21

Seventeenth Amendment, 69

Sherman Anti-Trust Act, 100, 242–43, 245

sin, 211–14

slavery, 77–87, 88, 89, 90–91, 138, 211, 231

Smith, Adam, 11, 99–100, 199–200

social contract, 118

social programs, 9, 119–21, 203, 232–37. *See also specific program*

Social Security, 64, 120, 202, 237, 238

socialism, 110–11

Socrates, 189–91, 193

Soviet Union. *See* Russia/Soviet Union

speaking out, 256–57

special interests: and dominance and hierarchy, 148, 154; and elections, 248; and environment, 242; and erosion of democracy, 4–5; and free markets, 115; and health care, 228; and labor, 231; and modern democracy, 203; and political parties, 89; and regulation, 124–25, 126, 127; and spread of corporatism, 181; and taxation, 100; and usurpation of rights, 220; and what is democracy, 23; and working for change, 258, 259

states: ballot initiatives in, 18

states rights, 88

Stinkards, 150–51

"struggle for existence," 113–14

suffrage. *See* voting

suicide, 105

Supreme Court, U.S., 20, 69, 94, 162, 177, 178–79, 181, 246, 247

"survival of the fittest," 138–39, 147, 265

T

Tacitus, Cornelius, 30, 31–34

taxation, 91, 92, 258; benefits of, 116–19; and Boston Tea Party, 41, 44; and corporations, 64, 100, 117, 237, 238; double, 99–103; and elections, 248; and energy, 245–46; and influences on Founders, 37, 38, 39, 41, 44; and middle class, 237–38; and religion, 248; and Republican Party, 229–30; and socialism, 110; and tax cuts, 118, 230, 245; types of, 101; and wealth, 99–103, 199

Ten Commandments, 165, 171–72, 173

terrorism, 4, 56–59, 60, 61, 62, 158, 222–24

theocracy. *See* religion

Thirteenth Amendment, 88

Tiananmen Square (1989), 22, 216

Tocqueville, Alexis de, 65, 122, 164, 244

Tracy, Antoine Louis Claude Destutt, Comte de, 99–101

trade, 127–29, 231–32. *See also* free trade/markets

tribal societies, 141, 148–53, 183–88, 198, 202, 211–14. *See also* indigenous cultures; Native Americans

U

unions, labor, 129–30, 201, 230–31, 234, 236. *See also* labor

United Kingdom, 40, 171–72, 174, 206, 223, 233

United Nations, 8–9, 18, 208, 214, 252–53

United Nations Development Programme, 8–9, 206–7, 209–10

V

voting, 92, 220, 253; and accuracy of vote, 251–52; among animals, 143, 144; and corporations, 251–52; and electoral college, 251; in England, 206; and erosion of democracy, 6, 7; "instant runoff," 249, 250; and modern democracy, 21, 191; of women, 69, 87–88, 92, 206

voting machines, 6, 252

W

wages, 69, 107–8, 129–30, 223–30, 234–35, 236, 237, 238

Wal-Mart, 230

war, 39, 199; and Congress, 221–24; and democracy in world today, 215, 216–17; and elections, 221; and failure of democracy, 61–63, 64; Kant's views about, 10–11, 12; preemptive, 61, 215, 223; and presidency, 221; on terrorism, 222–24; and tribal democracy, 149–50, 151–53; and what is democracy, 10–13

Washington, George: and American Revolution, 53, 54, 160; and Constitution as work in progress, 92; and Constitutional Convention, 39–40, 76; and economic interpretation of Constitution, 76; and Hewes, 45; and influences on Founders, 29, 38, 39–40; and presidential power, 157, 159; reelection of, 161; and religion, 165, 167–68; wealth of, 72–73; and what is democracy, 17

wealth, 92, 110, 112, 138, 200, 230, 257; and democracy in world today, 210, 217; and dominance and hierarchy, 153; of Founders, 67–76; and government as evil, 94; and Kirk's conservatism, 135; and political parties, 89, 91, 135, 159, 160; and power, 121; and taxation, 99–103, 117, 119, 199, 237; and tribal democracy, 148; wolff's comments about, 265

West, Thomas G., 81, 83, 87

wolff, robert, 184–85, 186, 188, 261–65

women, 69, 77, 87–88, 92, 104–7, 206. *See also* gender

working poor, 130, 154

worldview: and definition of democracy, 17–18; and dominance and hierarchy, 140–54; and people as evil, 17, 205, 213; and people as good, 213

About the Author

THOM HARTMANN is a bestselling, award-winning author and nationally syndicated radio talk-show host, who lives in central Vermont and can be found on the Internet at www.thomhartmann.com.